Living in
America

April, 1995

Lekha & Herman

"Tvameva bandhu"

Mugdha & Raj

LIVING IN AMERICA

Poetry and Fiction
by
South Asian American
Writers

EDITED BY

Roshni Rustomji-Kerns

with an Introduction by Rashmi Sharma

WESTVIEW PRESS

Boulder • San Francisco • Oxford

Special thanks are owed to Mangla R. Oza for creating the mandala used on the cover and in the book.

Published in 1995 in the United States of America by Westview Press, Inc., 5500 Central Avenue, Boulder, Colorado 80301-2877, and in the United Kingdom by Westview Press, 12 Hid's Copse Road, Cumnor Hill, Oxford OX2 9JJ

A CIP record for this book is available from the Library of Congress
ISBN 0-8133-2379-7. ISBN 0-8133-2378-9 (pbk.)

Printed and bound in the United States of America

The paper used in this publication meets the requirements
of the American National Standard for Permanence of Paper
for Printed Library Materials Z39.48-1984.

10   9   8   7   6   5   4   3   2   1

This book is dedicated to:

The South Asian American writers whose voices
are heard in this anthology

The many South Asian American writers who
submitted works that we could not include
because of space and focus

Members of the Advisory Board for *Living in America:
Poetry and Fiction by South Asian American Writers*:
Chitra Divakaruni, Pia Ganguly, Ashok Jethanandi,
Arvind Kumar, Kashinath Pakrasi, Javaid Qazi,
Rashmi Sharma, and Neera Kuckreja Sohoni

Charles Kerns for his constant encouragement and support,
for assuring me that it is usually the computer that
is at fault when carefully saved manuscripts disappear,
and for retrieving the lost manuscripts

Contents

Contents   ix

Acknowledgments

I have received invaluable assistance in the course of compiling this anthology. I wish to acknowledge with gratitude: Arvind Kumar, editor of *India Currents Magazine* for setting up the first meeting to discuss this anthology and for having enough faith in me to nominate me as the editor! The members of the Advisory Board for their help in the final selection of works for this anthology and their constant support and advice; Susan McEachern, Senior Editor, Westview Press, for her enthusiasm for this project, her wise counsel, and her appreciation of South Asian American literature; Susan McEachern's assistants, Jon Brooks and Jennifer Barrett, for their help; Libby Barstow, Senior Production Editor, Westview Press, for guiding me, once again, through the intricacies of putting together a book; Emilie Buchwald, Milkweed Editions, and Karen Braziler, Persea Books, for their advice and support during the initial stages of the project; Eric Gotfrid of Dimensional Computer and Bill Daniels and Darin Raffaelli of Mail Boxes Etc., without whom the works in this anthology would not have been typed, FAXed, Xeroxed, and mailed off to contributors, readers, and Westview Press.

Roshni Rustomji-Kerns

Credits

South Asian Literature (University of Michigan), 21 (Winter-Spring 1986). Reprinted by permission of the author.

The selection on p. 235 is an excerpt from *An American Brat* by Bapsi Sidhwa (Milkweed Editions, 1993). Copyright © 1993 by Bapsi Sidhwa. Reprinted with permission from Milkweed Editions.

Living in America

Introduction

Roshni Rustomji-Kerns

Life in the United States and Canada. Coming to America as an immigrant, an expatriate, or a refugee from South Asia.[1] Being born in America into a family of South Asian background. Experiencing birth, relationships, death in America. Studying and working in America. Encountering memories of South Asia in America. Weaving the memories and the realities of the South Asian diaspora across continents and centuries into the fabric of American life. And, of course, writing in America. These form the focus of this anthology, *Living in America: Poetry and Fiction by South Asian American Writers*. Although works by some well-known, widely read South Asian American writers are included, the majority of the works presented in this anthology are by new and emerging authors and by authors whose works have not yet gained an audience beyond the world of scholars and enthusiastic readers of South Asian American literature. Most of the works are published here for the first time and were written in English; others were written in America in a South Asian language such as Gujarati, Hindi, or Urdu and translated into English.

As the accompanying essay by Rashmi Sharma points out, the history of South Asians in America begins before the twentieth century. To place this anthology within the context of South Asian American literature, we might argue that the history of South Asian American literature should be traced back to the oral histories and stories and to the diary and journal entries of the earliest South Asian immigrants and expatriates in America. Unfortunately, these are not always easily available.[2] The poems and songs published in the Gadar Party (the Party of Revolt) weekly newspaper were most probably the first systematically published and widely

read literary works by South Asians in America. The Gadar Party was
founded in San Francisco in 1913 by people from the subcontinent of
India living in America who were actively involved in the independence
struggle being waged in India against the British colonizers. Nand Kaur
Singh, who came from the Punjab to the United States in the 1920s, still
recites some of the poems and songs of the Gadar Party for her children,
her grandchildren, and her great-grandchildren in California.[3] A list of
well-established and influential twentieth-century writers of South Asian
descent living in America could begin with the names of writers such as
Ved Mehta and Santha Rama Rau, followed by Meena Alexander, Agha
Shahid Ali, G. S. Sharat Chandra, Rienzi Crusz, Anita Desai, Chitra
Divakaruni, Zulfikar Ghose, Amitav Ghosh, Bharati Mukherjee, Uma
Parameswaran, Raja Rao, Sara Suleri, Vikram Seth, Bapsi Sidhwa and
Shashi Tharoor.[4] In and with this anthology we gratefully acknowledge
the important contributions and influences of these and other South Asian
American writers. Acknowledgment is also due to the writers of South
Asian descent whose writings about living in America, bringing South
Asia to America, still lie hidden in personal journals, diaries, letters,
unpublished stories, poems, essays, and memoirs. We recognize as well
the women and men of our communities who have continued to tell their
stories and to sing their songs. The publication of this anthology, with its
specific focus, is an introduction to the richness and the diversity of South
Asian American literary voices. Hopefully, the anthology will encourage
writers of South Asian descent living in the Americas to make their voices
heard as often and in as wide an arena of literature as possible.

A number of the works in *Living in America* can be read as dealing
with familiar themes, presented in recognizable literary styles. Not to
explore these works further in order to understand and appreciate the
unique cultural and historical literary backgrounds, influences, and traditions embedded in them would be a disservice to the authors and readers alike. But to read these works as "merely ethnic" or as "ethnic docu-
mentaries," to keep them somehow apart from our serious readings and
discussions of twentieth–century American literature, would be shortsighted. After all, any literature can be read as ethnic literature. But it is
usually only the dominant, dominating, mainstream literatures in most
cultures, especially in America, that escape this designation as well as the
limitations and the marginalization it often signifies for readers and crit-
ics not conversant with or interested in the cultures and histories of specific nondominant, nonmainstream literatures.

South Asian American literature, like the literatures of the other non-
dominating ethnic, racial, or cultural groups in America, contributes to
as well as complicates and changes the complexion, the traditions, and
the mythologies of American literature. The writers included in this

anthology certainly show the influences of Western literature and the Western literary traditions, especially as they exist in world literature written in English. But as they recreate in their writings the visions of their particular experiences of America, they bring their own very diverse South Asian cultural voices to the traditions and expectations of Euro-American literature. Some South Asian American writings can be woven into the traditionally accepted tapestry of American literature without disturbing the tapestry very much. Other writings disturb this tapestry. To some extent they may even deliberately de-form the tapestry by refusing to follow the expected patterns of language and writing and by destroying the accepted mythologies that have surrounded "traditional" American literature. But by their very presence, these voices participate in the ongoing process of re-forming twentieth-century American litera- ture to reflect twentieth-century life and society in the Americas. To look at these aspects of South Asian American literature and to hear the first- and second-generation voices that do not always fit the academic norms of "correct" or "standard" English does not "marginalize," "deAmericanize," or "exoticize" this literature.[5] On the contrary, it stress- es the diversity of literary and cultural traditions and voices of American literature that go beyond a Eurocentric American literature. A Eurocentric literature that of course carries within itself its own diversity of European traditions and history.

The South Asian voices that are gradually becoming an intrinsic part of American literature have a long and distinguished literary history. Echoes and influences from the classical and folk literatures of South Asia, from South Asian Islamic literature, and from the flourishing tradi- tions of South Asian oral literature appear in the writings of South Asian Americans whether or not they are conscious of the connections. In this volume, for example, works such as Moazzam Sheikh's "Kissing The Holy Land," Ranbir Sidhu's "Border Song," and Jyotsna Sanzgiri's "Azalea" reflect the aesthetic traditions of classical Sanskrit *Kavya* (highly ornamented court poetry) with its insistence on the importance of *rasas* (the construction of emotions, moods, and sentiments) and its recogni- tion of the fluidity of form and style, the lack of rigid boundaries between literary genres. The South Asian Islamic traditions of poetic prose and of intensely lyrical poetry that explore abstract ideas and ideals and portray the yearning for lost homes and lovers are revealed in works such as Naseem Hines's "The Dew and the Moon," Tahira Naqvi's "All Is Not Lost," and Agha Shahid Ali's "I See Chile in My Rearview Mirror." The South Asian cadences of oral literature, the poet-story- teller's voice, can be heard in G. S. Sharat Chandra's "India Association Plans a Newsletter," Rajesh Oza's "Dr. Mango and Johnny Fish," Rajini Srikanth's "You Live on Your Side," Tahira Naqvi's "All Is Not Lost,"

Uma Parameswaran's "Darkest Before Dawn," Rashmi Sharma's "What's in a Name?", and Neera Sohoni's "Close Encounter." Darius Cooper's "I Have Been Offered My Country's Begging Bowl Again," Saleem Peeradina's "Reflections on the Other," Boman Desai's "This Thicket," Rienzi Crusz's "Conversation with God about my present whereabouts," Litu Kabir's "The Return," and Meena Alexander's "Mandala" are reminders of the classical and folk epics and romances of South Asia in which the recitation of poetry and the narration of stories are very quickly transformed into philosophical discussions.

An acute awareness of time and space pervades much of South Asian American literature. The landscapes and histories of Africa, the Americas, Asia, and Europe appear in the works of writers of South Asian descent who live and write in Canada and the United States. And at this point of South Asian American literary history, the choice of locale—the physical, geographical, and cultural landscapes that form the backgrounds and contexts of works by most of these authors—generally falls into what can be termed four categories. In the first category are works set in Asia and about Asia without any overt references to the writers' lives in America. In the second category are writings about protagonists (real or fictionalized) who are returning from America to South Asia as visitors or residents. Works in the third category feature South Asian protagonists' lives in America. And in the fourth category are writings in which South Asian American authors portray landscapes, characters, experiences, and events with no reference to Asia or the Asian experience in America.

The literature that falls into the first category reminds us as South Asian Americans and our audience of where we came from and the experiences and landscapes that we carry with us regardless of where we choose to live and write. Works such as Rohinton Mistry's *Swimming Lessons and Other Stories from Firozsha Baag* (1989), Bapsi Sidhwa's *Cracking India* (1993), Meena Alexander's *House of a Thousand Doors* (1988), and Gita Mehta's *A River Sutra* (1993) fall into this category. Writings in the second category often present the confusion, bewilderment, and frustration of realizing that memories of the motherland seldom mesh with reality when South Asians return to South Asia from America or Europe. This category would include Santha Rama Rau's *Home to India* (1945) and Bharati Mukherjee's *The Tiger's Daughter* (1972). In this literature a process of remembering seems to begin, an attempt to put together the fragments of memories and of the present situation that make up both areas of the world, both homes. In the third category the re-membering continues and is used to explore ourselves, our lives, and the lives of others around us in America. Bharati Mukherjee's *The Middleman and Other Stories* (1988), M. G. Vassanji's *No New Land* (1992), and most of the works in this anthology fit into this category. In the fourth category writers of South Asian descent living in America use their prerogative as writers to select any landscape, character, experience, and event they wish to, without any reference to South Asia or South Asian America, for their works. Zulfikar Ghose's "Brazilian trilogy," which begins with *The Incredible Brazilian: The Native* (1982), is one of the best examples of this category. And of course there are works such as Amitav Ghosh's *In an Antique Land: History in the Guise of a Traveler's Tale* (1992) and Suniti Namjoshi's *Feminist Fables* (1984), which can be placed in more than one of the categories selected for this discussion of South Asian American literature.

The title of this anthology reflects the focus of this particular collection of works by South Asian American writers. Members of the advisory board and I have selected writings mainly from the third and fourth categories because we felt that at this time of discussion and debate within the South Asian American communities regarding their place, their identities, and their roles in the multicultural societies of the United States and Canada, it is important to present the views of and from the Americas by writers of South Asian descent. The "American" in the title is definitely not restricted to residents of the United States. It refers to writers from the continent of North America, mainly Canada and the United States. Although Central and South America appear in some of the works, the writers of South Asian descent who submitted their works for this anthology live and work for the most part in North America, as residents of Canada or the United States.

While weaving literary and cultural traditions from South Asia into twentieth-century American literature, the writers of the South Asian diaspora also bring into American literature the literary, political, historical, and socioeconomic issues they carry with them as they travel across continents and cultures. As the introductory headnotes to the individual pieces in this anthology show, many of these writers and their families have gone through multiple migrations and diasporas. South Asian American literature is therefore also an important part of the broader literature of twentieth-century diasporas. And as South Asian American literature becomes recognized as an integral part of American literature, it in turn actively involves American literature in the complex and rich international literature of the diasporas of this century.

Notes

1. According to current geopolitical and academic terms, South Asia includes Bangladesh, India, the Maldive Islands, Nepal, Pakistan, Sri Lanka, and, increasingly, Afghanistan and Myanmar. The use of *South Asia* as a descriptive designation for a political and cultural identity is vigorously debated and discussed

within the various communities that fall under this rubric. See the essay by Naheed Islam, "In The Belly Of The Multicultural Beast I Am Named South Asian" in *Our Feet Walk the Sky: Women of the South Asian Diaspora*, edited by The Women of the South Asian Descent Collective (San Francisco: Aunt Lute Books, 1993). The members of the advisory board for *Living in America*, a number of the contributors to this anthology who also helped in locating writers, other members of the South Asian American community, and I tried to reach as diverse a population of South Asian American writers as possible to request them to contribute to the anthology. We are aware that the anthology is still not as equally representative of the different South Asian cultures and communities in the Americas as we had hoped. But we feel that we have been successful in presenting an example of the range and the diversity of voices of South Asian American writers.

It is important constantly to keep in mind that neither South Asians nor South Asian Americans are a homogenized, "unicultural" people. As this anthology reveals, South Asians in America reflect the profoundly different cultures, histories, languages, literatures, religions, philosophies, customs, and socioeconomic backgrounds of the people, communities, and countries of South Asia.

2. Some sources for South Asian American articles, essays, and interviews are included in Jane Singh, ed., *South Asians in North America: An Annotated and Selected Bibliography* (Berkeley: Center for South and Southeast Asia Studies, University of California, 1988). The socioeconomic struggles of a South Asian family in America during the early years of this century are narrated in Kartar Dhillon's "The Parrot's Beak" in *Making Waves: An Anthology of Writings by and About Asian American Women*, edited by Asian Women United of California (Boston: Beacon Press, 1989).

3. See Jane Singh, "Interview With Nand Kaur Singh: Gadar Indian Nationalist Poetry In America" in Miriam Cooke and Roshni Rustomji-Kerns, eds., *Blood into Ink: South Asian and Middle Eastern Women Write War* (Boulder, Colo.: Westview Press, 1994).

4. See Appendix B for a bibliography of selected authors and works.

5. See the introduction in Sau-ling Cynthia Wong's *Reading Asian American Literature: From Necessity to Extravagance* (Princeton: Princeton University Press, 1993).

Appendix A

In order to make the works in this volume more accessible to readers and to avoid rigid categorization of the works, we have organized the anthology into two parts, Poetry and Fiction. The works appear according to the alphabetical order of the authors' names. One of the images that emerges from this collection is that of the circular mandala. The works that evolve around individual experiences move outward to include relationships with family and then to other members of the South Asian American communities, expand to the larger arena of non–South Asian communities in America and other communities and cultures of the world, and then seem to reach out to spheres not always dominated by familiar human beings. And while the pattern moves outward to larger circles of concerns, characters, and landscapes, it also constantly calls attention to the center, the stories and poems that deal with a specific individual's experience and voice in America. It is a pattern difficult to show in a table of contents. But in the process of putting together the anthology, it also became apparent to members of the advisory board and the editor that many of the selections could be organized by certain central issues, themes, and concerns for readers who may be interested in reading and studying the works according to categories. The following are some of the categories and the works that fall into them. Many of the works belong in more than one category.

I. Chronology

First Impressions
Chitra Divakaruni, "The Founding of Yuba City"
Ved Mehta, selection from *Sound-Shadows of the New World*
Moazzam Sheikh, "Kissing the Holy Land"
Bapsi Sidhwa, selection from *An American Brat*

Surviving: The First Generation
Qiron Adhikary, "Nosey Nakshitka's Adventures in America"
Agha Shahid Ali, "Résumé"
G. S. Sharat Chandra, "India Association Plans a Newsletter"
Rienzi Crusz, "Conversations with God about my present whereabouts"
Chitra Divakaruni, "Yuba City Wedding"
Naseem A. Hines, "The Dew and the Moon"
Tara Menon, "The Perfect Host"
Tahira Naqvi, "All Is Not Lost"
Kirin Narayan, selections from *Love, Stars, and All That*
Usha Nilsson, "What a Big Lie"
Saleem Peeradina, "Reflections on the Other"
Javaid Qazi, "The Laid-off Man"
Sarita Sarvate, "Law of Averages"
Neila C. Seshachari, "The Bride Comes Home"
Rashmi Sharma, "What's in a Name?"
Ranbir Sidhu, "Border Song"
Neera Kuckreja Sohoni, "Close Encounter"
Neera Kuckreja Sohoni, "De-privileging Liberty"

Continuation: The Multiple Generations
Meena Alexander, selection from *Fault Lines*
Darius Cooper, "I Have Been Offered My Country's Begging Bowl Again"
Lakshmi Gill, "The Student Teacher"
Anuradha Gupta, "Crystal Quince"
Minal Hajratwala, "Twenty Years After I Grew into Your Lives"
Anu Mannar, "You can't give God a granola bar"
Diane S. Mehta, "The History of Language"
Tahira Naqvi, "All Is Not Lost"

Rajesh C. Oza, "Dr. Mango and Johnny Fish"
Uma Parameswaran, "Darkest Before Dawn"
Javaid Qazi, "The Laid-off Man"
Jyotsna Sanzgiri, "Requiem"
Sarita Sarvate, "The Law of Averages"
Neila C. Seshachari, "The Bride Comes Home"
Jyotsan Sreenivasan, "The Peacock's Mirrored Eyes"
Rajini Srikanth, "You Live on Your Side"

Appendix B

Anthologies and collections of South Asian American Literature:

Aziz, Nurjehan, ed. *Her Mother's Ashes and Other Stories by South Asian Women in Canada and the United States.* Toronto: Toronto South Asia Review Publications, 1994.

Katrak, Ketu H., and R. Radhakrishna, eds. *Desh-Videsh: South Asian Expatriate Writing and Art.* Special issue of *Massachusetts Review* 29, no. 4 (winter 1988-1989).

McGifford, Diane, ed. *The Geography of Voice: Canadian Literature of the South Asian Diaspora.* Toronto: Toronto South Asia Review Publications, 1992.

Mukherjee, Bharati, and Ranu Vanikar, eds. *The Literary Review: Writers of the Indian Commonwealth* 29, no. 4 (summer 1986).

Ratti, Rakesh, ed. *A Lotus of Another Color: An Unfolding of the South Asian Gay and Lesbian Experience.* Boston: Alyson Publications, 1993.

Rustomji, Roshni, ed. *South Asian Women Writers: The Immigrant Experience.* Special issue of *Journal of South Asian Literature* 21, no. 1 (winter-spring 1986).

Vassanji, M. G. *A Meeting of Streams: South Asian Canadian Literature.* Toronto: Toronto South Asia Review Publications, 1985.

The Women of South Asian Descent Collective, eds. *Our Feet Walk the Sky: Women of the South Asian Diaspora.* San Francisco: Aunt Lute Books, 1993.

The following two volumes are an excellent source of information on South Asian American writers:

Nelson, Emmanuel S., ed. *Reworlding: The Literature of the Indian Diaspora* New York: Greenwood Press, 1992.

————. *Writers of the Indian Diaspora: A Bio-Bibliographical Critical Sourcebook.* Westport, Conn.: Greenwood Press, 1993.

Journals and magazines such as those listed below consistently include South Asian American fiction and poetry:

India Currents Magazine (San Jose, California)
Journal of South Asian Literature (Michigan State University, East Lansing)
Toronto Review of Contemporary Writing Abroad (Toronto South Asia Review Publications)

Crossing the Dark Waters

Rashmi Sharma

This introductory segment is written from the immigrant's perspective. Recognizing that there is no dearth of academic reports and fiction on the subject, written primarily from an American perspective, few Americans have read or heard the voices of those struggling with questions of assimilation. Yet these struggles around what it means to be an American rejuvenate the dream that is this country.

For immigrants, the transition to becoming a U.S. citizen is made up of poignant, individual crises of identity in varying degrees. Each struggle to become American is the personal life of an individual—therefore this personalized historical perspective on history as "his-story" and "her-story" that are the lives of some of the "newer" Americans.

The old paradigm that the East is the East, the West is the West, with no possibility of the two meeting, is challenged by the stories of these immigrants from South Asia.

First, a perspective on immigration to North America from South Asia. Living in America. As an immigrant. As a visible minority that does not belong to the mainstream in religion, language, food, ethnicity, or culture. A daunting prospect, but I knew not the obstacles before I came. So much promise, yet such shrill acrimony directed at me from those seeking a scapegoat for their problems. Will I ever be part of that which I was not born into, this United States of America, this land that was "made for you and me"?

I am told that I can. That I have something of value to contribute. That viewing the United States through the less cynical eyes of the "newer" Americans is refreshing and of value. But who will listen to our sometimes inadequate words in our nonnative language of American English?

True, the experiences of those who have "crossed the dark waters," the *kālā pāni* of Indian lore, are of interest to all of society, since such assimilation (or lack of it) is also a reflection of what kind of a society the United States has become. "Who am I" through immigrant eyes parallels "who we want to be" as a society; and both, measured against the backdrop of what it is to be an American, will help us all—immigrant and nonimmigrant alike—to deal with who we are, and what we want to be.

As one observer aptly notes, "Telescoped as it was into a few years, the Indian migration to North America and the response of various groups to it provide a case study of immense importance, in which one can see the clash of interests of the employer, immigrant worker, native worker, official, and politician gradually evolving into public policy."[1]

Often, we are all lumped together en masse as "aliens," "foreigners" from India. Should I remind people that the term *India* refers not only to the geopolitical modern nation but to the region historically? That the name *India* is itself a foreign name given to the colonial and postcolonial nation; and that in about four thousand years of known history of the nation there are only five times that there has been a single, unified "nation" on the subcontinent? And that the modern nation of India alone has as much diversity in language, culture, religion, and ethnicity as does all of Europe?

Even in attempting to correct a wrong (as, for instance, in education) by including the culture and history of about a sixth of the world's population, we select inadequate educational curriculum materials representing my heritage and history. Should I speak up or be subserviently grateful for mere inclusion? Am I no more than the quintessential residue of colonialism, forever relegated to the backseat of the bus, watching helplessly in silence while others decide how to define my history, culture, and values? But I am in the "New," not "Old," world. Surely I, too, have a chance at freedom, dignity, equality, and my own voice?

Such discussions are not new to any group of immigrants. Yet, more than that of other groups, perhaps, immigration from South Asia is anything but typical. It defies neat statistical tables and criteria. Take, for instance, the case of this composite family that came to the United States: The father was born in Mandalay in 1917, while it was still part of British India, but that later became Burma and is now Myanmar; one child was born to this man in 1938 in Bombay, before India's independence in 1947, and the other child was born in Karachi in 1948, after Karachi became part of the new nation of Pakistan in 1947. In the

United States these three persons, from the same family, would be classified in three separate categories by nationality based on place of
birth—the father would be classified as Burmese, the older child as
Indian, and the younger child as Pakistani.

To ask the next generation of the family in the United States to pick
one single country of origin for affiliation, by checking one box on a
form, is inadequate, at best. The map of South Asia as drawn by the West
may be fine for an atlas, but this Western method of classification, and
somewhat arbitrary divisions imposed from the outside, do not take into
account the lives of individuals such as the composite family discussed
above. When it comes to self-identity issues, neat boundary lines drawn
on paper in colonial times seem inhumanly constrictive.

Based on individual background, people from South Asia are very different. These differences stem from ethnicity mired in race, caste, class,
economic background, complicated by urban or rural, intellectual or working class, age, religious affiliation, and a host of other factors. People from
urban backgrounds are grounded in a reality different from that of people
from the rural areas of the subcontinent. The growing middle class perceives its separate identity based in their unique worldviews as Muslims,
Hindus, Sikhs or Jains, Parsis, Christians, Jews, and so on. Add to this their
individual personal histories as immigrants to the United States, and the
result is a dizzying myriad of diverse images of these new Americans.
Why then are we all labeled homogeneously as South Asians?

Based on gender alone, there emerge a multitude of images. Self-identity is very different for men and women: While many men see their self-
worth or self-esteem primarily in the workplace, ratified by a paycheck, the
issue is not as simple for women. Women who primarily stay at home find
themselves cut off from the extended-family, *jati*, and other social support
systems they grew up with; but life is, apart from the changed setting, still
centered around husband, home, and children. But for those women who
have entered the work force, by choice or otherwise, the "second shift"
adds more than the usual second burden: There is an increased awareness
of the differences between traditional Indian and Western value systems.

Such issues of identity for South Asian women are much deeper than
mere choice between Western and Asian clothes, or hours spent in the
kitchen over the preparation of traditional foods, or the language spoken
at home. It is part of the push and pull between East and West, between
the self-denial and sacrifice of all the Sitas and Savitris[2] from the East,
who find themselves living in a society that values individual fulfillment
and believes in the individual pursuit of happiness. Such identity crises
can often reach schizophrenic proportions, although we sometimes pretend we don't see this painful attempt at balance by women between their
parents' values and those of the society in which they live now.

Further, when multigenerational families (patterned after the traditional family unit in India) occur here, we see women, as primary caregivers, perform an even more complicated tightrope act, often with tragic loss of self-identity. Elderly parents, equally vulnerable to this feeling of loss of family and community, pull women in one direction, while at the same time, their children pull women in the opposite direction! At both ends of the age spectrum women find themselves pulled in opposite directions: from elders who seek refuge in everything Indian, to their young children, born in the United States, struggling to hide their Indianness with a loud embrace of everything overtly American.

Accuracy and self-identity issues of the people from the Indian subcontinent were moot academic questions, probably, while South Asians remained in South Asia. However, once South Asians become part of the human family—from the many corners of the globe—that is now the United States of America, accuracy of the history of this group of Americans is no longer irrelevant. We need to move beyond looking at South Asia only in esoteric doctoral dissertations and romanticized tourist posters.

To gain an understanding of South Asian Americans, one has to look beyond the shell of sanitized essays and fictionalized accounts written by those wishing to cash in on yet another fleeting fad in the public eye of mainstream America. The writing of South Asian Americans themselves may be of help.

Our life experiences, whether in our native homes or in our adopted homes, do not easily fit the labels and categories that Western society places on our Eastern experience and identity. Even the assigned boxes of spaces for name on simple forms may not fit a traditional name. When they say "last name" at the end of the line for name, what do I do if my family name comes first?

Distinction is sometimes made between economic migrants and those who came to North America for more than financial gain. This distinction is not quite clear in U.S. history itself, and often the two goals did and do overlap. In the context of South Asian immigration to America, however, this distinction is quite valid: Economic migrants keep to themselves, avoid assimilation, and put up with discrimination in their attempt to earn enough money. In retirement, they return to their own community. Their touchstone, while "abroad" or in India, remains their own culture and values of their native country. Although it is seldom the only cause, this aloofness sometimes leads to discrimination and attacks on South Asians, as in the case of "Dot Busters" in New Jersey, where women wearing a "dot" (*bindi*) on their foreheads have become targets of violence.

Those of us who seek more than economic freedom in the United

States are forced to come to terms with our own changing identity in the context of the larger, fluid, and changing picture of what it means to be an American and to be included in the participatory democracy that is the United States.

We need to remember that economic hardship has always evoked antiimmigrant sentiment, for every new group. As South Asian immigrants, we have often stood out among Americans with our distinctive dress, culture, religion, and food. We have been easily visible targets for those wishing to find "foreign" scapegoats. We have felt this bias in being, at best, shut out of the society in which we live. This alienation often occurs not just from our old homes but in our new homeland, for legal "Aliens" and for naturalized citizens alike.

This feeling of not quite belonging to society as a full participant also cuts across all income levels. Outside of work, the struggling student and the wealthy M.D., female or male, elderly or young equally feel a sense of disconnection from mainstream America. Such transplantation shock for immigrants reaches across all age groups, socioeconomic distinctions, and gender. Sociologists and historians tell us that migration, since time immemorial, has meant movement of people for greener pastures. This displacement has probably always extracted an emotional price from all those who have moved, voluntarily or otherwise.

For South Asians, society in both our new and old homes is based on an agrarian or an industrial model, yet many of us are functioning (with varying degrees of success) in the Information Age. It is hard enough when these changes occur from one generation to the next; in the case of the "newer" Americans of South Asian descent we see this massive, daunting leap occurring within the span of a single generation.

Placing ourselves in the historical context of immigration, we see that at least since 1790 the United States has had a legal, organized system of immigration. True, it is not a perfect system, and in its origins it certainly was unashamedly racist—a product of its time and history. Thus, despite the unprecedented and enviable ideals of the framers of this nation's Constitution, until 1965 the Federal Immigration Law reserved naturalization, citizenship, and thus equality for people of the "white" race.

American trading ships had first reached India in 1784, and there was some trade between the two countries (not to mention a few other interesting connections such as the appointment of the same British general Charles Cornwallis, who was defeated in the American Revolution, to a post in India to flex his power for the benefit of the Empire). A few Parsi and other Indian merchants were apparently successful as traders in the United States in the nineteenth century, but merchants were not perceived as a threat in the same way that workers were, and their experiences doubtless were different from those of less affluent immigrants;

they certainly did not face the same discrimination as the turbaned Indian laborers and farmworkers.

For the most part, despite the fashion of naming girls "India," planting crepe myrtles from India in the American South, and using terms such as *Boston Brahmin*; despite the familiarity of intellectuals, such as Walt Whitman, Ralph Waldo Emerson, and Henry David Thoreau, with Indian philosophy, the spread of Theosophy, and the 1893 World Parliament of Religions (where Swami Vivekananda spoke eloquently on Hinduism), Americans were really not familiar with Indians of India in the nineteenth century.

Indian goods such as calico, lacquer, and spices were well known and used, but workers from India were still strangers to be frowned upon and kept out of the United States. Sentiments such as those expressed by Ulysses S. Grant when he visited India in 1878, that there was no despotism more absolute than that of the government of India, were not widely echoed in the United States. Although India and North America were subservient to the same colonial master at one time, the freedom sought by Americans was (it would seem) merely for themselves. Application of the same principles of freedom and equality did not extend to other subjects of the British.

Keep in mind that at this time in the history of the world, especially in European reality, colonialism by Europeans was alive and flourishing. India was part of the British Empire. Despite the United States' independence, the groups in power in the United States remained closely allied with the rulers of the European nations whose people had been the original colonists in North America.

The typical tactic of the British colonists was to keep the local people from dispossessing the outnumbered masters by using Gurkhas, Punjabis, and Sikhs to maintain security of their Empire in Asia and Africa. One ethnic group was used to manage and control another ethnic group within the Empire.[3]

Once the practice of slavery had been abolished by Britain in 1834, this gap in demand for labor and lower-level managers was sometimes filled by Indian "indentured servants" who were "imported" from India to colonial plantations in Guyana, Mauritius, Trinidad, Fiji, and South Africa. Most Americans were like Theodore Roosevelt, who had no compunctions about Imperialism, British or American. There was nothing remarkable, at that time, about Teddy Roosevelt, who in the presidential campaign of 1900 asserted the need to keep the West free of Asians, or about the many newspaper editorials (in papers such as the San Francisco *Chronicle*) bemoaning the presence of and warning against the turbaned "yellow blight" of the "inferior, brown Caucasian" from Asia.

In the Indian subcontinent, in the early 1900s, famine, drought, and epidemics caused shifts in society. Indians were starting to look for change ranging from landownership to a greater share in their own government. Many Indians had joined the British Armed Services, and went to the various far-flung corners of the Empire in service to the British Crown, breaking the taboo about "crossing the dark waters."[4]

Increasingly smaller landholdings also led to migration from India, particularly from the Punjab, where caste and other religious strictures were not as deeply embedded as they were in other parts of India.

Except as slaves and indentured servants or as curiosities to exhibit at fairs, few Indians came to the United States before 1906. The 1900 U.S. census reported 2,050 people from India. (See Table 1 for U.S. census reports.)

The story of an early immigrant to the United States perhaps began in the Punjab, in a village in the Doaba region of Jullundur. On a cart or tonga, he traveled to the nearest train station, where he said goodbye to his young wife, kids, and family. He boarded a small, slow, local train to a larger train junction such as Jullundur; there he transferred to another train for the long ride to Delhi. Then came another transfer to a Howrah-bound train for Calcutta, which took almost twice as long as the train trip to Delhi from the Punjab. By now he had been on the road for about a week. In the bustling city of Calcutta, he spent a small fortune of about 35 rupees on a boat ticket. He boarded the next steamer bound from Calcutta for Hong Kong. There, after a short rest at the Hong Kong Sikh *Gurdwara*, or if lucky, with friends of friends, or relatives of relatives, he spent another fortune, about $50 in gold, for steerage to Vancouver aboard a Japanese or Canadian boat. After this steamer heaved its way across the vast Pacific Ocean and reached port on the American continent, he began the real journey of finding his way in the foreign land, full of people who looked upon him, at best, as an unwelcome guest.

This journey took him to wherever work was possible. For safety as well as to keep from feeling totally alienated, he probably met up with and became a part of a small group of Indian workers. Typically, he went from the sawmills and timber industry in Washington State, to railroad construction jobs in northern California, and then became a migrant farmworker in the central valley farms of California, eventually saving enough money to become a farmer in California.

Unless he married a similarly complexioned woman, often a Mexican immigrant, his lonely sojourn was not eased by the presence of a wife or children, since even if he had been able to afford to pay for their travel and other expenses, U.S. law prevented them from entering the country. If, by any stretch of the imagination, a family overcame all these barriers, there was still the hurdle of literacy tests and physical examinations.

Most first-generation immigrants to North America have faced the same kind of discrimination as did and still do people from South Asia.

TABLE 1 Immigration to the United States from India, by year[a]

	Number of Immigrants	
1820	1	
1821–1830	8	
1831–1840	39	
1841–1850	36	
1851–1860	43	
1861–1870	69	
1871–1880	163	
1881–1890	269	
1891–1900	68	
1901–1910	4,713	
1911–1920	2,082	
1921–1930	1,886	
1931–1940	496	
1941–1950	1,761	from India; 20 from Pakistan
1951–1960	1,973	from India; 929 from Pakistan
1961–1965[b]	2,602	from India; 846 from Pakistan
1966–1970	27,859	from India; 4,045 from Pakistan.

[a]Until 1947 "India" included the areas that are now Pakistan and Bangladesh.

[b]In 1965 U.S. immigration laws were reformed to do away with preferences for Europeans and whites.

Indians were British subjects, a fact that complicated their legal standing. Further, in addition to the complications mentioned earlier, the category "Indian" refers to people born in "India," whether of European, Indian, or mixed ancestry. Numerous "Indians" who have come to the United States and Canada via East Africa, Fiji, and so on and who have also retained their Indian culture and lifestyle even though they gave up their Indian passports have felt the brunt of discrimination against Indians as much as any person born on the subcontinent. The point I would like to make here is that these statistics are imperfect indicators. The impact of Indians in the United States is not completely understood within the limited Western scientific methodologies of classification and compartmentalized enumeration. India, as ever, defies neat, mechanistic categorization!

In the Northwest lumber town of Bellingham at the turn of the century, union workers drove out Indian workers and the "turbaned coolies" who had helped construct the railroad in the Northwest and the Panama Canal. The migrant Indian farmworkers in California were subjected to

"No Japs or Hindoos" on signs in windows of stores and homes during World War II. Nor has such racism completely disappeared, as we see from the evidence of the recent "Dot Busters" in New Jersey or less overt cases such as an underemployed Silicon Valley engineer.

History cannot be denied. The Federal Immigration Law of 1790 reserved U.S. citizenship for "whites" only. The Chinese Exclusion Act was passed in 1882, to keep out Asians. In 1907 an Asian Exclusion League was formed. The head tax on Asian immigrants to the United States went from $50 a head in 1885 to $500 in 1903. The Indian Nobel laureate Rabindranath Tagore commented, when he faced similar road-blocks before being allowed to enter the United States for a lecture tour, that even Jesus Christ would not be allowed to enter the United States under existing conditions, because not only was he poor, he was also Asian.

In 1910 the U.S. Supreme Court held that Indians were Caucasian and therefore could not be excluded from citizenship based on race. But in a reversal in 1923 the Supreme Court ruled that *white* did not refer to the Caucasian race but to the European landmass attached to Asia; there-fore Indians could not become U.S. citizens, and citizenships granted on the previous ruling were null and void. In 1924 Congress passed an act that denied entry to those who were ineligible for citizenship. These laws, combined with the 1920 California Alien Land Law prohibiting landownership by noncitizens, devastated the few Indian immigrants who had toiled through twelve- and fourteen-hour days of back-break-ing labor in the fields to earn a piece of the American dream. Between 1920 and 1940 about 3,000 Indians returned to India. The 1940 census showed 2,405 Indians in the United States, 60 percent of them in California and 65 percent in agriculture.

In 1965 Lyndon Johnson pushed through Congress legislation that changed the degree of European bias in immigration laws. The second wave of South Asian immigrants to the United States—the legal immi-grants in the first decade after immigration laws finally became free of racial and ethnic bias—were not the "huddled masses" but often highly skilled, educated, and not especially poor. This so-called brain drain (as if this immigration left South Asia bereft of any "brain power") from South Asia means that the economic status of these immigrants remains among the highest in the United States. Yet these "successful" immi-grants have also faced discrimination. The discrimination against them is based on skin color and their Asian background. And more attacks are made against the turbaned Sikhs, even though the Supreme Court ruled in 1994 that their turbans have the same significance for them as yarmulkes do for the Jew. And the myth of the "model" and the "well-off" minority placed on South Asian immigrants ignores the realities of the racial and class discriminations directed toward South Asian and other minority farmworkers and laborers.

As an immigrant from South Asia, I feel that we need to understand the real meaning of what it is to be American. The real grandeur of our adopted nation lies not in economic opportunity but in the ideals it was founded on, in the vision of the Bill of Rights. This grandeur is not static; as Jefferson pointed out, every generation has to learn and reaffirm the founding principles if this unique experiment in liberty is to survive. I agree with Daniel J. Boorstin's argument in *Hidden History* that we have been putting so much emphasis on the diversity of the peoples of America that we have forgotten the importance of community, of people's willingness to work together, in the building of the United States.

Yet some of us, including some "model" newer Americans, are not aware of the history of our adopted nation or the significance of the first sixteen words of the Bill of Rights, which provide the underpinning to the rest of our freedoms; much less do we know of a recent reaffirmation of and return to our "common compact" as expressed in the Williamsburg Charter, which says that "one of America's continuing needs is to develop, out of our differences, a common vision for the common good. . . ."[5] Instead of focusing on the invisible values that unify Americans, some have always found it easier to stay mired in our visible diversity, loudly claiming their "share," based in their minority status, irrespective of the common good of all.

A community of common good, based on common needs, building upon democratic principles, includes everyone, in all our diversity. The Bill of Rights protects the rights of the smallest minority, of the least popular persons, no less than those of the majority.

Many of us who are defined as minorities are still trying to grapple with the concept of reverse discrimination, and most understand that minority rights are for inclusion of those previously excluded. But that does not mean the denial of anyone else's rights. No matter what our ancestry, we all need to remember that this nation is the proud inheritor of a long American tradition of inclusion: Rhode Island was formed to accommodate the "riff-raff" deemed unfit for the Massachusetts Colony. In a democracy, we are perhaps always playing catchup with our grand ideals and vision.

Older societies had a monocultural stamp,[6] but what distinguishes American society is its unique idea of a new society forged not by the dictates of birth but by a unique establishment of the principles of unity in diversity, by shaping the principles of liberty and equality into a historically unprecedented new mold of a free society.

Yes, this model has its flaws, and our ideals are not always transformed into reality, but in this model of participatory democracy, none of us can sit on the sidelines, content to stay suspended in our Little Bombays and Little Delhis. If the principle of forging a society beyond one grounded in Old-World homogeneity is to flourish, every generation—certainly every newer American—needs to understand the history of this nation and contribute to it positively.

Thus, recent curriculum changes in education to extend the study of the history of humankind and civilizations to include non-Euro-American, nonwhite, non-Judeo-Christian cultures, despite many detractors, are laudable and worthwhile for both the majority and the minority communities. Just as inclusion of Jews, Roman Catholics, and Irish led to a strengthening, not destruction, of this nation, broadening the spectrum to include Asians and others will further benefit the country. Whatever dire predictions there may be, an expanded interpretation of who is an American will help, not harm, the United States.

Whether we, as South Asians turned Americans, sit by on the sidelines or participate in our communities is our choice. As immigrants we perceive very clearly that in our new homes, choice is the way of life. Without the safety net of our "homes" in India and the Indian community here, what choices are we going to make? They will not be simple.

As a new American I ask myself, How far do I assimilate? Should I keep quiet when well-meaning individuals refer to my clothes as my "costume"? Am I no more than a legal "alien"? After giving up my native citizenship and becoming American, how do I reconfigure my personality? Can I erase my sense of who I am? Am I forever trapped as an "Indo-American," a split personality, neither here nor there, incomplete and trapped in my partially metamorphosed state?

If my children feel more excited about Christmas and Thanksgiving than Diwali, have I been an inadequate parent?

Given all the rapid Westernization that is occurring in my birth-homeland of India itself, in forcing myself to stay Indian, am I creating some kind of an aberration of an "India" that exists only in history and in nostalgia?

Is there a "culture war" in the United States in which I am automatically included, despite no desire on my part to wage war on anyone?

Even if I can figure out who I am and what I want to become, what kind of a society am I becoming part of? I hear the questions sociologists and historians are asking: Have we lost a sense of who we are as a society?

Don't freedom and the idea of inalienable rights of each individual pose a contradiction to the idea of majority rule?

Is the metaphor of a "melting pot" preferable to that of a "salad bowl" or are both inaccurate and demeaning? Do we all have to fit into a homogenized American society? Is greater assimilation required of non-European, non-Christian immigrants than other groups in history?

Is it necessary for Americans to dress, act, and think a certain way? And what is that? Who should decide this process? What, after all, is a real "American"?

We are fortunate to be fulfilling a dream of equality, living in freedom to follow our individual pursuit of happiness, in a cultural spectrum beyond that which the country's founding fathers could have envisioned. Surely the best testimony to the ideal of the United States, despite all its faults, is that it can include all of humanity and allow a flowering of the best inalienable aspirations of people from anywhere.

People from the Indian subcontinent, or South Asia, historically adept at assimilation, find that living in America offers a new twist to living with people from different faiths and cultures. This time our experiences are based not on yet another invasion of South Asia but by our exit from the land of our birth. Will our crossing be successful?

Will spicing of American society from the real "Indies" that Columbus set out to "discover" prove too exotic and foreign, or will our *masālā* add to the whole?

Certainly, the spirit of America's frontier expansion is alive and well—even though we reached our physical boundaries generations ago. In a strange twist of finally acknowledging that, yes, the world is round, we find our constant westward frontier push is now leading us back to the East, across the Pacific! Not merely in trade, but in values and worldviews as well. This is a decided shift in the underlying paradigm of What is American.

Notes

1. Joan M. Jensen, *Passage from India* (New Haven: Yale University Press, 1988), 1.

2. Sita and Savitri are two well-known women from ancient Indian literature. In the Sanskrit epic-romance, the *Ramayana*, Sita follows her husband, Prince Rama, into a fourteen-year exile, into the forest. Savitri is one of the most complex women protagonists of the Sanskrit epic, the *Mahabharata*. She brings back her husband from death with her cunning use of command of language.

3. Since the War of Independence of 1857 (sometimes called the "mutiny" of 1857), diverse groups were used to control other groups within the Empire.

4. "Crossing the Dark Waters" was the original working title of this book and deserves a word of explanation. Over the centuries traditional Hindu society had become decadent to the point that migration was frowned upon, and elaborate schemes were devised to enforce this stricture. In his autobiography Mahatma Gandhi talks of how he had to be "purified" for having gone to study in England, for having crossed the barrier of the Dark Ocean Waters, the *kālā pāni*.

5. The Williamsburg Charter: A National Celebration and Reaffirmation of the First Amendment Religion Liberty Clauses (Fairfax, Virginia: First Liberty Institute at George Mason University, 1988.)

6. Strictly speaking, India is not a monocultural society. Even in the five times that there has been a unified nation of "India" in the region of modern South Asia, diversity—linguistic, racial, religious, and that based on caste and jati—has abounded. However, in that birth is the determining factor in defining who a person is, India, too, shares with Europe and all older societies a more monocultural stamp than does the United States.

Bibliography and References

Boorstin, Daniel. *Hidden History*. New York: Harper & Row, 1987.
Daniels, Roger. *Coming to America*. New York: HarperCollins, 1990.
Guiness, Os. *The American Hour*. New York: Free Press (Macmillan), 1993.
Hitchens, Christopher. *Blood, Class, and Nostalgia: Anglo American Ironies*. New York: Farrar, Straus & Giroux, 1990.
Jensen, Joan M. *Passage from India*. New Haven, Conn.: Yale University Press, 1988.
Takaki, Ronald. *Strangers from a Different Shore*. New York: Penguin, 1990.
———. *A Different Mirror*. Boston: Little, Brown, 1993.

Brief Chronology

| 1790 | The federal Immigration Law passes, reserving U.S. citizenship for "whites" only. |

1790   The federal Immigration Law passes, reserving U.S. citizenship for "whites" only.
1828   Ram Mohan Roy founds the *Brahmo Samaj* (a Hindu reform movement) in India.
1834   Slavery is abolished by Britain. A need for other forms of cheap labor surfaces. Indentured laborers from India recruited for the West Indies, Fiji, Kenya, South Africa, and other parts of the British Empire.
1835   English language is introduced as a medium of instruction in India. Emulation of British leads to education of status-conscious, privileged Indians to be educated in Britain. Such travel lifts the taboo against crossing the *kālā pāni*, or foreign travel.
1848 and 1849   Punjab finally is "won" by the British in India. Prince Ranjit Singh and is removed from India and raised at a safe distance in Britain with Queen Victoria's children.
1851   Half a dozen Indians march in the Fourth of July parade in Salem, Massachusetts.
1857   Indian War of Independence (the "Mutiny").
1858   East India Company is purchased by the Crown (paid for by Indians). All pretense of British intentions in India restricted to mere trade come to an end.
1865   Hawaiian Board of Immigration examines the possibility of recruiting laborers from "East Indies."

1868   Walt Whitman writes poem "Passage to India."

1870s   Singh Sabhas start in the Punjab with a view to cementing Sikh brother-
          hood. Political ramifications of such a movement alarm the British, who
          had relied on the principle of divide and rule to govern India.

1877   Queen Victoria is proclaimed Empress of India.

1882   The Chinese Exclusion Act is enacted to keep Asians out of the United
          States.

1885   The Indian National Congress is founded in India.

1892   Mohandas K. Gandhi arrives in South Africa and starts to organize
          Indians for their political rights.

1893   Swami Vivekananda speaks to the World Parliament of Religions in
          Chicago.

1897   Queen Victoria's Jubilee is celebrated amid great pomp and expense in
          India.

Late   Discontent in the Punjab against landlords, moneylenders, and taxa-
1800s   tion.Population pressures. Exodus of Punjabis from Punjab; some opt
          for service to the British in various parts of the British Empire in mili-
          tary capacity; others migrate to California and the Northwest Coast of
          the United States. Indian workers become part of the laborers working
          on the California railroad and on the Panama Canal.

1902   Khalsa Diwan is formed in Punjab.

1905   Viceroy George Curzon attempts to partition Bengal. Demand for self-
          government in India by Gopal Krishna Gokhale.

1906   Indians start a boycott of British goods in India.

1907   Asian Exclusion League is formed in the United States.
          Bellingham riots in Washington State. Indian workers run out of town
          by organized labor. Attempt made to keep out Asians based on means
          testing.

1908   Taraknath Das, a student at the University of Washington, starts pub-
          lishing *Free Hindustan*.

1910   U.S. Supreme Court, in *United States v. Balsara*, maintains that Indians
          are Caucasian, therefore cannot be excluded from citizenship based on
          race.

1913   Gadar Movement starts among Indians living in San Francisco, with a
          view to gaining freedom for India.

1914   Many Indians leave for India to work on the Gadar Movement there.

1917   U.S. government, under pressure from British government, prosecutes
          and imprisons Gadar Movement members for their political activities.

1919   Jalianwalla Bagh massacre by the British of a peaceful rally in Amritsar.
          Worldwide ramifications against British rule in India.

1920   California passes the Alien Land Law prohibiting landownership by
          noncitizens.

1923   U.S. Supreme Court rules in *United States v. Bhagat Singh Thind* that
          "white" in Immigration Laws does not refer to the Caucasian race but
          only to the European continent or landmass attached to Asia, therefore
          Indians cannot become U.S. citizens. Further, the Court rules that citi-
          zenships granted on the previous ruling are null and void.

1924   The Immigration Act is passed, denying entry into the United States to those who are ineligible for citizenship.

1940   The census shows 2,405 Indians in the United States, 60 percent of them in California and 65 percent in agriculture.

1947   India's Independence; Pakistan created which causes large–scale displacement of people.

1956   Judge Dalip Singh Saund elected to the U.S. Congress from California.

1965   Immigration reform pushed through Congress and signed into law by President Lyndon B. Johnson. European bias in immigration laws removed.

PART

1

Poetry

Meena Alexander

Statement: I arrived in the United States fully formed, or so I thought, in the fall of 1979, but the world split apart. My poetry, *House of a Thousand Doors* (1988), *The Storm* (1989), and *Night Scene, the Garden* (1992); my novel, *Nampally Road* (1991); and my memoir, *Fault Lines* (1993), have been ways of working through memory, into this new world.

In a paper titled "Piecemeal Shelter: Writing, Ethnicity, Violence" presented at a colloquium at the University of Pennsylvania in 1991, Meena Alexander says that for many years she "has been haunted by the sense that the act of writing makes up a shelter: allows space to that which otherwise would be hidden, covered over, crossed out, mutilated." This statement by Meena Alexander seems especially true for many of the writers in this anthology.

The poem "Mandala" reveals Meena Alexander's awareness of the different landscapes of geography and cultures within which she lives, and it presents her central concern regarding the encounters between cultures as they exist in these last years of the twentieth century. This poem as well as the later selection from her memoir *Fault Lines* demonstrates the lyrical qualities of her writing in all the genres she uses.

Mandala

I can see you now: behind your head a hole
where a bird flies in, flame in its beak
all cut in silk from the robes of a Chinese emperor.

At his death the silks were borne
over the mountains to Tibet, parti-coloured threads
stitched into the borders of blessedness.

The Kalachakra Mandala (Wheel of Time Mandala), a figuration for the Blessing of Time, was created by Tibetan Monks in the Museum of Natural History, New York City. The entire intricate surface was formed by the patient pouring out of multicoloured sands. It was the first time that this sacred form was created outside Tibet. Upon its completion the sands were poured away.

Our city is all glass: trees, streets, horses
with ice in their manes dragging open carts
glass towers in fractions.

The Tibetan tanka rests on a dealer's wall
on a side street off Madison Avenue.
On it a bird of paradise with no name
except that, a calling which in darkness cries out

Pomegranate streaked wings dragged to the right
against corn coloured silks, a stiffness
of bird flesh swallowing its own shadow.

Closer at hand
in the Museum of Natural History
the Kalachakra Mandala shivers under arc lights.

You have taught me this:
the figuration of blessedness is never tranquil,
it is singular not to be cast away.
Later for us that very day, sunlight, shame

Your pipes all seven of them laid
in a semi-circle beside a mirror;
in a book you had, a stele with flying figure
female, Indic in origin
palms clasped to a beloved throat;
bedclothes in a heap
toothbrush on the floor
spurts of smoke drifting to a high window
no wings visible.

The city locks us both into a hole:
the past's a scratch
against the density of framed silks,
a seizure in the heart.

This yearning almost spends me —
harsh, impenitent, naming names and streets
and meeting places no one we live with will ever know

Ourselves a crooked hieroglyph,
two wings snapped into a sail

as time scrapes itself together
in fiery, stunted waves.

I stand at the window
as sunlight crushes glass into a rose
and men in turbulent rings,
not gods but as gods might be, tousled, muscular
punch ears and bloody nose and leap
over the wall at Central Park South

Into the spew of cars, fast hooves,
the asphalt of a road bordered by winter trees,
black river almost

Love's trajectory
where a silken thing centuries old
flies in courting death, and natural histories
cast into skin, nipple and nail

Prevail, solving time's compassion.

Agha Shahid Ali

Statement: Agha Shahid Ali writes that he is, by virtue of being a subcontinental, the product of three major world civilizations/cultures—the Hindu, the Islamic, and the Western. This very rich situation, the result of various historical "accidents," is further textured by his status as an "exile" in the United States. From the point of view of his poetry, he considers his site a lucky, even a privileged one, for he feels he, like other writers in English from the subcontinent, has the "right" to redefine the language, "discover" it for the "first" time.

Agha Shahid Ali's poems suggest the diversity of themes and styles that are found in the writings of South Asian American writers. The poet shows his awareness of being an "exile," even an "alien" in "Résumé." In "I See Chile in My Rearview Mirror," his portrait of the beauty of multiple countries and continents serves to emphasize his role as a poet who uses his own site, his view within his particular rearview mirror, to craft a poem.

Résumé

I
an applicant
to the water's green offices
sign my name above a thin horizon

below it reflections
of temples and mosques
a postscript on God

I wait for the sapphire
gossip of stars

but those who promised
to recommend me

place the moon's blank sheets
in my hands unsigned

Who are these authorities
with files of xeroxed rumors?

I hear orders

The clerk of climates
tears up my forms

no opening he says
no vacant reflection

only the rusted wars
and jets dissolving

in a smoke-red twilight

but if I will accept—and I say Yes

Maybe he says Maybe—and I say Yes

above me a quick ceiling of ice
I the secretary of memory
in chambers of weeds

the water's breathless bureaucracy

I See Chile in My Rearview Mirror

> By dark the world is once again intact,
> Or so the mirrors, wiped clean, try to reason . . .
>> —James Merrill

This dream of water—what does it harbor?
I see Argentina and Paraguay
under a curfew of glass, their colors
breaking, like oil. The night in Uruguay

is black salt. I'm driving toward Utah,
keeping the entire hemisphere in view—
Colombia vermilion, Brazil blue tar,
some countries wiped clean of color: Peru

is titanium white. And always oceans
that hide in mirrors: when beveled edges
arrest tides or this world's destinations
forsake ships. There's Sedona, Nogales

far behind. Once I went through a mirror—
from there too the world, so intact, resembled
only itself. When I returned I tore
the skin off the glass. The sea was unsealed

by dark, and I saw ships sink off the coast
of a wounded republic. Now from a blur
oil tanks in Santiago, a white horse
gallops, riderless, chased by drunk soldiers

in a jeep; they're firing into the moon.
And as I keep driving in the desert,
someone is running to catch the last bus, men
hanging on to its sides. And he's missed it.

He is running again; crescents of steel
fall from the sky. And here the rocks
are under fog, the cedars a temple,
Sedona carved by the wind into gods—

each shadow their worshiper. The siren
empties Santiago; he watches
—from a hush of windows—blindfolded men
blurred in gleaming vans. The horse vanishes

into a dream. I'm passing skeletal
figures carved in 700 B.C.
Whoever deciphers these canyon walls
remains forsaken, alone with history,

no harbor for his dream. And what else will
this mirror now reason, filled with water?
I see Peru without rain, Brazil
without forests—and here in Utah a dagger

of sunlight: it's splitting—it's the summer
solstice—the quartz center of a spiral.
Did the Anasazi know the darker
answer also—given now in crystal

by the mirrored continent? The solstice,
but of winter? A beam stabs the window,
diamonds him, a funeral in his eyes.
In the lit stadium of Santiago,

this is the shortest day. He's taken there.
Those about to die are looking at him,
his eyes the ledger of the disappeared.
What will the mirror try now? I'm driving,

still north, always followed by that country,
its floors ice, its citizens so lovesick
that the ground—sheer glass—of every city
is torn up. They demand the republic

give back, jeweled, their every reflection.
They dig till dawn but find only corpses.
He has returned to this dream for his bones.
The waters darken. The continent vanishes.

Indran Amirthanayagam

Statement: All exiles and immigrants go beyond the land where good and evil live side by side in separate provinces with a peace agreement carefully preserved. Is there any good in leaving your grandmother, or evil in forgetting her as you walk the streets of New York looking for a face, a gait that in some way reminds you of a place you can't quite, and don't want to, and must not forget?

Elephants, friends, famous writers, music, and politics from all over the world are brought together in this poem where memory and metaphysics are presented in the form of questions. Although memory in Panna Naik's poem "Illegal Alien" seems to overwhelm the narrator, memory in this poem becomes a part of the poet's questions about his own life, about the lives of other people and places, and about the contradictions that may exist in Elysium or on the sun.

What Happened to All My Life?

What happened to the elephants?
the conversation goes on and on
What happened to the elephants
and Rangoon, where does the rhino roam?

Hey, what happened to M and I
I want to know what happened,
the talking goes on, I'd like
to take part, present my paper Rushdie
What's happened to Salman?

Where is Marianne?
And who shall inherit
London. . . . why does J disappear
in the evenings and return
in the early night
as a hooded horseman?
Where is Tagore? And who
is the sweetest lyricist

in Serendip? And who
is the best bomber in Lanka
And how is G keying the concert
grand in downtown L.A.
And how hot are the waters
of Elysium, how cool
the center of the Sun?

G. S. Sharat Chandra

Statement: I have been in the United States for more than two decades, but I haven't ceased to be an Indian poet. It's essential for us to keep our identity here, and it's even more essential to expand this literature of ours in English for future generations.

G. S. Sharat Chandra's statement and the poem that follows address issues of maintaining one's identity as a South Asian in America and of passing on the inheritance of South Asian cultures to future generations of South Asian Americans. These issues are constantly debated and discussed by South Asian Americans in academic conferences, in classrooms, and in their homes, among strangers, friends, and family members. In the narrator's voice, his tones, and the rhythm of his speech, G. S. Sharat Chandra, an important South Asian American poet, echoes the conversational tone of an Indian poet storyteller.

India Association Plans a Newsletter

Gentlemen, good ladies,
how you take care of your children is world famous.
We are all from India here
but India is not all here,
I, the editor of the new newsletter said this,
don't forget because this will be my motto:
to make India over there to become India over here,
for this I need God's grace,
your help in generous support and sympathy.
If not for us, who is left
but for our children who were never born
like us in old India?
Every day we see them more and more Americanized.
What about our great Indian culture,
I asked one day while walking
followed by thinking.
I also asked Patil,
Bhose, Ghose, Kutti Nair and Muthu Iyer,
we are all Indians though we come from different parts and
argue.

On this everybody agreed.
We cannot let our great country go to waste.
So, I am planning this newsletter.
Your name will be printed boldly
next to your story, joke, idea, gems of thought,
anything worth printing, even poetry.
I'm editor so don't worry,
I'll print only noble things good for our children,
not like Penthouse or Playboy,
I've good family background,
my father is famous journalist in India
before and after death, ask anybody.
But I'm modest, I'm only seeking your co-operation.
We require a name
so suggest a name and win a prize.
No American names please.
Also, not your children's names please.
I encourage minors, majors, Hindus, Muslims, Christians,
what matter, even domestic ladies ought to enter.
So, good luck with your inspirations,
I begin publishing newsletter as soon as our combined
efforts produce results.
In the meanwhile, may Goddess Lakshmi
bless us with a smile wider than usual.

Darius Cooper

Statement: I arrived in the United States of America as an immigrant. I am living as an exile. I am scrutinizing from my particular position of inbetweenness my own culture (India) and my host culture (USA) with the anthropological skills of an artist and a critic.

In "I Have Been Offered My Country's Begging Bowl Again," Darius Cooper, the immigrant-exile, transports a part of the mythology and legends that surround Gautama Buddha's life to the United States and to his own life in his new home. According to Buddhist legends, the first people the Buddha approached with his begging bowl after he had become the Enlightened One, the Buddha, were his wife and his son, whom he had left behind when, as Prince Siddhartha, he had started off on his quest for enlightenment. The begging bowl and the act of begging are often the symbols of humility and compassion that connect all of us as human beings, rich or poor. In this poem the echoes of Buddhism are woven together with the Adam and Eve story. Families and children, as part of the quest of finding one's place as South Asians living in America, appear very often in South Asian American literature written by women as well as men.

I Have Been Offered
My Country's Begging Bowl Again

As darkness falls,
I look at my son's
beautiful sleeping face,
his tiny palms
firmly closed
over the weight of his world,
and think of my parents
as they dream of holding him
in their arms,
in a small town
far far away.

My wife is sleeping next to him,
Mersault's convincing frown

firmly embedded on her forehead,
and I wonder
if I can ever go home again,
after these long long years abroad.

Yesterday,
in some other darkness,
a friend
blew a speck of my country's dust.
It now enters my eyes, tonight,
and myths
that I once threw
in the waters
like painted Gods
at the end of a festival,
suddenly get revived.
Like those paper Gods
on pointed sticks
I rise and prop myself up,
and with banners
flying in the noisy forehead
of my sky
I suddenly notice
that my son is smiling
in his sleep
and slowly opening his palms.
As I watch, even
the frown EVEaporates
from my wife's
calm bodhitree face.

I have been offered
my country's begging bowl
again.

Rienzi Crusz

Statement: I sing (among other things) of exile, the "encounter," the unfolding saga of the Asian immigrant in Canada. I plead, I dream of a happy synthesis of cultures, a fashioning of a new mythology. I'm seduced by language, its endless possibilities for syncopation. My well-springs: memory, and an "undogmatic religion of life"; Neruda's "man of bread and fish" who "learnt the infinite" from ordinary men and women. Writing for me in Canada (in terms of challenges and reward) seemed almost to move in sympathy with the seasons: the long cold winter, then spring's green openings, the fire-dance of summer.

In "Conversations with God about my present whereabouts" and "Remains of an Asian poet writing in Canada" the memories of the physical landscape of Sri Lanka, the gentle as well as the harsh beauty of the land, the plants, the animals, the birds, and the seasons, are brought into the reality of the poet's life in Canada in the form of poetry. Instead of remaining in the domain of nostalgia, the poet's memories are transformed into a part of the poet's sense of who he is in his new homeland. The refrain "But I am perfect now" in "Conversations with God about my present whereabouts" echoes some familiar aspects of the philosophies and the poetry of South Asia.

Conversations with God
about my present whereabouts

True, I have forgotten
the terraced symmetries
of the rice-paddy lands.
How the gods underfoot
churned in time
a golden bowl of rice.
A loss of aesthetics, perhaps.

But I am perfect now.
They have crushed the ears of corn
to feed my belly
white slice by slice,

and all imperfections die
with One-A-Day and vitamin B complex.

True, I now walk
without the lumbering skill
of the elephant, the way
he smells the slaughter of mud and hole,
the precision of stars
in his thick legs.

But I am perfect now.
Snow and ice
embrace my horned boots,
skates and skills,
the bones uncracked,
the butterfly's muslin wings
untorn among the thorns

True, I sometimes ask:
where's the primal scream,
the madness of sun,
the dance of hands and pebbles
by the ocean shore?
And where's the sea-shell horn,
the words of angels under the sea?

But I am perfect now.
The chameleon
has muted my rowdy scream
to the whisper of a white-boned land,
and stretching in silence,
I am a king of silence.

True, I often miss
the sensuous touch of fingers
on the shying touch-me-not,
the undergrowth's pink badge of bruise,
cacophony of crows,
the rain that pelted my thin bones.

But I am perfect now.
Seduced on shaven grass,
my barbecue glows

like a small hell,
the pork-chops kindle,
the Molson cool,
I wear the turban of urban pride.

True, I have changed dead history
to now,
turned my father into me,
the long gone daddy
now skating on a rink
of clowning children.

But I am perfect now.
I have switched the time and place
of the womb,
my lungs free to scream
though disciplined to whisper,
free to trap the robin in my eyes,
if not the strident crow.

I AM perfect now.

A brown laughing face
in the snow,
not the white skull
for the flies
In Ceylon's deadly sun.

Remains of an Asian poet writing in Canada

About the butterfly
that flapped
amber
in the cerebral land

How winter
was made equal
to summer
and the skin glowed
like an oiled Brahmin
and bangles grew
on naked trees

And summer
blew orioles
salad of mango
and the Bird of Paradise
draped its wings
on the concrete land

They found
saffron wings
raw
on a smooth stone

The skull
separate   still green
in the dark wound
of a tree

A thigh
bronze warm
with the maul
of thorns

And they found
the sun   dead
under the snow

Chitra Divakaruni

Statement: Living and writing in America is for me at once a challenge and an opportunity. The challenge lies in trying to bring alive, for readers from other ethnic backgrounds, the Indian—and Indian American—experience, not as something exotic and alien but as something human and shared. It lies in getting my own community to see the subject of my work (often the plight of women of Indian origin struggling within a male-dominated culture, even here in America). It is necessary and important and not, as many have complained, a betrayal of my people, an exposure of secrets that create a "bad impression" of Indians in American society. But the opportunities are more important: to be able to straddle two distinct cultures and depict both with the relatively objective hand of the outsider; to destroy stereotypes and promote understanding between different sectors of the multicultural society in which we live; to paint the complex life of the immigrant with its unique joys and sorrows, so distinct from those of people who have never left their native land. The possibility of achieving even one of these through my work makes me glad to be an Indian writer in America.

Chitra Divakaruni's familiarity and skill with the classical Indian form of the poetic narrative, the telling of a story using poetic language and imagery, as well as her interest in the early South Asian immigrants to the United States are revealed in a series of five poems and poetic narratives, titled "The Yuba City Poems." Yuba City, settled by Punjab farmers around 1910, is now a thriving Indian community in northern California. Until the 1940s the Alien Land Laws largely precluded nonwhite immigrants from owning land, and immigration restrictions prevented their families from joining them. A number of the original settlers were never reunited with their families. The two selections in this anthology, "The Founding of Yuba City" and "Yuba City Wedding," portray men from the Punjab who came to California to farm, to settle a city, and to set up new families.

The Founding of Yuba City

Let us suppose it a California day
bright as the blinding sea that brought them

across a month of nights branded
with strange stars
and endless coal
shoveled
into a ship's red jaws.
The sudden edge of an eucalyptus grove,
the land fallow and gold in their eye, a wind
carrying the forgotten green smell
of the Punjab plains.

They dropped back, five or maybe six,
let the line straggle on. The crew's song
wavered, a mirage, and sank
in the opaque air. The railroad
owed them a month's pay, but
the red soil glinted light.
Calloused from pounding metal into earth,
their farmer's hands ached
to plunge into its moisture.
Each man let it run pulsing
through his fingers,
remembered.

The sun fell away. Against its orange,
three ravens, as in
the old tales. Through the cedars,
far light from a window
on a white man's farm.
They untied their waistbands,
counted coins, a few
crumpled notes. They did not fear
work. Tomorrow they would find jobs,
save, buy the land soon. Innocent
of Alien Laws, they planned
their crops. Under the sickled moon
the fields shone with their planting:
wheat, spinach, the dark oval wait
of potatoes beneath the ground, cauliflowers
pushing up white fists
toward the light.

The men closed their eyes, faces
to the earth's damp harvest-odor.

In the Punjab noon, flame of red skirts.
The women, on their heads
sheafs of brown bajra,
rotis, jars of buttermilk
for their husbands' lunch.
Scented with hibiscus oil,
their black hair fell like rain, like
tears, on the faces of husbands
they would not see again.

A horned owl gliding on great wings
masked the moon. The men
stroked the soil, its
warm hollows, and unknowing
smiled in their sleep.

Minal Hajratwala

Statement: I'm the child of a strange generation that named all its daughters Lisa or Jennifer. I was the only Minal, which means "fish," and writing helps me swim through these strange waters. After visiting South Africa recently, I am convinced that the biggest task facing the Indian community in the United States is to fight our own bigotry and prejudice—toward gays and lesbians, other people of color, women with short hair, and various castes and classes among ourselves.

Minal Hajratwala transforms the tension between generations, her life across different continents and histories, and the ancient stories surrounding the concepts of duty and women's roles into her own sense of duty in the twentieth-century United States. Recognizing that even those who gave her life cannot accept her "brown, bisexual body," she fights valiantly for human rights that transcend cultural and geographical borders.

Twenty Years After I Grew into Your Lives

I tell you who I am
or rather, you discover
secrets hidden in mistaken boxes,
papers published in other worlds

Twenty years it took me to grow into my own
courage to speak as myself
or rather, to whisper
half-sentences and mostly-truths
but somewhat better than utter silences

You grew up in simpler times and foreign nations,
such distances have always gaped between generations
and those places live in me still—
my tongue that savours fish you fried at Sunday barbecue
on the Fiji Islands,
my body whose form India's clothes
still flatter

And it is my body, after all,
that is the site of your confusion—
sexual, bisexual, feminist
but still brown-skinned, black-haired
red-blooded

Alive with the pure heart of our warrior caste,
nevertaintedby outmarriage,
descended from the Kshatriyas—
men who died for duty
and killed for gods-know-what

I, too, am militant
in my battles for human rights,
for health over hunger, not Pandava over Kaurava,
for freedom to be
other than mother of 100 sons*

And the hushed battlefield of our epic
is my brown, bisexual body,
which even you, who made it, cannot accept.

---

*The Pandavas, five brothers, defeated their 100 cousins, the Kauravas, in the
Hindu epic *Mahabharata*. The Kshatriya duty to fight is among the
religious/metaphysical topics enumerated in *Bhagavad-Gita*, a dialogue that takes
place during that war.

See also *May You Be the Mother of 100 Sons: A Journey Among the Women of India*, by
Elisabeth Bumiller (New York: Fawcett, 1991).

Diane S. Mehta

Statement: Growing up in America has been complicated by the fact of a mixed Indian and Jewish ancestry. For me, writing verse is an act that accepts both cultures and pursues a feeling of inclusion and rootedness.

In her poems Diane Mehta explores the landscape of America, with its multiple languages and its different cultures. Her questions about which fragments of history the future children of America will inherit appear in "America" and "The History of Language." "The History of Language" portrays a woman of European descent in Asia, while the poet in "America" reflects upon the migration of languages. It is a theme that is very appropriate for this anthology, which includes writers of South Asian descent who are very aware of the multiple languages that they have inherited.

America

The future is a train of immigrants
    dressed in prophecies,
circling the mountainside like drumbeats.
    They come like a romance:
the Cuban dancers in the park,
    shoulders quarrelling
like the conversation of knives over steak,
    and that woman
twisting her dress around her knees like fire.
    But nothing stays this way.
On these unmeasured streets we buy despair
    like wild roses,
a lament rises earlier than dawn,
    arousing
the familiar promise of a foghorn
    in a landlocked town:
something left behind, something
    like the ease of language—
our hearts filled patriotic verses long
    beyond the schoolyard,

surf revised its line to an excuse
        for eager sands at dawn.
Our good intentions know no paradise
        here,
dreams become confined to mattresses,
        strange nouns
like the long, unsettled phalanxes
        of light on crowded streets.
Our footsteps become printed devotions,
        negotiating grace
despite the time of day, the invocations
        of hills beside the road
(the dead in narrow rows of rectangles).
        Hurrying home,
our hearts among our broken oracles
        below iambic waves.

The History of Language

Darkness spreads its roots below our time zones.
        Colored signals over
rear-view mirrors queueing by the curbstones
        repeat for no one. Liesel
reads her German at the seder table.
        Language migrates east
to Canaan, reverses at the Second Temple,
        Torah on its shoulder,
and turns to speak the German that survived:
        paragraphs unable
to define their words, nouns capitalized
        and moving through
exiled communities because you cannot
        banish languages like people.
And when the hieroglyphs of Egypt
        rose up through Sinai,
worshippers, hearing holy, holy, holy
        stood on their toes again
as if angels could defend a country.
        When the rain falls
in empires it buries sounds among
        their destinies: the still
of silence becomes rhythmical if sung
        in the heart.
Would anybody know if what we saw
        was merely what
we imagined sight to be? A cinema
        scrolling through our corneas,
the unreliable kaleidoscope
        of lines, a memory?
Amnesiacs will barter any trope
        to retrieve the past
from an idea of what the past could be.
        I would love you with ideas
but have no way to release history
        from its repetitions,
the future from its past, which has the same
        atomic frame
as yesterday. In language this is how an M
        divides the Mediterranean

into Roman, Greek and Semitic time.
     Or how bands pound out marches
till Wagner rises. How will you react,
     when in your child you see
the history of the world turning back,
     repeating someone else's life?

Panna Naik

Statement: As an Indian woman in America, I do not feel marginal. If anything, I feel very confident. I do things in the United States that I would not dare to do in India. Indeed, I started writing poetry in America. More than that, the theme, the content, and the expression for my poetry, which came rather uninhibitedly to me in the United States, would have been risky back home.

If America gives me freedom and flexibility to write whatever I want, it also takes me away from my readers. My fundamental problem as an immigrant poet comes from the fact that I write in Gujarati—the choice is consciously mine—which is neither read nor spoken in the society in which I live. My readers, however few, are not around me.

Thus it is a double jeopardy for me. To reach a wider audience, I do translate my poems into English, but much is lost in translation.

"Illegal Alien" was translated from the Gujarati by the author. Even though the poem was originally written in Gujarati, the images and the concerns presented in the poem are rooted in the alien culture and in the constant fears of deportation and the overwhelming feelings of nostalgia faced by many immigrants in America.

Illegal Alien

It has been years
since
I deported Memory,
once my constant companion,
to where he belongs.

Now,
suddenly,
in the dead of the night,
there is a whisper in the air.
He is trying to sneak back.
Feeling suffocated,
I open the window
shut down for years.

Hearing someone knocking,
I open the door
to find
just the wind hissing
through the cracks.
Banished memory,
I reassure myself,
wouldn't come this openly.

But did he really try
to slip in clandestinely?
I feel enraged at the thought.
Doesn't he know
that in America
an illegal alien
is arrested,
handcuffed,
jailed,
tried in court;
and when found guilty,
once more deported?

When I enter the room
I find him
spread over bed sheet folds
disguised as silver moonlight
that shines through the open window.

Police tell me:
"opening that window
was your first mistake."

Saleem Peeradina

Statement: My dislocation in the Midwest is only external; the real place of fertility resides elsewhere. I continue to draw from the richness of my Indian origin and sources while, at the same time, maintaining a global perspective. I should say that I've always produced out of a double consciousness—from having multiple allegiances to place, language, religion, and ideology. I was bicultural in a different way even in Bombay, my birthplace. Every place remakes itself into an environment of exile that can be an extremely stimulating condition for a writer. I live, teach, and write the conflict itself.

The two poems by Saleem Peeradina included in this anthology are from a series of four poems titled "Reflections on the Other." Selections III and IV are skillful variations on the theme the poet sets up at the beginning of the first poem, "There are always two kinds/of people, two states of mind, two voices." In III the poet speaks of the frustration and the anger of a nondominant/dominating group that is looked at, and located at a distance, as "the other" by a patronizing, dominant group. In IV he expands this awareness of alienation, of "being looked at," to concerns that include and yet go beyond the traditional discussions of "the other." In "Reflections on the Other," not only does the poet portray the concerns of being "the other," he also shows how the sense of being dislocated can be turned into a changing of positions and transformed into a sense of power, of a recognition of one's self.

Reflections on the Other

III

When you refer to the other, you say

We must think of the other
We must hear the voice of the other
We must empower the other—

Thereby expressing your largesse
your concern for that which has suffered

neglect, that you imagine
you are ready to redress. The moment
You think 'other', you position yourself
in a place from which no one can budge you
simultaneously situating the other
in an inextricable spot.

You approach, but only out of
incurable curiosity, unable to close the distance
you measured out before you got there.
It's your boundary, a kind of safety net

You can climb back into on the way out
once your gesture is completed.
Your return was written into your failure,
a loss well understood by those

You leave behind. The dignity
of those you shame is a fate
you will never know, not until you're forced

To change places with the other.

                          IV

The other is a new taste, an echo
from a distant shore, any place you have
not been before, a country that insists on
occupying the map, an unforeseen epic
journey.

The other is a neighborhood beyond
your skin's barbed wire fence; an uninvited
guest from a future age who could have been
your rescuer before your memory betrayed
his origins.

The other is a smell you disapprove of,
as strong, sensual, homely
as your own; a dark secret you enter
as you would an abandoned path in search of
misplaced dreams.

The other is an unclimbed mountain
veiled in mist; a poem that baffles;
yourself in a story minus your heroics; a haunting
melody, someone else's pain whose trail leads
to your door.

The other is not always born condemned
to die as the other. It could switch sides
when no one is looking, yet keep the other
company: its own inescapable other, not the self's
sloughed off other.

The other is the truth
continually denied, a lie only a shade deeper
than your own. If there were no other
to pick on, you'd have to invent one. For there is never
a final solution

To the other, no easy transfusion of blood
to alter the course of your life. Only the hope
of being smitten by a familiar; standing mirrored
enveloped in a greater mystery, a far more
intimate estrangement.

Jyotsna Sanzgiri

Statement: Jyotsna Sanzgiri writes that she immerses herself in many poetic forms, both Eastern and Western, and hopes to develop a voice that synthesizes these influences. She draws on classical Indian literature, as well as formal Western verse—such as sonnets and sestinas—to work on her poetry and fiction. Living in California, with its many cultures and languages, gives her a unique opportunity to experience the processes of immigration and assimilation that are crucial to her writing. Over time, she hopes to integrate all these influences so that her Indian roots and her American experiences can serve to develop poetic moods that include the comic, tragic, heroic, erotic, and so on.

The two poems included in this anthology are from a series of poems titled "On Living in America: In Four Moods—Comic, Tragic, Erotic, Heroic." "Requiem" is from the section titled "Tragic" and "Azalea" from "Erotic." In this series of poems, Jyotsna Sanzgiri skillfully uses the concept and techniques of *rasa* from the traditions of classical Indian Sanskrit literature and art to portray in a variety of poetic forms her experiences as a South Asian living in America. The poems speak of friends and strangers and of landscapes from all over the world. The concept of *rasa* is found in the classical Sanskrit poetic (verse and prose) genre, the *kavya*. *Kavya* is a linguistically elaborate and ornamented genre of courtly literature in which the communication of the very essence of universally recognizable emotions, moods, sentiments—the *rasa*—often becomes the most important element.

Requiem

For Robert who died of AIDS

> The plum tree's
> torn limb reminds
> me your seed
> can no longer
> bear fruit.

Withered branches,
brown crackling
leaves enclose
me. Eyes blur,

I cannot see
the sunlight
touch healthy
shoots, their
greening leaves
their flowering
buds.

Friends gather
round. Trembling,
I see them prune this
ceased life,
your
silenced song.

Azalea

I.

Eyes gleaming, you murmur,
Azaleas cover the hillsides in my land.
One perfect flower before you,
and you speak of Asian abundance.

My mind lifts, soars. Fragrant
temples, jasmine-filled. Women
glide, saffron flowers thread
dark braids. For generations
red-gold gul mohurs offer shade.

II.

I glance at the crystal vase,
its azalea like white silk.
Back in the West, I converse,
bathed in the lush foliage
of my land.

Rashmi Sharma

Statement: Rashmi Sharma writes that the conflict of identity among Indians living in the United States, as part of the interplay of various cultures and ethnicities into "what is American," has always been of great interest to her. She hopes, some day, when her hectic life slows down a bit, to get a Ph.D. on a facet of this subject.

Rashmi Sharma's concerns with the cultural as well as the socioeconomic and political history of South Asian immigration to the United States can be seen both in the poem that follows and in her introductory essay, "Crossing the Dark Waters," in this anthology. The issues she raises in her essay on the history and the contemporary reality of South Asian Americans are crafted into a poem in "What's in a Name?" In the poem she explores the identity of South Asian immigrants through their names. Her essay and her poem present points of view and questions that are explored in many of the works in this anthology.

What's in a Name?

Am I Krishnamurthi or Chris?
Vardhamana* or 'R.D.'
Vijaya[†] or Victor?
Markandaya or Mark
Shailendra or Shelly?

What's in a name, you ask?
My very identity, the genesis who I am.
But who am I?
Am I Indian or an American?
Or the hyphenated, split personality of 'Indo-American'?

---

* Vardhamana is the name of one of the major proponents of Jainism, a religion perhaps older than Buddhism, remarkable for its creed of nonviolence and sound ecological balance; a name any child should be proud of. Yet, in the American context, shortened to V.D., it could be embarrassing and inappropriate in a name, as are many perfectly good names from other languages and cultures. Thus the American abbreviation of R.D. instead!
[†] Vijaya refers to victory, hence the translation to the similar name of Victor.

My parents name me
but society renames me.
Which am I to be?
Should others define who I am?
Should I, could I, figure out who I am?

My heritage and my future
are the poles that pull me apart,
Wrenching me in half.
Doomed forever to never really belong completely in one culture.
I know not whether I am part of a 'melting pot' or part of a 'fruit salad'.

My parents' value of their cultural heritage, and mine,
Are what's in my name.
I am no more nor less than others who also came
To this unique experiment in freedom, this nation of immigrants.
I am who I am.

Neera Kuckreja Sohoni

Statement: I have lived in America variously as student, worker, home-maker, and mother. Each phase has been enriching in some ways and alienating in others. But the experience of being here has never been dull or ambivalent. It has made me more willing to try out uncharted territory.

Asking America to give the same privileges to people from Asia as it does to people from Europe takes different forms and different tones in South Asian American writings. In this poem the tone moves from a request to a quiet statement that leaves no room for any question that people from Asia are an integral part of America: "We live here now." Although the poet mentions the "ancient east," she is not concerned with memories as is Panna Naik in her poem "Illegal Alien." Instead, Neera Sohoni confronts derogatory terms such as "pollen skins" and "rag-heads" and stereotypes that many Americans use against people from Asia while withholding privileges from them.

De-privileging Liberty

America
do not turn your back on me
take me
homeless weary
huddled into your
caring arms though I hail not
   from west
  but the ancient
mellow east
Brown and yellow
  Autumnal race
  Not White
  Nor Cauc-asian
  Merely Asian.
America, turn not your
  back, as the Liberty
   Goddess,

      facing Europe
        sheltering
        privileging
          white,
        filtering
          East.
America, we live
      here now.
We pollen skins
rag-heads tanned
      coolies farmers
      garment-sewers, makers of
        Silicon chips we
who weave our dreams into
      your tapestry.
Unfold
behold
hold us. Do not turn
      away, America.
Stay
Let us belong.

Amita Vasudeva

Statement: When I first began to share my writing with others, I feared that no one would understand it because it was so particular to my experiences. Only recently have I recognized that my writing has the ability to transcend such boundaries as gender, place, nationality, and age. While my writing is still very personal and spontaneous, I appreciate the special connection I make with someone who reads my work and tells me, "I relate."

The stereotyping of people and the ignorance regarding the languages and gestures of those who do not belong to the dominant culture are captured in Amita Vasudeva's "Can You Talk Mexican?" Although in the previous selection, Neera Kuckreja Sohoni, as a South Asian American woman born in India, mentions the stereotyping and the derogatory terms used for Asian Americans in her poem, Amita Vasudeva, born in the United States, presents the voices behind the stereotyping, cruelty, and ignorance toward minority cultures in twentieth-century America

Can You Talk Mexican?

"Can you talk Mexican?"
    They used to ask me.
"No, I'm not Mexican I'm Indian, and besides they speak Spanish,"
    I used to reply, waiting eagerlessly for their best
    attempt at doing a "raindance."
"Owwow ooh ow ow." Smacking outstretched palms to their little
    mouths and hopping around.
"Not THAT kind of Indian—Indian from India,"
    I would correct, as soon as they finished whooping.
"Oh. . . . Can you talk Indian?"

PART

2

Fiction

Qiron Adhikary

Statement: When asked how she feels about living and working in America, Qiron Adhikary is quick to point out that although other South and Southeast Asian writers may be threatened with death and dismemberment for their creative work, she has only been threatened with imminent eviction and hunger—a clear demonstration of the superiority of the "First World" and a tender mercy for which she is, in her own vinegary way, grateful.

"Nosey Nakshitka's Adventures in America" is the story of a South Asian woman's encounters with different people and with herself in the multicultural world of America. Nosey does not come to America for higher education or as a member of an immigrant family or as a bride; she comes to America because she has been seduced by American media. And once in America, she undergoes various changes and of course in the process she manages to change some of the people she encounters in different parts of America.

Nosey Nakshitka's Adventures in America

At the age of 25, without a word to anyone, Nosey Nakshitka packed her bags and left for America. It had, admittedly, been a long time coming. All her friends—and Nosey herself—had seen this particular move hovering over the horizon of her early life.

For one thing, there were the American TV programs Nosey watched endlessly. In these programs, everyone and thing was whiter than white, cleaner than clean. Nosey, heartily sick of the endless bars of strong-smelling yellow laundry soap with which the washerwoman thrashed her white school blouses, leaving them a defeated shade of gray, was ready then and there to abandon both the washerwoman and her home for those boxes with the cheerful names and bright colors, and the pretty blonde women whose sole purpose in life seemed to be doing their families' dirty laundry, and making it all come clean. Perhaps she thought using Bold! or Spotaway, or Loud! would make her thin, tall, and blonde, the blueness of her eye rivaling the sky.

Imagine, then, her utter disappointment on landing first in Hawaii, then in Los Angeles, to find that a goodly portion of the citizenry was far from white, and even when white, far from clean.

Possessed of little Korean and less Spanish, she found herself living in the barrio of that truncated city, with its sonorous Spanish name—La Ciudad de Nuestra Dama, La Reina de Los Angeles—the City of Our Lady, the Queen of the Angels, reduced beyond recognition to its initials, two letters that conveyed none of the magic or mystery of the last lot of conquerors to troop through its naturally smoggy valley.

Nosey, with her brown skin and dark hair, and her velvety brown eyes, with that conquistador nose marching across her face, was mistaken for every variety of Hispanic (and they were legion) by everyone. It seemed Indians—of her kind, anyway—were a rare commodity in those parts.

In a Greyhound bus station in Bakersfield, an ancient Cubano spoke to her in a friendly Spanish, tipping his hat. The more she replied in English, the angrier he apparently became, finally cursing her (she knew that, even though she didn't know what he was saying exactly), his frail, bony hands trembling on his walking stick. till she cried in desperation, "Indian! India!" whereupon he beamed broadly and exclaimed in a tone of blessed relief, "Ah! Los Indios!" Despite her lack of Spanish, she had a powerful feeling that he still didn't get it, but it's impossible to argue with someone when you don't speak a word of their language.

In Bakersfield she visited a friend of hers, a white woman from Georgia who had married a Singaporean Nepali. Apparently, the police in Bakersfield, who were also mostly white, had just enough experience with brown people to repeatedly attempt to arrest the man for the crime of being Mexican—tantamount, in Bakersfield, to being an illegal alien, or some other type of scofflaw.

Nosey returned to Los Angeles—which the Hispanic inhabitants cheerfully pronounced Los Ang'hay-layss, confident their Anglo neighbors would be unable to do likewise—shaken by her first taste of life in America. Left to herself, she would probably have become a charter member of the Republican party, despising those less fortunate for their disinclination to get out there and hustle for a few bucks, as her American, and also mostly Republican, friends were fond of saying.

But America gnawed at her as a wolf-cub at a young Spartan; it refused to leave her alone. It chewed at her grimly, it shook all her senses with its vast and complex systems, and the many-colored people those systems oppressed. Rushing back to Los Angeles in search of the cosmopolitan, Nosey discovered instead her neighbors, young and pretty Hispanic women who complained bitterly to her about the disgusting condition of their apartments, the holes in the bathroom walls, the rats that bit their babies. "Ay!" they would sigh, showing her the marks of a vicious rat bite on a tiny foot or hand, crying over the injustices of their life in a language so beautiful in its rhythms and tones that often she would stand listening, quite lost.

They must have thought her an idiot, for she never responded with anything intelligible, just nods and hand-waves and shakes of the head. Nosey herself began to feel like those old Indian women, her grandmother's friends and her mother's, who, it seemed, punctuated every conversation with repeated shakes of the head.

"I'm turning into what I most despise," she would mutter to herself, staring at her reflection in the mirror. Locked in her tiny, cramped room—with its ancient, spotty silvered mirror; cheap tacky plywood cabinets; and two-burner stove; its worn carpets saturated with generations of cooking odors, stale cabbage, rancid bacon grease, ancient onions and garlic; its cheap, battered black-and-white TV, which nonetheless received every channel in the world, its lumpy mattress and sagging bed with thin gray sheets worn by countless bodies—she would lie awake late at night staring through the grimy window at the gray concrete wall that comprised her view.

Her bathroom wall, too, had holes through which rats and cockroaches crawled. She bought rat poison and cockroach motels ("Ha!" she cried bitterly, when she first saw those ingenious devices. "This whole goddam place is a cockroach motel!"), and left them lying around strategically. She stuffed the holes with newspapers and broken bits of brick and concrete found on the road. And she took to writing "Cockroach Motel" as her return address.

Friends come to visit noticed that she was unhappy and gaining weight. "Come home," they pleaded, "we'll pay your way. Come back, we miss you." But Nosey set her jaw, grimly determined not to return a failure. "I came to America to find something," she would say, "and I'm not leaving till I find it."

No one asked her what she'd come so far to find, which was just as well, for she no longer knew. Seduced by 66 channels of truly terrible daytime TV, she lay about smoking clove cigarettes and making weak cups of tea, and wishing she could find a job, but not really doing anything about it.

Luckily, she had some meager funds to live on, for in the City of the Angels, nothing is free. And she was young enough not to be troubled by the future, still slim and pretty, with her firm, high breasts and narrow waist, and her ridiculously high-heeled shoes that gave her a streetwalker's exaggerated gait.

Where did she go on those warm, sunny days when she ventured out of her tiny room in the barrio? Why, to the library, of course. The main branch of the Los Angeles Public Library, an enormous building stacked floor-to-ceiling and wall-to-wall with books, periodicals, magazines, papers, reference works of great import and scholarly worth, and—the homeless. This library proved to be the beginning of the

Education of Nosey Nakshitka. Within its solid walls, she learned to repudiate her conservative political roots, to reshape, painfully, her point of view to progressive. For at every table and bench sat or lay or lolled yet another person, indistinguishable in gender under layers of clothing and grime. In fact, they were often indistinguishable in race as well, for who could tell if this was a black man's (or woman's) face, or a white, yellow, or brown person's, darkened by wind, sun, and dirt, hair matted into pseudo-Rasta locks?

Not Nosey, whose experience with those of the white or black persuasion was limited indeed. Having grown up mostly among those as brown as she, or only slightly lighter or darker, she found herself greatly disadvantaged by her lack of knowledge. She felt sorry for those people, as only a member of the bourgeoisie can. She had no idea who they were, or why they were there. Clearly, it was not for the purpose of increasing their store of knowledge. And some were obviously mad. Those, for instance, who wore heavy wool coats over several layers of tee-shirts, sweatshirts, sweaters, leggings, pants, and jackets, in the muggy Los Angeles heat.

Others seemed defeated, dispirited, as if they had fought once too often or too long in a world which cared little and noticed less. They had grown accustomed to being invisible, and now shuffled past others, seeing as little as they were seen.

In her middle-class way, Nosey despaired at having to sit next to these filthy wretches, then despised herself for having such feelings, and sat next to them out of guilt, in the end, holding her breath for long periods.

She tried to talk to them from time to time, even when it was obvious that they were neither interested in, nor capable of, conversation. "Are you okay?" she would ask in faint tones, the result of having to hold her breath against the mighty stench that wafted from some ripe and seasoned unfortunate or the other, which, seizing her by nose and throat, assaulted her senses with vigor. The stupidity and meaninglessness of the question never dawned on her. She was like one of those society ladies who descend among the poor, armed with a conscience, and determined to do good. She noticed less about the creature sprawled next to her than she hoped others would notice the goodness of her heart. And all for naught, for her magnificent nose, the foundation of her nickname, responded with greater sensitivity to the accumulation of odors upon the bootless and unhorsed, it seemed, than their dainty retroussé American counterparts.

So it was that, out of the goodness of her heart, real or imagined, she turned one day when hailed on the Santa Monica Boulevard by a tall black man in tattered clothes. "Hey, hey, sister," he called, waving a thin, but elegant, arm. His trousers were held up by a cord, his long feet bare. "C'mere, I got something to show ya."

What could it be, she wondered, the poor man's obviously one of the downtrodden, but he called me sister, maybe he needs help, I'd better go see what he wants. One could hardly blame her for being shocked into immobility when the man pulled what seemed like an enormous penis out of his pants and waved it at her.

True to her middle-class background, Nosey's first thought was, "In broad daylight! And on a crowded street, too!" Fortunately for her, the man's attention soon turned towards fresh victims, so that he hardly noticed her standing there, panting and clutching her rather flat bosom in horror.

She went home thinking, "He called me sister! What kind of son-ofabitch would do that? I've been gulled, had, tricked! What did he mean, sister? What kind of bastard waves his penis at his sister? Aren't I his sister under the skin? How could he? How dare he?"

It's probably safe to assume that the penis-waving man spared Nosey no further thought after registering her shocked expression. But it was not the baby-biting rats, the use of the public library as a homeless shelter, the viewing of parts normally concealed behind clothing, the view from her room, not even the smog that settled in that still valley, that finally drove Nosey northward to Berkeley. It was the police in the barrio, and—believe it—the crime.

For Nosey lived in the one part of town where the police had virtually free rein to do as they pleased. Most of the other inhabitants of that dismal sector were illegal aliens, people without papers who had come there to escape certain death at the hands of American-trained death squads in their own countries, or slow starvation, or any of a hundred other evils. She saw it in their narrow, frightened faces, their timid downcast eyes.

It seemed to Nosey that only the adolescent boys looked angry, growing up in that wasteland far from hope and home. They resisted. The others suffered, usually quietly. They complained to Nosey about the rats that bit their babies and the bosses who didn't pay their wages, the sweatshop conditions they worked in, their constant fear of La Migra. But to those bosses and landlords and officials who harassed them, they said nothing. They lowered their eyes so even their expressions would remain neutral, and they suffered without complaining.

Nosey, understanding one word out of ten, somehow managed to realize that these people felt they were victimized. "By what?" she wondered. "After all, this is America, the land of opportunity. I mean, my god, at least in this country they have jobs and a place to live. If things were that bad, surely they would go home." To say that she failed to see the parallels between their situation and hers would have been a resounding understatement of fact. The Los Angeles Public Library had educated her, but not enough. She still felt more affinity with the wealthy denizens of Santa Monica and Malibu than the poor ghetto- and barrio-dwellers.

It was left to the Los Angeles Police Department to complete her education. For it was not till she saw a police raid on the barrio that she finally began to understand the fear oppressing her neighbors. Walking home on a sunny afternoon after purchasing a pack of expensive clove cigarettes, Nosey turned down a dead-end street that gave onto a little alley she often used as a shortcut.

Before she had taken five steps, several police cars, sirens screaming, lights flashing red-blue-yellow, screeched to a halt behind her. Four, maybe five policemen in full uniform leapt out of the cars and sur- rounded a group of Hispanic youths who were playing some sort of game on the sidewalk. Truncheons swinging, they slammed the kids up against the dead-end wall. "Wider, I said, you little spic bastard," one of them shouted, swinging at an unprotected dark head, his face red with a combination of rage, physical exertion, and twisted sexual gratification. "Spread 'em, motherfucker!" They kicked at the boys' legs, tripped them, pushed them face first down onto the dirty road or pavement, kicked their exposed bellies, faces, heads. Teeth broke and went flying, bones snapped, and the truncheons rose and fell, rose and fell.

"They won't do that to ME, surely," she muttered to herself. "I'm an educated person, I speak English, I'm not illegal like them. They wouldn't do that to me." She called her friend, Michael Murphy—actually, Michael Mohammad Mustapha Murphy—in San Francisco to tell him about the incident. His response was sympathetic but curt. "You better hike your fanny outa there fast, girl. Them Migra folks ain't gonna ask if you speak English 'fore they throw your ass in a van and schlep it out to Tijuana. And if you think not speaking Spanish is a disadvantage now, I don't need to tell you, you ain't never gettin' out of Tijuana without you know a few words, you get my drift?"

She got his drift. "For an educated individual, Murphy, you talk like street scum," she said, hanging up. She was angry, because she felt he wasn't sympathetic enough. And also because, as much as she hated life in the Los Angeles barrio, she hated change even more. She thought about how she could hike her fanny out of the barrio without getting killed, waylaid, or sidetracked to Tijuana en route.

"Christ Criminy," she said, using her latest and currently most favorite expression, "where in the name of a bleeding saint am I going to go?"

Was it fate that reminded her of an old friend in Berkeley? Beautiful Berkeley by the Bay, known to the smaller-minded among us as the

People's Republic of Berkeley, or Berserkeley, depending on political persuasion and current dietary inclination. It was the perfect place for a Nosey Nakshitka. Only think (as her mother might have said), think only! Of the plethora of twelve-step programs that awaited our Nosey, of the dabblers in the occult and practitioners of Wicca, of the radical feminists, the lesbians, the drag queens, the jackboot-and-flannel-shirt set, the fag-hags, the Castro Street clones, the dwellers in the Swish Alps, the hippies, Yippies, yuppies, guppies, the widespread political activism, and the enthusiastic factional hairsplitting! What more suitable medium for the growth and development of a Nosey Nakshitka?

Unaware of these subtle permutations, Nosey got on the horn to her old friend and fellow-Singaporean Netty John. "Netty," she said, "I don't think I want to live here any more. Where are you living? What town, I mean?"

"Berkeley," said Netty, delighted at the thought of a fellow-sufferer to share American agonies with.

Nosey, studying her map of the United States intently, failed to find anything like "Berkeley" listed there. "How you spell that?" she asked tentatively.

Netty spelled it for her. "Are you coming? Come, nah, it'll be great. I don't know what-all you think you're doing in Ellay. Terrible place, I'm telling you. People getting killed and all kinds of things, there. Come here, lah. We'll have fun."

Nosey melted at the familiar sounds of Singlish. How musical one's own tongue always sounds! "Ai-yah," she cried. "What to do? I'm telling you only, this place is making me mad. Chih! Crazy only everybody is, here."

"Ah, you, why you never call me? I could have told you. You also, one kind only." Netty, feeding off Nosey's loneliness and longing, cued her again.

"Alamak!" Nosey exclaimed, "tell me how to come only, I'm coming. Now already want to come."

"Ha," said Netty nasally. "Greyhound only, take, take the Greyhound bus."

"But where to take?" Nosey, despairing. "This Berkeley is not on the map, even."

"Hai-yah, hopeless! Listen, lah," Netty, annoyed. "Tell the bus driver Oakland or San Francisco, whichever one, we will come and pick you."

Nosey, studying the map again, was beside herself. "This Oakland is where?" she asked. "Only San Francisco on this map. San Francisco can or not?"

"Can, can," said Netty. "Call and say only what time to come and pick you."

"Okay," said Nosey. "Long distance very expensive, okay, so I hang up now. When I get the ticket then I call. Okay?"

They exchanged expressions of mutual affection, loneliness, and regret before they hung up.

Still Nosey was reluctant to take the next step—to actually locate the Greyhound bus station, and buy a ticket for San Francisco, several hundred miles away. She went to dinner with her lover and a mutual friend. She did not tell them her intentions. The relationship with her lover was falling apart, he had been unemployed for nearly a year, and had run out of money, and it seemed all their words had turned to knives so that they could not speak without wounding each other.

The mutual friend was also having problems with his marriage, though he didn't like to discuss them. He was a soft-spoken man in his sixties with thick silver hair and a passion for roses. He grew different varieties, and often brought her a single perfect bloom, or tomatoes from his garden, as a gift. He pretended not to notice when she quarrelled with her lover. Sometimes he gallantly came to her defense. "Drop it, Jim," he said, "you ain't treating the lady right."

Times like that, Nosey wanted to kiss him on the top of his silvery head, but she restrained herself. Tonight, however, he was strangely demonstrative and affectionate. He insisted on taking them to an excellent restaurant, picking up the tab with a practiced twist of the wrist. He danced with her, a couple of slow numbers. "I'm an old man, darling," he smiled, "I can't do that fast stuff. Besides, to me that ain't dancing anyway." He called her Princess, and kissed her hands. At the end of the evening, he hugged her warmly. "Goodbye, little girl," he said. "Take care of yourself. You take care of her, Jim. She's a beautiful lady." And he kissed her on the cheek.

They parted shortly after midnight. He returned to the office. Three hours later, he was shot dead in the parking lot by someone with a high-powered rifle, who didn't even bother to take his wallet.

Nosey took the next Greyhound bus to San Francisco. True to form, she left without a word to her lover.

If you think life in Berkeley was any better for Nosey Nakshitka than life in Ellay, you're wrong. You're right, too, of course, but that's what life is all about, isn't it? Plain old complex as hell. Life was better because she had more friends, live ones, none of whom died of gunshot wounds in the following years. Life was not as good because she ran out of money and actually had to get a job, and the people she worked for exploited her every bit as mercilessly as the barrio bosses in Los Angeles exploited their poor illegals. Life was better because she didn't HAVE to speak Spanish to get by. It was worse because, although she spoke perfect English, flawless, the Queen's English, no less, she was surrounded by people who told her she talked real funny, or didn't understand a word she said, or thought she was a dreadful snob and putting on unaccept-able airs, or didn't believe those accents should be coming from such a brown face, and asked her, among other things, if she was English, awak-ening her all-too-familiar streak of sarcasm.

Invariably, to such a question, she replied, "Irish, actually. You've heard of the black Irish, to be sure," and was greeted by stupefied expressions and blank looks. Some people who hadn't seen her brown face assumed she was an exotic white foreigner and were dreadfully dis-appointed when they came face to face with her. These mostly made her aware of their disappointment, in no uncertain terms.

Others, however, like landlords, in Berkeley's rent-controlled and rental-hungry market, were perfectly happy to rent to a dark-skinned foreigner apartments they would never have rented to a dark-skinned compatriot; so life, taken altogether, was not so bad.

Occasionally, Nosey would experience some culture clash or culture shock; as, for instance, when someone presented her with a cake of *blachan*, that wonderfully funky concoction made of tiny shrimp that are crushed by trampling (rather like wine grapes, and with the same under-lying idea—that unwashed feet contribute marvelously to the body and flavor of food products), then fermented, then dried in the sun into hard little cakes that can fracture a skull on careless contact. She placed the *blachan* in the refrigerator and promptly forgot about it, being, as it were, too occupied with the process of keeping body and soul together to spend her time cooking.

At least, she forgot about it until the refrigerator broke down, one sunny August. As the cooling powers of the refrigerator waned, the nose-destroying odors of the *blachan* waxed ever more powerful, till even the usually preoccupied Nosey could not fail to notice them. Having been raised by some of the world's greatest champions of denial, Nosey simply lit incense and called the landlord. This charming individual, who often stalked the backyard with a loaded rifle, uttering pleasantries such as, "I'll be damned if I let a kike or a nigger in my backyard," came over immediately to examine the fridge.

He looked it over from top to bottom, then pulled out tools and set to work, a faint expression of distaste growing on his face. Finally, he turned to Nosey, who was watching him, fascinated. "Y'know," he said. "I don't know how to tell you this, but I think a rat died under your refrigerator."

"Oh, no," said Nosey, eager to be of assistance, "that smell isn't a dead rat. It's something we eat, back home. We call it *blachan*."

Fortunately she was not so stupid as to keep on blabbing when she saw the look on his face. It was a mixture of equal parts of disgust, incredulousness, and downright contempt. He left immediately and ordered her a new fridge.

Later, Nosey was to remember her early adventures in L.A.—as, for instance, when she had her first run-in with the Oakland Police Department, which, to her great surprise, were mostly white. That the mostly black inhabitants of Oakland seemed not the least bit surprised by this fact surprised Nosey even more.

Arriving in America full of faith in rags-to-riches and Horatio Alger stories, she ended up calling herself a godless Communist and a confirmed radical. She had cut off her long, beautiful hair when she left Singapore. "It won't look good in America," she said to her friends. "I'll look like some kind of stupid Third World woman."

After a couple of years, she began growing her hair again, eager to look as Third World as she could. "As long as it'll get," she replied when people asked her how long she would let her locks grow. She took to catching the 15 Stockton bus that ran through San Francisco's Chinatown and eavesdropping on the conversations of old Chinese ladies; she began to haunt the markets of Oakland's Chinatown, buying bowls of noodle soup at Vietnamese restaurants and sweet cakes made of sticky rice and coconut milk or red beans with raw sugar. And once she followed two Bengali women down a Berkeley road for nearly half a mile, almost crying at their familiar tones.

She even took to eating soggy *dosais* covered with *tovel chaatni* made from freeze-dried coconut. That's how low homesickness can make you sink, she thought, as she scraped her plate clean. "I owe it all to George Bush and Ronald Reagan," she would say. "I can't imagine despising anyone more. Those turkeys have cured me forever of my naive belief in America, the home of the free and the land of the brave." They hadn't, of course, though they'd gone quite a way to doing so. For example, she still thought "the brave" in the national anthem referred to a young man of Native American descent.

But she had come a long way, baby.

Meena Alexander

Statement: I arrived in the United States fully formed, or so I thought, in the fall of 1979, but the world split apart. My poetry, *House of a Thousand Doors* (1988), *The Storm* (1989), and *Night Scene, The Garden* (1992); my novel, *Nampally Road* (1991); and my memoir, *Fault Lines* (1993), have been ways of working through memory, into this new world.

Meena Alexander's narrative-discussion, in the following selection from *Fault Lines*, on the bearing and nurturing of children who have inherited multiple cultures is echoed in this anthology in short stories, such as Sarita Sarvate's "The Law of Averages," Naseem Hine's "The Dew and the Moon," and Tahira Naqvi's "All Is Not Lost." This selection from Meena Alexander's *Fault Lines* and the selection from Ved Mehta's *Sound-Shadows of the New World* are the only two works in this anthology that are from published autobiographies. We decided to include these two selections because they give a background of the kind of historical autobiographies and memoirs against which much of South Asian American "fiction" is written.

Fault Lines

Svati Mariam was born in New York City, late at night, on May 12, 1986, almost born in the taxi cab. I will never forget the full moon behind the Guggenheim, a pale lemony color as the cab raced down Fifth Avenue. David didn't know I was fully dilated, nor the cab driver, whistling through his teeth. I bit into my lips to stop the pain. One red light, I thought, and that will be that and the child will be born here, now. But we got into the emergency room and I was on the stretcher, and in another half minute she shot out all blue and gray and mottled, my little one, and I trembled and laughed, all at the same time, an experienced mother now. "What is her name, her name," Dr. Wolf asked, when he got there. "Here she is, she must have a name." I took the strength of speech into my own lips and said, "Svati, Svati Mariam is her name."

She was all mottled and discolored then.

"That was before you became a beauty," I tell her, when she asks me what color she was when she was born. "I am varnish now," she replies or sometimes she fixes herself a color change: "peach." And then continues: "You are brown mama, papa is blond papa, Adam is brown Adam, and I am peach Svati."

What shall I be for her, my little one? I push her each day towards Broadway. The days pass. She is still so young, packing in her years, one, two, three, four. Sometimes I worry for her, a little Indian-American girl-child. Whenever I can I hold onto the reality of mechi and mechan, her grandmother and grandfather in Kerala, her aunts, her cousins. Another soil, another earth. But what might she wish to be, that other soil cast into invisibility years down the road, when her small breasts flower and boys line up for her? What will she make of me, her South Indian mother? Will she recall I loved her, loved her brother too, throwing my arms around them, trembling at the sound of trucks roaring past, ambulances that halt to the stench of burning rubber at Saint Luke's emergency room?

In a dream Adam comes to me, as he did when he was a little child. "Mama, I am losting," he cries out, making me blindfold him and then twirl him around. His little arms stick out, he wanders around the room, relying on me to steer him away from tables and chairs and books lying in heaps, all the while singing out in his deep little voice, "Losting, Mama, losting," and when he signals, flapping his arms up and down like a pigeon might, I know he's had enough and I hug him to me, shower kisses on his cheeks. With my free hand I tug off the blindfold and watch him, pleased and anxious all the same time, rubbing his eyes, staring at me, once again, as if we had just met, he and I, for the very first time. He used to play that game all the time when he was three, even four. Was it to repair a memory he could not bear?

I cannot forget Adam just before he turned three. He lay on the air-port floor at Trivandrum. Words tumbled out of his mouth, mixed in with the tears. He beat at the cold floor. "No. No. Don't take me away, no, no." He was a well-built child with rosy cheeks. His tears made a mess on the floor. He could not bear to leave Kerala and his grandmother and grandfather and the rough and tumble of all that love, scents of cows and chickens and goats, the safety of so many arms to hold him.

I bent to pick him up, preparing for the passage through the metal detectors and body searches, then over the tarmac into the plane, all ready for the first step, in long return to New York. But as I stooped I felt myself dissolving, a sheer bodily memory I have no words for. I was all tears. I cupped his struggling little form to my breasts and looked at my mother's face. Through her tears, she looked back at me quite steadily.

A few days after Adam returned to New York, he lay on the floor in his American grandmother's house and drew a little picture: his map of the world. On the brown paper there were squiggles running up and down and a square shape somewhat at an angle to the up and down lines.

"Kozencheri, Delhi," he explained, reading his map to us, "India, sixth floor."

"What's the sixth floor?" We peered over his shoulder.

"Grandma's house, right here."

He beamed in delight at his own creation, the hereness, the honey of life included in it. Looking at him, I learnt to forget the little clenched form on the airport floor, the pain, the refusal. How close to danger we so often are, I think to myself, how little the present reveals the complicated amassing discord out of which alone our words can rise to music. In the little kitchen behind us, Toby was warming up a zucchini preparation she had cooked for our homecoming. That tangy, alien fragrance, and the sweetness of bread pudding steaming on the stove top distanced me from those thoughts and I shifted my weight in the new shoes I had bought for our return to this island city by the Hudson.

A little over a year later, when Adam was four, the doorman at Toby's building on Riverside Drive leant over and engaged him in conversation.

"What are you?" asked the lean black man from the South, bending towards my child. A few days earlier Frank had complained bitterly to me about white people and how all they thought was that blacks chewed watermelon. He had grimaced, elegantly spat out the bit of tobacco he had chewed into a bit of silver foil, and folded the whole caboodle up into a triangle, tossing it into the bin at the foot of the marble fireplace in the foyer.

"So what you, child?"

Adam, shy as ever, had just looked at him.

"You American, child?"

"No," said my son very boldly.

"Indian then. You Indian, child?"

Adam shifted his weight "No." He stuck his fist into his little mouth as he sometimes did. I was growing tense. What did my firstborn wish for himself? Some nothingness, some transitory zone where dreams roamed, a border country without passport or language?

"What you, then?" Frank insisted, his old man's voice growing tetchy as he waited.

Raising himself to his full height Adam replied, "Jedi, I'm a Jedi knight!" His head filled with Luke Skywalker and Darth Vader and the citadel of Death Stars, planets of lost origins, Adam knew exactly what he was talking about. Perhaps Frank knew what the child was saying, perhaps he didn't. But his face creased in smiles and he pressed a silver nickel into Adam's grubby little hand. The next time I saw Frank was several months later. He had moved to another apartment building. He was limping now and visibly aged. His cough was worse too. "How's the Jedi knight?" he asked me in a hoarse whisper. "How's the little knight?" "He's fine," I replied, "growing taller by the minute."

Svati too is growing taller. Born six years after her brother, she is now the age he was when he thought of himself as a Jedi knight. Just the other day she came home from preschool with a picture she had made of her Indian grandparents: mechi, mechan and her aunts Anna and Elsa and the dog and cat, all in the Tiruvella house. Her grandparents had round bodies and round eyes. Her grandfather and her two aunts had short crisp hair colored in with crayon strokes, all dark. Mechi had a sari, her hair drawn back in a bun. But through her bun, poised on top of her round head, ran a stick. At least that's what I took it to be.

"Svati, what's that?" I pointed.

"Bone."

"Bone?"

"She's my bone-and-arrow mechi, you know that. Bone-and-arrow Indians, mama."

Her voice rose in the utter certainty that sometimes grips her. I bent down and picked her up

"Darling, mechi and I and you are a different sort of Indian. She doesn't have a bow and arrow running through her hair like that. Who told you?"

I carried my child into the living room and turned my palm as I often do, into a map of India.

"Look, Svati, India is here—America there." I pointed a little to the right of my palm, somewhere near my ribs. "And Native Americans live all over this country. They were here first."

"And mechi?"

"Mechi lives in India. You know where she lives in Tiruvella."

"And Mechan?"

"Yes, he too."

"And the well?"

"Yes, the well and the guava trees and your aunts. And know something else? Native Americans don't wear their hair like that."

The next day I went into school and spoke to the teacher, an attractive young woman, filled with good projects for the children. Had she really thought I was Indian from the plains somewhere west of Manhattan? "I am Indian," I said, "from Asia. Heard of Columbus?" "Sure." I spoke about Columbus and his obsession with finding India. How he thought when he landed in America that he had struck the Indian coast. And then I mentioned Vasco da Gama, searching out the spice trade in the ancient kingdoms on the west coast of India. A child like Svati, I added, was caught in the crossfire of the white man's naming patterns. All of this took about a minute as children entered the classroom.

"Come and tell a story to the children, will you?" she invited. I promised I would. A week later I went back to tell the children a tale of India. I opened up my palm once again and drew invisible pictures on it. Two weeks after that the teacher invited a Native American from the Community House, and he came with a peace pipe and pictures of herbs and headdresses and ancient rites and talked to the children of his people who had once inhabited Turtle Island. That sacred geography all built over, bits and pieces of burning, I thought to myself as Svati told me of the visitor to her school.

Boman Desai

Statement: The author writes that his literary works constitute his statement.

"This Thicket" is an excerpt from Boman Desai's forthcoming novel, *Asylum, U.S.A.* The novel is structured as if it were a drive in a car, taking the reader/traveler from one point to another. According to the author, all successful novels and drives get the reader/traveler from one point to another. In "This Thicket" the author leads us from one technique of storytelling to another, from a straightforward narrative to a narrative that becomes a philosophical discourse (a technique used constantly and brilliantly in the Indian epic the *Mahabharata* and other classical Indian literary works). From the story of the protagonist's marriage to an American in order to get his green card, we are led to the protagonist's encounters with racism within his family and within the different cultures he has lived in. We are then drawn into his struggle to find a solution to end racism within all cultures and races.

This Thicket

One more Uturn: Two weeks before I got married I had written to my parents about the crazy reasons people got married: duty, money, security, pregnancy, excitement, oneupmanship, tohaveababy, togetawayfromhome, tohavesexwithoutguilt, hewasthefirsttoaskher, theywerenotgettingany-younger, theyhaddoneeverythingelse, alltheirfriendsweregettingmarried, wantingwhattheyweresupposedtowantwithoutaskingwhattheywanted-forthemselves—and, of course, love. What did Socrates say about love? Only a fool married when in love because when in love you did foolish things, or words to that effect. It was a Catch 22, losing proposition by definition. Socrates was, perhaps, bitter. Was he also, perhaps, the wisest of fools but still a fool? or the most foolish of wise men and still wise? He married Xanthippe, but her shrewishness might have been directly proportional to his Ripvanwinkleness, or maybe vice versa. Besides, he loved boys. But I've made too much of a turn already and I'm ploughing into a thicket, and it's not the one I had anticipated.

The day after I got married I wrote to my parents that I was married. I didn't want to say more until I had my green card and divorce when I would have said only that it didn't work out, but it was not to be. They sent congratulations, they sent gifts, they wanted pictures. What could I tell them? I could fill a book (this book) with the things I couldn't tell them, but what could I tell them? I couldn't and didn't tell them she was gay. I couldn't and didn't tell them we lived with her girlfriend. I told them everything else. My father wanted us to make the best of it. She must like you or she wouldn't have married you. My mother had known something was wrong from my two letters. First you said people were stupid to get married, not even a week later you said you got married. My grandmother sent money; because the boy showed courage. But I'm stalling now in another thicket, and it's still the wrong thicket. This is difficult to say. My father wanted pictures, but Barb did not want pictures taken. It would have been a sham, and she was right, but how to tell my folks? My father thought I wouldn't send pictures because Barb was a black woman, a negress as he knew to call black women. First, I laughed; then, it was not so funny.

You begin to understand the nature of this thicket. Is this turn necessary? or would I be pusillanimous for racing past the beast? the skin cancer for which no doctor will find a cure, for which the cure is under our own skin. Is it possible to understand a problem without appearing to condone it? Is it merely gratuitous to believe that understanding a problem is the first step toward overcoming it? What did Marx say? The problem is not interpreting the world but changing it, or words to that effect. My grandmother said I should scrub myself (scrape myself) with pumice stone when I bathed; otherwise, I would turn black like our servants. My father was even more a product of her wisdom than I was. Everyone wants to feel superior to someone. Even blacks subscribe to hierarchies of blackness. Why are blacks more than browns or olives or yellows or whites at the bottom of society's totem pole? I do not know. This is not the question as much as What is to be done? Let me be kind to my grandmother first. She had not access to the world from her Indian village as we have today. She had not television, she had not movies and radio except within the narrowest limits, she had not even electricity when she'd been a gamine trolling narrow dusty streets with her brothers. It was difficult for her to measure her provincialism. Let me also be kind to my father. He never acted on his worst instincts. He would gladly have helped those to whom he found himself superior. He would have been the staunchest yankee rather than a rebel. If I had married a black woman he would have raged against her until he met her, then she would have become his daughter-in-law (always assuming other things equal—education, intelligence, common interests, that sort of thing) because he prided himself on his liberality.

This is still not good, but it's the best that can be said, and it's better than what might be said. Am I any better myself? If I were to marry a black woman it would not be without thinking: But she is Black! and How am I going to explain this? Perhaps the liberalization process progresses with generations. My grandmother would not have allowed such a marriage, my father would have needed an explanation, my child will not have to provide an explanation, and so on until perhaps a twenty-first century descendent will emerge enlightened enough to recognize that the darkness under which his forebears labored was darker than their pigmentation, enlightened enough not only not to recognize gradations of pigmentation but not even to see them, enlightened enough to be blind, less an unlikelihood than might once have been imagined in this late browning stew of America. As diverse ingredients continue to find their way into the stew, color becomes increasingly common, and America provides more possibilities for a rich stew than any country in the world.

What am I saying? He is not a nonracist who says he is a nonracist. He is a nonracist who doesn't know he is a nonracist. Have I said enough? Have I said too much? Is it time already to come down from the mountain? Yes, yes, and yes again. Irony has more currency than a bully pulpit in the increasingly hardboiled egg of today's globe, but before I waft down from my star, my cloud, or is it merely my pedestal? let me add a corollary. Racism is not notched in the skull, spine, and pelvis, not even in the carpals and the tarsals. Respect the man, not his racism, and there is hope. What did Nietzsche say? If we succeed in making people hate themselves we will have to seduce them into loving themselves again or we will all become victims of their revenge, or words to that effect. Let me also add a caution. The eradication of racism will not mean the eradication of strife; racism has less to do with color than with class, status, inequity, insecurity—but I'm ploughing more deeply into this thicket than I'd intended, that's another book, and I don't know that I'm the man to write it.

What am I saying? At the moment of truth the joke was on us, on all of us Indians who laughed with the English at the expense of other Indians, we were laughing at ourselves, victimizers and victims at once, because while we might have laughed with the English at the babus, the natives, we could never be the English, only sad English Wannabes. We're all schmucks. We're also all beautiful. It's up to us which way we want to go, and I want to get out of this thicket.

Chitra Divakaruni

Statement: Living and writing in America is for me at once a challenge and an opportunity. The challenge lies in trying to bring alive, for readers from other ethnic backgrounds, the Indian—and Indian American— experience, not as something exotic and alien, but as something human and shared. It lies in getting my own community to see the subject of my work (often the plight of women of Indian origin struggling within a male-dominated culture, even here in America). It is necessary and important and not, as many have complained, a betrayal of my people, an exposure of secrets that create a "bad impression" of Indian in American society. But the opportunities are more important: to be able to straddle two distinct cultures and depict both with the relatively objective hand of the outsider; to destroy stereotypes and promote understanding between different sectors of the multicultural society in which we live; to paint the complex life of the immigrant with its unique joys and sorrows, so distinct from those of people who have never left their native land. The possibility of achieving even one of these through my work makes me glad to be an Indian writer in America.

Poetry, in South Asian traditions of literature—both oral and written— is seldom seen as a specific literary genre existing only in a strictly defined rhythmically patterned literary form. The use of descriptive language, of linguistic ambiguities and nuances, of extensive imagery as well as the presence of *rasa*, the re–creation of emotions, moods, sentiments, have been seen as the essence of poetry (regardless of the literary form) in South Asian art from the earliest times to the present. If we had kept strictly to distinctions of forms according to South Asian literary traditions, it would have been difficult to organize this anthol-ogy into the more Western (and more accessible) divisions "Poetry" and "Fiction." Works such as the following could easily be included in a "poetry" section. Chitra Divakaruni's skill as a poet who uses both verse and narrative forms is seen in the two works by her in this anthology.

Yuba City Wedding

Empty kitchen. Only a few smudges of yellow across the colorless sky, like paw-prints of a dog that's stepped in piss. I want to be asleep, like the others, but someone is driving a nail, a huge iron one like we used to use on the railroad ties, into the top of my skull. That, and the coming wedding.

The thin walls shiver with the snores of the five men I share this place with. A train tears through the morning, flakes of plaster fall from the ceiling to coat my hair. The floor is slanting away from my feet. I hold tight to the coffee mug, but it's cold now and no help, the swirling inside it thick and muddy like my mind.

I close my eyes and try to picture Manuela's face. Nothing comes.

They took me out last night. My last taste of freedom, they joked. We went to Pepe's Diner by the tracks. The other places—the ones owned by the white men—don't like us Indians, even when we pay ahead for our drinks. But that's O.K.; I like Pepe's. The packed mud floors and the smoky oil lamps remind me of the *dhabas** back home, and the other men, Mexicans mostly, leave us alone.

I knew a lot of people there last night. Gurpreet was there, and Surinder, and the man who works the signals at the station house. My housemates, of course, and some of the Jat farmhands who pick lettuce with me. Avtar Singh called out a toast in Punjabi, good times in bed, many sons, something like that, and we all drank tequila. It's taken me a long time to like tequila, bitter and burning, not like the rice-toddy we made back home, sweet with a full, ripe smell. But now I can drink it with the best of them, throwing back my head, then sucking the salt off my fist. Some of the Mexican pickers I knew raised their glasses, and Manuela's cousin Roberto, who'd tried to knife me when he first found out we were seeing each other—it seems a long time back now—came over and threw his arms around me and gave me a beery hug. I should have been happy.

But I couldn't forget the ones who weren't there. The older men, turbaned and grizzle-bearded like the fathers we had left behind, the ones who chanted every week from the *Granth Sahib*[†] at the *Gurdwara*[‡] ceremonies I was no longer permitted to attend. Baldev Singh, who shared my coffin of a cabin through that miserable voyage to America, who held my head when I threw up on the floor. Rajinder Mann, who bought me my first pair of American pants and talked to the foreman

---

* *dhaba:* roadside cafe
† *Granth Sahib:* holy book of the Sikhs
‡ *Gurdwara:* Sikh place of worship

for me because I didn't know English, who got me my first job clearing land for the Central Pacific Railroad Company. I'd known they wouldn't be there. Still, it hurt to look at the empty row of stools at the bar where they usually sat.

They hadn't wanted me to marry Manuela, of course. It had been O.K. while we were going out. A young man needs these things, they said. But when I told them we were planning a wedding, it was another matter. *A Christian, a woman who speaks a different language, who eats pig's flesh and cow's? Unclean,* they said. *How can she bring your children up as good Sikhs?* They said, *She will leave you for another man, one of her own kind. They always do. Look what happened to Tejinder. Be patient,* they said. *One of these days the immigration bans will be lifted and you can go back to your own village and marry, a fine girl, one who has never known a man. She'll cook you roti and palak-dal, bear sons with your nose, your forehead, your skin. Nurse you in old age.*

Nights, I lay in bed and pictured her, my bride, in a shiny gold *sal-war-kameez*,* long braids framing a face where the features shifted like sand when the Lu wind blows. Only her eyes were clear, black and bright and so deep I could dive in. I smelled her jasmine hair-oil. Her skin was soft as lotus petals. But when I opened my eyes there was only moonlight, thin whiplashes of it falling through the blinds across a mattress that sagged like my heart was starting to. I knew I couldn't be like them, couldn't wait and wait while time burned through my flesh and left only trembling. So I filled my lungs with the smell of Manuela's cinnamon breath, the ripple of her laugh deep down in her throat, her fingers flying like wings over my body, and in the morning I told them.

Now there is nothing left to wait for but the wedding. Late in the afternoon, when the sun has pulled in some of its burning and breath is not like a hot wet sponge inside the chest, we'll put on the black pants and white shirts we've rented for this day and make our way up the hill, my friends and I, to the Iglesia Santa Maria. There will be a lot of raucous joking and back-clapping along the way, partly because they hope it will be easier, now, for them to do what I am doing, partly because the old stone church, looming up dark and domed against a bleached sky, fills us with nervousness.

I've never been inside the church. I try to think of it now, holding the cold mug in my hands, pressing my throbbing forehead against it. Stained glass windows the color of blood, gutted smoky candles in front of the shrines and the dead smell of wax they leave behind, the wooden Christ with twisted limbs and tortured eyes who looks down

---

* *salwar–kameez:* Indian tunic and pants for women

from the Cross and sees everything. Manuela has told me all of it. The stone basin from which they will sprinkle water on my forehead. I can feel it, cool, the drops smelling of the shadows in the corners of the church. The warm red wine already turning a little sour, the week-old wafer that will crumble in my mouth, gum up my throat. The new name Padre Francisco has chosen for me, Ysidro, which sounds a little like Surdeep, so I will feel at home.

I hear voices upstairs. Laughter, things falling over. They are talking of the party tonight, the torches, the guitars and flutes, the big roasting pits that must be started already. There'll be lots of drinking, chilled beer, of course, and sangria in pitchers with sliced oranges floating in them, tequila and rum brought up special from Sacramento. And lots of dancing. Men with hair slicked back and sombreros dusted and boots polished to shining with pig's grease, farm girls turned señoritas for an evening, giggling behind fans decorated with black lace, hiding their chapped hands in the folds of their white gowns. My housemates have already picked out partners. Slim-hipped Margarita, Rosa of the flashing eyes, Isabella whose plump lips taste better than tequila. The names fall at me through the ceiling, along with hoarse bedroom jokes. Before the night ends, there will be a few fistfights, maybe a knifing. Or perhaps a wedding or two in the works, if my friends are lucky.

But I'm not really thinking about them now. I'm picturing the end, the wedding procession winding its way along the narrow stone path to the room in the back of Doña Inez's tailor shop which will be our new home. More singing and toasts and jokes about brides and grooms, and then the two of us left alone in a bed smelling of crushed flowers, while outside the cheers and yells mingle with the sound of bottles breaking. Manuela opens her arms and I look down at her, but suddenly there's nothing there, nothing except black emptiness like a crack in the earth after years of no rain, pulling me down into it.

I stumble to the sink. A fist around my heart, squeezing. Red spots behind my eyes growing into a wash of blood. I plunge my head into the bucket, and water fills my nostrils like cool silver so I don't have to think, at least for a little while. I hold my breath and it grows into a chanting inside my chest, the passage we always start with from the Granth Sahib. And then a scene comes to me, from a childhood story I thought I'd forgotten, of a man who enters a magic cave in search of treasure. As he steps forward, the walls close in behind him. It is very dark, like behind my eyes now, and he is afraid. But then a door opens in the rock in front, and he sees a light. He steps through, the walls close in again, again the dark, but then another fissure opening, another light, brighter this time, as though shining off diamonds. I forget how the story ended. But the chanting is gone now, and in its place a quiet rustle, like wind in tall trees. Last week Manuela told me she felt the baby move for the first time. I open my eyes in water and imagine what he sees, the dark swirl and flow, his tiny hands opening and closing. I hear footsteps coming down the stairs. I lift my face and breathe in the bright waiting air.

Because of immigration laws, most of the original Sikhs who settled in Yuba City could not bring their families with them or, in the case of single men, go back to get married until the 1940s. As a result, in the 1920s and 1930s several men married local women from Mexico.

Lakshmi Gill

Statement: I've lived in North America now longer than I have lived in the country of my birth. Nevertheless, I haven't become a North American. I didn't choose to be a Punjabi-Spanish-Filipina, but I have chosen not to be a North American. There's an entire planet to roam in, a universe, a world of imagination.

Lakshmi Gill has selected her prerogative as a writer to write about characters, landscapes, and stories that are not specifically South Asian. The student teacher of the story does reflect the author's awareness of an entire planet in which she can roam and the wealth contained in the world of imagination that her protagonist tries to nurture in at least one of her students.

The Student Teacher

He woke up at 5 a.m. with the cows. Getting them out to pasture was not easy; sometimes he'd beat a cow that kicked him until he was tired out. But his father expected the chores completed before Allan could go to school—at Junior High down in the village of Dorchester. To catch the bus, he'd not had time to change every morning for the past two weeks.

"He stinks," Susan said.

"Of cow-shit," Jimmy added.

Mr. Michener, their Grade 8 teacher, exclaimed, "You don't judge a man by that," and proceeded to lecture them for 20 minutes on the worth of a human being. After class he spoke to Allan, who was brushing the odd muck off his pantlegs.

"Couldn't change again?"

"No." Allan spoke in his soft, hardly audible voice. He moved away, thinking furiously: *I hate being a farmer.*

> My name is Allan Fielding. I am native to Upper Dorchester and have lived here all my life. I have two sisters. I earn my living in the woods with my friend who is 18. I am 13. I am a farmer.

Mrs. Callaghan went through the 3 x 5 cards slowly, trying to remember names and details. A farmer. What a quaint word. That tall child who stared at her with his clear grey eyes throughout class from the back of the room; who answered questions quickly and intelligently; who came up to her several times during the day speaking softly, trying to make friends, was a farmer.

"They're at that age when they're feeling their straps. Breaking through," Mr. Michener filled her in on the rest where the students left off on their 3 x 5s. "Allan's father—he's a fundamentalist Christian— keeps a tight hand on him, his only son. The two girls—older—got away."

"It sounds like his mother is in the shadows."

"Very much so. Quiet. She has no say."

The students got all excited filling out the Peer Nomination Form. They had all been together eight years but had taken themselves for granted. Now when it was crystallized for them, they had to think. Who was friendliest? Best dressed? Can we put our own names down, Mrs. Callaghan? Sure, why not. Smartest kid? Allan's name came up 18 times for smartest kid; the 19th was Judy. It took Mrs. Callaghan two hours to tally the names, but it was worth it—she now had a sociogram. She was determined to know them.

"Highest in Math, Science. Good kid all around. Just had this one problem. Used to come to school smelling of cow—I had to give the class a good talking."

"They made fun of him."

"Yes, made him feel bad."

Mrs. Callaghan remembered something a Scarboro Father once said to her. *You don't have to go to the Third World; the mission field is here. Here in the First World you will find the apathetic, neglected children.*

"His father's farm. I visited there once. He doesn't keep the place well. Dirt. Garbage all around. Doesn't treat his animals well. Doesn't treat his children well. The two daughters got away. It's funny how that happens. He's a fundamentalist—so children go the other way."

In the schoolyard, two Grade 1 children danced around Allan, his tall figure like a Zen Master's staff. Mr. Michener had said that he never played with anyone when he was a child; he was just kept out there on the farm. "So when I see him playing with the younger children. . ." then his eyes nearly misted over. He had taught some of these children's parents in this same old school building. Mrs. Callaghan watched from the Grade 8 window the children going round and round, holding on to his outstretched arms, Allan, still, at the centre.

> I have changed from last week since you came because I have gained more self-confidence. Since I live on a farm, if I go to the city to get something for the machinery, I am not ashamed of what I am carry-

ing because I am a farmer and I am proud of it. I have also learned that when a cow kicks me, I will just hit it once to make it understand.

"So, how much land do you have?" Mrs. Callaghan asked Allan during her five-minute conferencing with individual students. Since it was 3 p.m. they had extra time. He had said that he could take the late bus that came in from Sackville.

"Two hundred acres, some wooded, some cleared. I help my father. Sometimes I come to school straight from work. I had a bit of a problem here in school because of it." Then he explained what she had already heard many times.

He never missed school. Unlike the others, he seemed to want to come everyday. The Grade 7s had shown her their journals which were full of "school is so boring" that she was puzzled by Allan's persistence. Perhaps, home was worse?

Most ambitious: Allan, 18 nominations.

"You're a good, serious student."

His expression—a veiled eagerness—didn't change. "I want to go on to university. I'm saving my money."

"If you keep up the good marks, you might try for a scholarship."

"Yes," he murmured, a slight catch in his voice betraying his hope.

"Well, you don't mind now being what you are."

His clear gaze fell steadily on her smiling face.

"I must bring you a Thomas Hardy book to show you how fine it is to be a farmer."

The next student popped her head in to see if their conference was over. As Allan rose reluctantly, Gwynn came in next. That day they had gone over Hugh Garner's "A Trip for Mrs. Taylor" and to introduce the theme of loneliness, she had played *Eleanor Rigby*. While Paul McCartney's voice rang out "All the lonely people/Where do they all come from" she had watched their concentrated faces. At the corner, near the window, 14-year-old Gwynn sat with lowered eyelids. Her parents were divorced, just as most of the children's in the class were, and she missed her father. When she had looked up, Mrs. Callaghan saw the depths of her hurt.

"I like the *Northanger Abbey* you gave me to read," Gwynn began. "But some words I don't understand."

Mrs. Callaghan had paired her with Allan for a Reading Group Activity. The class had never done such an activity before, so it wasn't going very well. But, at least, Mrs. Callaghan thought, they were reading. There was so little time to be with them—they could only touch and then it was over. While they were together, it would matter.

"I really want to get out of here," Gwynn was saying. "I hate Dorchester. There's nothing to do. I like going to Sackville. At least there's a movie house there."

Mrs. Callaghan felt a twinge of guilt. To those who lived in even greater isolation, Sackville, New Brunswick, at the pit of the marshes, at the edge of the border, must feel like a haven. And yet, to her, who had seen gay Paree . . .

"Yeah, every chance I get, I go out to Sackville."

Just like the Dorchester boys. The Sackville boys would get together and ridicule the Dorchester boys who would come up occasionally for some "civilization." She could never figure it out since they all looked alike—typical, plaid-shirted, blue-jeaned, tan big-booted kids with long, unkempt hair. The Typs, her own child dubbed them. The Typs would cruise the drag in their beat-up half-tons, packed in the back, drunk, loud. But apparently there were distinctions. Mr. Michener said, "Our kids go down to Sackville for shop class at the Junior High on Day 6. Over there they're taught how to build miniature cox engines; over here, these boys can put together a whole car, engines and all, right in their backyard."

Unlike Allan, who was poised to awaken, Gwynn showed no hope of moving out of her desperation. Mrs. Callaghan could not offer her any platitudes or promises. In silence they sat together, breathing in and breathing out.

On the third and last week of her practicum, it rained during the Monday lunch hour. Mrs. Callaghan looked out the window and remarked under her breath, "It's raining."

Allan, who hovered near her, said, "What do you want? I'll get it for you."

Was she allowed to send a student out to do something for her? She hadn't had a drink all morning.

"Coke?" He inquired. All the students teased her for drinking Coke every lunchtime: *Mrs. Callaghan, you're a Coke addict!*

She nodded.

Allan said, "I'll go to the store for you."

"Maybe not. It's raining." She moved away.

He followed her around the classroom. "That's nothing. I have a jacket."

She handed him a $2 bill. "Put something on your head."

Since she was on duty, she walked up and down the hall and in and out of classrooms. Jimmy and Don were arm wrestling in the Grade 7 room surrounded by their fans. In Grades 5/6 some children clustered around a Math game on the computer, others glued cotton onto a

Christmas collage at their desks. She glanced out the window once in a while. Soon she saw Allan's head come up the rise of the road and then the rest of him slowly walking towards the school, alone, like a traveler in his worn-out beige jacket and blue jeans, looking up at the building as to a mountain. The slight rain fell about him, covering everything with a fine mist. Watching him, Mrs. Callaghan made up a poem:

> Behold, the farmer! I wait at the market-place
> Deflecting questions.

She walked quickly to the side door, pushed the handlebar, and called out his name so that he wouldn't have to go around to the front door. He ran through the yard and handed her the bottle and her $2 back.

Mrs. Callaghan's brows lifted. She pushed the bill to his hand.

"No, I had money." Then he gave her two candy canes. His face was flushed from his run and his hair was wet. His eyes were two star sapphires that gazed down at her, distant and lost in a cosmic loneliness.

"Thank you," she responded. Ah, *carry away the farmer's oxen, and make off with the hungry man's food.*

At home, Mrs. Callaghan took down *The Return of the Native* from the bookshelf and asked her own 13-year-old son if he thought it was suitable reading for their age group. "I don't know. Too old, probably." He handed it back, his interest lay in Tolkien.

She went to the porcelain shaft on her desk, applied glue to its side and fitted it firmly but gently on the broken pagoda. Hong Kong images rushed through her mind. She had summered there in her childhood, a short jaunt from the Philippines, the country where she was born. The Philippines—where her own father had become ensnared by marriage when he meant only to visit this new and exotic land he had heard of as a child in India. Because she had seen how desperately he had wanted to get away, she had left early and lived everywhere else, even if only in hotels and roominghouses. Paris, San Francisco, Toronto. The restless list went on: a year here, a year there. She had got used to leaving her things in boxes, because even if she lived in one city for longer than a year, she would transfer from apartment to apartment. She left furniture behind, carried only the most modular and portable.

Then she got married, followed her husband to the town of Sackville, where they had stayed for 14 years. And time, an eternal present feeding the past, was no longer fed by the future. Wherever she turned, it was Sackville, like a mountain climbed because it was simply there. Each day she would go out because one foot lunged at the rockface and the other found a foothold. All inspiration had gone; it was only a matter of assiduous avoidance of the fall.

Her eyes glistened as if with tears as she set the figurine on its side, a tiny blue and gold tomb of some dead Empress, the pile of shafts like pitons driven into its rigid body. It was so much easier to build than to repair.

She thought about the book all night. He would not be ready for the passionate Eustacia, but Hardy was so good with rural life. There would be connections. From his bedroom in Upper Dorchester, he would fly to that other Dorchester in Wessex. The gulf bridged.

It was Friday, the last day of her practicum. She drove out early, passing by homes with painted names on mail boxes that she recognized. That was where Judy lived! And sweet little Kenny over there. In the 14 years she had lived in Sackville, these houses were just that to her—architectural wonders, stately old stone mansions, wooden shacks, colonial dwellings—but now, they suddenly spoke to her: "Good morning, Mrs. Callaghan." They had faces, smiles, frowns, thoughtful looks. She wondered where Upper Dorchester was. She took a side road which twisted up and down hills, out to where houses thinned out. This was Hardy country. She gazed in amazement, she had never really looked before: stretch of sepia fields broken by dark green woods that loomed suddenly, dry sedge on the marshes, cracked mud-flats extending toward the gently flowing river. When she reached Dorchester Cape, lost, she turned around to get back to the school.

The students milled around her to say good-bye. The atmosphere was light, pleasant—she was leaving them with good feelings. The boys drew lots for *A Man for All Seasons* and the girls for *Jane Eyre* which she had picked out of her bookshelf the night before.

"You're to share these books with the whole class," she exhorted the winners. She passed by Allan's seat. "See me after class."

She gave him *The Return of the Native* as some students came up to the lectern to say more good-byes. He clasped the book and read the card: "It's great to be a farmer!" she had written. He stood rigidly nearby, like one in attendance, as she moved around to accommodate the others. From her peripheral vision she could see that he was pleased.

"Give me your address," his soft voice reached her in the din. She scribbled it while Gwynn was saying how she wished Mrs. Callaghan would be teaching at university in five years' time, so that she could be taught by her again.

Mrs. Callaghan, touched deeply, smiled back at Gwynn. "Yes, that would be nice. Five years from now."

Anu Gupta

Statement: I am thrilled to be a second-generation South Asian American woman living in the United States. This is an exciting time for our community. We are in the midst of challenging ourselves and others to define what it means to be South Asian *American* and to negotiate and reconcile the two spheres of beliefs, values, and thoughts in whose intersection we find ourselves. Amid this energetic confusion, writing reveals answers and raises new questions; it provides perspective and insight into who I am.

In "Crystal Quince" the protagonist not only gives the reader a glimpse of her life within her family and her Indian American community but also shows how she, as a young, second-generation South Asian American, learns about the beliefs and expectations regarding a wife's role in Indian tradition. The issues regarding living between cultures that this generation faces are presented in the following story through images of different places, clothes, and rituals. Priya Agarwal in her book *Passage From India: Post 1965 Indian Immigrants and Their Children* (Palos Verdes, CA: Yuvati Publications, 1991) discusses some of the issues that second-generation South Asian Americans encounter.

Crystal Quince

The main street of Little India in Jackson Heights comes to life as doors are unlocked and shopkeepers rush to get their stores ready. Women change the saris on the mannequins while others return jewelry to their display cases. Fragments of Hindi, Punjabi, Gujarati, and Tamil fill the air like the sound of an alarm clock radio, signaling the start of a new day.

The calmness of this morning weekday scene strikes me, and I remember the weekends, when I usually came here with my family. At those times, the street was filled with people and families—grandparents, grandchildren, husbands, and wives. On Saturdays and Sundays, parking was an absolute nightmare, and to find a spot in front of India Sari Palace (ISP) or Sam & Raj, the two most popular stores, was considered a triumph. This Wednesday morning, however, there are only a few cars and the street is practically empty except for a handful of pedestrians. As my mother and I turn the corner, I look at the bare white wall of the Rockbottom, remembering the boys who would congregate there and shower women with wolf whistles as they walked by.

It has been many years since I walked down the streets of Jackson Heights. Coming back here with my mom is a disturbing yet peaceful experience. So much has changed. Landmarks like Sona are still here, but so many tiny stores have sprouted up here and there and on top of each other that I am overwhelmed by the newness of it all. At the same time I am calmed by the knowledge that they are all extensions of Little India that reinforce the feeling of community. The existence of Little India has been crucial to my development. As a child, it was a place where I could look out the window of the car when my dad parked illegally in front of a fire hydrant, and see other children like me, a place where I could run into friends who did not live in Long Island, a place where almost everyone was Indian. This street and I had grown and changed together. What started out as a few scattered shops soon became an entire street, then an entire block, and now almost a whole neighborhood. Likewise, I had "started" as a child who hated herself for being different, who then tried to be like everyone else, and who now, after college, is proud of who she is.

Across the street I can see the new grocery store with its big green letters shining in the sunlight. The owners are still unloading and unpacking vegetables while their children run around, adding to the chaos of "opening day." My mother grasps my arm to cross the street, but I stop her, as I recognize the woman approaching us.

"Look, Ma! It's Nisha Auntie."

The calm on my mother's face suddenly transforms itself into a tight smile. It has been a while since she has seen her old neighbor, and a chance meeting in Little India is not welcome. Nevertheless, I know she will be cordial to her former friend. It is the Indian thing to do—to make small talk, move along, and not ask any questions.

I wait patiently as they chat away, making excuses for why they have not kept in touch, trying hard to hide a truth that is so obvious to both of them, and to me.

Then I notice the lipstick, still wet and shiny, on Nisha Auntie's face, and I remember the pain of being a woman.

In the America of TV sitcom land, old neighbors welcome new ones by bringing over food as a means of introduction. The exact opposite happened with our new Patel neighbors. Nisha Auntie was the first to greet us with food, and subsequently, she would always bring over her newest concoctions. Although her food, and by extension, she, was shunned by my siblings, my daring parents would humor her efforts and never refuse her Gujarati dishes, which always had a sweet taste to them. The children lost interest in the Patels right away. Nisha

Auntie and her husband, Neil, didn't bring any kids for them to play with. My sister and brother, Srishti and Vikrant, didn't care why, but I had to ask.

"They can't have kids," was my mother's answer. She left it at that.

After the food came Nisha Auntie's requests to my mother. "Could you please take me to the store, Meena? You know that Neil won't let me drive." They went, the two of them, to the supermarket. While my mother bought cold cuts and sandwich bread for her children, Nisha Auntie bought the one thing that would ease her pain.

Months later, after strange calls at night and random visits by Nisha Auntie, I noticed the Budweiser cans with purple lipstick on them in the garage. Silently, my mother would throw them away in our garbage, with no explanation, despite my constant inquiries.

"We don't like her coming with us. She dresses funny . . . and wears too much makeup, especially that ugly purple lipstick." With these proclamations, Srishti and Vikrant refused to go to the store with my mother and HER. Their trips, then, were made silently, together, in the quiet of the morning or the laziness of the afternoon.

Two years later the only thing that was changed was the growing number of cans in the garage each week. "Ma, you shouldn't help Nisha Auntie buy alcohol. I know you don't pay for it, but it is illegal to help someone who is, uhm, a *sharabi*, an alcoholic. Ma, are you listening?"

"Radha, what do you know of the suffering of a woman? Let her be, she is not hurting you or me." Unlike me, my mother did know what suffering was. She understood all too well the solace that alcohol could provide. She knew the numbing effect one drink, two drinks, a few drinks could have on pain. Perhaps this shared understanding, this collective unconscious is why my mother helped Nisha Auntie buy beer. I will never know for sure. Besides, my mother was one of those women who did things without necessarily having reasons she could express for doing them. A "Why?" would have been answered with a blank look and a "Because."

Years later, however, the incomprehensible would become crystal clear. I now understand why Nisha Auntie locked herself in her house and drank herself into oblivion; why she watched for hours as Vikrant played on the driveway; why she hated holding newborn babies at social gatherings; why she was never home on Halloween and went away around Christmas; why the laughter of children in the street would bring tears to her eyes; and why she poured a case of beer into her frail 4'9" body hoping it would give her a child.

"We're getting late, Radha. Hurry up! I *know* you don't spend this much time getting ready in college."

"I'm coming, Daddy."

"None of this coming business, Radha *beta*.* We're going to miss the wedding."

With that, I snapped the clip in my hair. There. Quite pleased with my transformation, I took a long look in the mirror. My hair, usually disheveled and everywhere, was combed straight behind my back, with the sides clipped up and away from my face. My makeup was painstakingly perfect, and a *bindi*† could be found between my eyebrows but slightly higher than them. I had on big gold earrings to complement my necklace. The elaborate jewelry went well with the simple but elegant silk *salwar-kameez*.‡ On my feet were *chappals*§ to match. "So," I thought to myself, "the 'American' girl could really look Indian if she tried." I licked my lips, straightened out my *chunni*, ‖ and raced down the stairs.

In the hotel I met my "godparents." Ashok Uncle gave me the biggest hug.

"Radha *bitia*, is your *padhai*# going well? Do you like Brown?"

"Yes, Uncle, I'm doing well in school, and I love Brown."

"Good. So, Meena, when are you getting this one married? I need time to practice so that I can sing at her wedding."

"Ashok, *bhaisaheb*,** you know that Radha has her own mind."

I eased away, trying to avoid an ugly scene, and made small talk with my godmother, Preeti Auntie. Her latest craze, besides dieting, was home decorating. For her, alcohol was not the way to ease the pain of being barren.

"Are your parents getting anxious about marrying you off?" she asked.

"Yes, Auntie, but obsessed is probably more accurate." She smiled and gave me a wink.

"Do you have any plans to go away?" I asked.

"Just our usual trip to Virginia," she replied. With that I just nodded. For almost five years, Ashok Uncle and Preeti Auntie have been trying to have a child. Modern technology through the art of artificial insemination simply was not cooperating. Some of our friends had even specu-

---

*beta and bitia: son or child. Parents and other older relatives and friends will use this term to describe their daughters as well, usually as a sign of affection.

† bindi: a small circle worn on the forehead as a sign of marriage or for adornment.

‡ salwar-kameez: a South Asian piece of clothing consisting of a long baggy shirt similar to a tunic and baggy pants.

§ chappals: sandals.

‖ chunni and dupatta: both refer to a long scarflike piece of clothing that is worn with a salwar-kameez.

padhai: studies of schoolwork.

**bhaisaheb: bhai means brother and saheb means sir. This term is often used by women to address their husbands' close, older male friends.

lated that my godparents had faked a miscarriage two years prior just to save face in the community.

Ashok Uncle and Preeti Auntie were close family friends. Although they were not our formal godparents, they treated me, Srishti, and Vikrant as if we were their own children. When Vikrant was very little, Ashok Uncle would spend a lot of time with him talking about turtles and rocks. Once Vikrant, impatient at being ignored, called Ashok Uncle "Daddy," creating an awkward situation. Preeti Auntie would always take Srishti and me shopping. Even though they would never admit it, they were more excited about my getting married someday than my parents were.

We made our way from the lobby to the reception room where the wedding was to take place. My godparents were the oldest couple here without children. In fact, I was surprised to see them here since Preeti Auntie had not been invited to the premarriage bridal preparation ceremony. I bent down and whispered to my mother to find out why. She gave me a hard nudge with her elbow and told me she would tell me later. It had something to do with Preeti Auntie's presence being inauspicious for the bride-to-be.

During the ceremony I realized how intricate an Indian Hindu marriage is. Most of my non-Indian friends pictured their weddings out of a June issue of *Brides*. They worried about color coordinating their bridesmaids, at the same time complaining about their latest boyfriends. On the other hand, choosing between white or pink taffeta or what boy to date were not decisions in the forefront of my mind. This was perhaps the only chance I would ever have to see an Indian wedding before my own, which would probably be in a few years. Thus, I watched with wonderment and confusion as the bride and groom, the *dulhan** and *dulha*,[†] sat in front of a huge fire with their heads bowed, the end of his *sahera*[‡] knotted to the end of her *dupatta*.

Afterward I decided to be brave and ask my mother what those prayers and chants meant after all. Was it just another rendition of "Do you take this man/woman . . . Yes, I do. You may now kiss the bride"? At a loss, she referred me to Ashok Uncle. With an unexpected sadness in his voice, he answered my question.

"When a woman and a man get married," he began, "the woman can ask the man for seven things so that she can be assured of her happiness with him."

"And the man can ask her for seven things, too?"

---

* *dulhan*: bride.
† *dulha*: groom.
‡*sahera*: a scarflike piece of clothing, similar to a *chunni*, that is worn by the groom.

"No, Radha, the man can ask for only one thing."

"Well, what can he ask for?"

"The one thing that every Indian man asks for from his future wife, the one thing that only she can provide him with is . . . a child."

There was silence at the table. My godmother got up to get some water. As forks clanked against plates of Indian food, I looked at my mother and thought of purple lipstick on beer cans.

Crystal Quince is the latest fall lipstick color for dark-toned women. It is available at your nearest Clinique counter.

Naseem A. Hines

Statement: The memories of my childhood afternoons are still vivid and clear in my mind. There used to be a two-foot-high stone platform on one side of the jasmine trellis. I would pretend it was a dock. I would pull a camp cot close to the dock, put a wide board across the platform and my cot, and make my cousins walk on the board to the cot. This camp cot was my imaginary steamboat, the kind I had seen in the movies. We would have to make gestures with mock paddles to push ourselves away from the platform towards the sea. Little did I know that Nature in Her gentle way was preparing or even inspiring me to sail on, across the dark waters, and find my own new world!

And so it came to pass that eventually, in the spring of 1980, I came to the United States to find a new horizon and to strive to create a new destiny. "The Dew and the Moon" is not completely autobiographical. However, like the main characters in the story, I consider myself very fortunate that I, too, was blessed with a second chance to make something of my life.

My brief observation about living in America is as follows: The legend of America is a magnificent saga of the strong-willed immigrant. Each biography unfolds a series of adventures, struggles against discord and disharmony, and evolves into some aspect of metamorphosis. But only if one is lucky will one's endeavors result in triumph.

"The Dew and the Moon" is a variation on the theme of a South Asian woman married to a South Asian man who is in America and the sorrow and the problems that arise when the husband, for one reason or another, does not want to be married to the woman who has been chosen for him. Neila Seshachari's "The Bride Comes Home," another story in this anthology, deals with a similar theme. This is an issue that is very relevant in the South Asian American community today. The lyrical style of "The Dew and the Moon" and the philosophical stance of the female protagonist of the story are strongly influenced by the author's knowledge and love of Urdu poetry and Sufism.

The Dew and the Moon

Last summer my aunt from India came to visit me for a few days. It was a clear August evening and Seattle was absolutely gorgeous.

Twilight was approaching, and the golden yellow light, unique to the Northwest summer horizon, was giving way to softly spreading velvet darkness. The pale moon was now visible. This was Auntie's first visit to Seattle, and I believe that she was having a good time rejoicing in everything that was different from her previous experiences. She said to me, "Priya, did you ever notice that in this part of the world, even the moon rises differently, as if it is standing upright? In India the moon is somewhat horizontal, as if it is reclining on its back." I nodded in agreement.

I thought to myself, How strange that Auntie should notice the different angle of the moon! I remembered that when I first arrived in the States, it was April. Things seemed so new and different. I, too, had observed that the raindrops never seemed to fall in a straight line; whipped by the cold wind the rain always fell in a slanted manner.

How entirely different were those days when I first came to the States, a stranger in a totally strange country. But did I ever feel completely comfortable in my own country, India? Perhaps yes, when I was still very young. Life was not so easy once I left my father's house, but why was I recalling those days? It all happened such a long time ago. What a strange thing it was that of all the people in my family, only I saw my destiny changed by my father's heart attack.

I remember, I was about to graduate when one night it happened. Dr. Harjit Sigh, the heart specialist, lived quite close to our house, and his presence was crucial in saving my father's life. During the course of my father's recuperation, Dr. Harjit began to visit us more frequently. His wife had passed away a few years ago, and his only son, Lalit, had been studying in the United States for the past few years.

One evening, when I came back from the university, my Parjaiji, that is, my older brother's wife, told me that Dr. Harjit had come to visit my father. She handed me tea and a tray full of refreshments and asked me to take it to my father's room. I was about to enter my father's room when I heard Dr. Harjit say to my father, "Well, friend, your son is looking after your business, and I dare say that your daughter-in-law manages the household efficiently. Your older daughter, Priya, is bright and beautiful. The twin sisters, Jaspal and Balvant Kaur, are still young and in school. What kind of worries do you have to cause a heart attack?"

I stopped. I also wanted to hear my father's reply. What I heard pained me greatly. My father said, "Brother Harjit, it seems to me that my late wife is eagerly awaiting me to join her in heaven. If only I could find the right match for my older daughter, Priya, I could go in peace." I entered the room, greeted Dr. Harjit and my father, and began to pour the tea. When Babuji was alone, I confessed to him that I had overheard their conversation and implored him not to worry about me.

Things were moving along quite routinely, when one day Parjaiji told me that Dr. Harjit had asked for my hand in marriage for his son, Lalit. This was quite unexpected because Dr. Harjit did not belong to our caste. However, Babuji had accepted the proposal. I learned further that Lalit was coming back to India shortly for a week to visit his father. Our marriage was to take place during that week. Parjaiji said, "Lalit will go back to the States and send for you as soon as all of the necessary paperwork is completed."

It seemed to me that from that moment on everything moved at a breakneck speed. The wedding invitations were printed and mailed out, and the catering for the wedding reception was arranged. In preparation for the wedding, the house was freshly painted, and the paint was barely dry when the close relatives and guests began to arrive.

I heard from someone that Dr. Harjit did not have his own villa decorated for the wedding but was going to put us up at the same hotel where he had made arrangements for our wedding reception. Later, just before Lalit's return to the States, we were to move into the villa from the hotel.

I was shown a photograph of Lalitji. He was certainly very handsome. I knew that he was highly educated, and my family assured me that he had a pleasant and charming personality. However, I remained skeptical. I had heard that when Indian boys or girls go abroad, their style of thinking changes. They like to meet and talk with their proposed spouses before marriage. So one day when I could find my Parjaiji alone for a few moments, I asked her if she had sent my picture to Dr. Harjit for Lalit to see.

To my surprise, she laughed and informed me that it was not true. She said, "Lalit must have complete faith in his father's choice. He seems to be a very nice boy. In spite of living in the States for four years he has not given up his Indian values. I am so happy for you." I began to wonder what it would be like to go to a strange country and try to live there.

* * *

I am Lalit, Dr. Harjit's son. It does not seem so long ago that I also had to face the question of survival in a new country, the United States. I can tell you from my own experience that no amount of textbook learning can prepare you for the changes and adjustments one has to make in order to survive in a new and strange country. One has to adapt and get to know a different lifestyle, educational system, and much more. The few frenzied weeks before I left India for the States are vividly etched in my memory.

Babuji, my father Dr. Harjit, was so proud when I graduated from the Medical College with honors. Financially we were well off and he had no objection when I proposed to go to the United States for higher education. At that time we thought that I was going away for only a year or two at the most.

I had gained admission to a prestigious university on the East Coast and had some financial support. But after my arrival in the United States, I found out that I would need more money to meet my daily expenses. I got together with two of my friends and compatriots, Ravi and Shuja, who were also experiencing similar financial strains, and in a few weeks we opened a small cafeteria close to the university district that we manned as our schedules permitted. The three of us had never cooked before, and we had to learn to cook and to prepare good tea and coffee.

Luckily, our tea shop began to do good business, especially in the late evenings because most restaurants catered to diners, and we carried only light snacks and beverages. It was during our exams that we had to advertise for help for our tea shop because all three of us needed time to study. It was then that I first met Lisa. She answered our advertisement and came for the interview. She was a business administration major at the university. She had striking looks, pleasant manners, and above all she was willing to work flexible hours.

After the exams, when we looked at the shop accounts, Ravi, Shuja, and I realized that the shop was doing much better since Lisa had joined us, so we decided to let her stay on. Summer break followed the exams and I did not receive my full financial support and subsequently lagged behind in my rent payment. I felt embarrassed to write Babuji for more money.

One day I got a notice to vacate my dormitory apartment within a month. I was quite concerned and was perhaps a little absentminded at the tea shop. After we had closed for the evening, Lisa asked if she could help me with whatever was bothering me. I told her that I needed to move out of the dorm soon and did not have enough money to pay a couple of months' rent in advance and the hefty damage deposit that the apartment landlords demanded before they rented out to students.

When we were about to close the shop, she asked me if I could walk her home. Her apartment was not large but was quite sufficient for her and a roommate. Lisa then explained to me that living in a dorm was not the right choice for me to begin with because the students who lived at the dorm were required to buy their food passes as a package deal. She told me that she cooked for both her roommate and herself and it was much cheaper. I was quite touched with her helpful gesture.

After work we often walked together. Soon the term began again and I became extremely busy. At the end of that semester, one of my partners, Ravi, was ready to leave. When we did the accounts for the shop, we realized that Lisa had not cashed many of her paychecks. That evening, when I asked her the reason for this extraordinary favor to us, she laughed her carefree laugh and said that she was not in any urgent need of money and wanted to give us a break.

A few days later she invited all three of us to her apartment for dinner to say farewell to Ravi. It was a small and intimate affair. A few weeks later, after consulting with Shuja, I asked Lisa if she would like to become our partner in the tea shop and take Ravi's place. She readily agreed. Our friendship became deeper and deeper. She was interested in every aspect of my life and soon knew more about me than did anybody else in the United States. When the quarter came to an end, we decided to move in together.

My relationship with Lisa developed so easily and naturally that I never felt the need to write to Babuji about her. I had decided that when I'd see Babuji face to face I would tell him about us. Many days and months passed this way. Like Ravi, Shuja also graduated and moved elsewhere. Lisa managed the tea shop all by herself. It was mid-December and schools were closed for the holiday season. It is true that with Lisa my life was heavenly, but during the holiday season I often felt homesick.

To my surprise, Lisa had bought tickets for us to go to Las Vegas for the holidays. Lisa knew how I felt about the holiday season and so had planned this little vacation for us. It was a memorable vacation: We got married in Vegas!

Lisa was expecting our first baby when I received Babuji's telegram out of the blue. It said that he was very sick and if I wished to see him for the last time, I should do so immediately. In a state of panic and shock, I left for Delhi. I had forgotten how long a journey it was from the United States to India. Finally, when I arrived in Delhi, a burning wave of hot breeze slapped me across the face as I got out of the airport. My eyes stung and my body burned with heat. Immediately, I rushed to the railway station. I did not have a reservation but somehow I got into an overcrowded compartment of the first train leaving for my small hometown.

I prayed for an opportunity to hold Babuji's hand and tell him that he was about to become a grandfather! I felt sorry that I had not communicated with him as often in the past few months. When the train pulled in at my hometown, I saw a large wedding band and procession at the station. Noise pollution, I thought. In my mentally depressed condition, seeing such gaiety at the railway station piqued me. All of a sudden I saw a whole bunch of my relatives accompanying that wedding party. With a splitting headache, I staggered out of the train on unsteady feet. One of my aunts was right in front of me. Following a conditioned reflex I bent down to touch her feet. I was about to rise up and ask her if she could tell me how my father was doing when Babuji himself appeared before me.

I was stupefied. We embraced each other for a long moment. He had aged somewhat, but I was relieved to see him alive and well. Babuji insisted that he began to feel better the moment he learned that I was coming home. In the car, besides Babuji and myself, there were some other people, so the conversation remained quite formal. When the car came to a halt, I noticed that we were not at our villa but at a newly built hotel that I had never seen before.

I was looking forward to being alone with Babuji. I asked him why we were not going home and also who was getting married, but he only smiled mysteriously and pointed to a room, asking me to take a shower and get ready to go to the wedding. I did not want to go to the wedding. My head was spinning from jet lag, heat, and exhaustion, but I was so relieved to see Babuji alive and fine that I thought to myself, What could be the harm in going to a wedding? After all, I am already here. So I got ready and went downstairs to the lobby, where Babuji and some other members of my family were waiting for me.

To my complete shock and dismay, the thought flashed through my mind that it was my own wedding to which I was being taken. I had to talk to Babuji alone and urgently. I waved at him, but he simply kept looking at me with great pride. Perhaps he was a trifle inebriated. He called out once more, "Lalit will always remember what a surprise I gave him." Before I knew it, I was being ushered into a car decorated with flowers and balloons. I was frantic for an opportunity to be alone with Babuji just for a few moments to tell him what a big mistake this all was, but he was already in another car. I did not want to say anything to my friends who were riding with me, for fear of creating a big scandal. I felt completely numb and helpless. My headache grew worse and worse. All I could feel now was a loud pounding at the back of my head. The wedding band, other music, and the surrounding din made me completely deaf. Like a zombie, I followed wherever I was being led.

Suddenly, I realized that it must be dark. I could feel the silence now. Where did all the din go? Where was I? Where was Babuji? I soon realized that I was sitting on a sofa of an air-cooled bridal suite. I looked around me. Surely I must be dreaming. A dream that every Indian youth often dreams. The bridal bed was bedecked with fragrant flowers. The bride was sitting on the bed, her veil still shading her face. Like a robot I walked toward her. However, my fatigue got the better of me, and I slumped on the bed. A soft voice asked me if I was alright and I answered somewhat roughly, "I am tired and I have a bad headache." I closed my eyes.

I must have dozed off, because when I opened my eyes, my shoes and socks had been removed and I was lying on the bed. My tie and collar had been loosened and my head rested on a woman's shoulders. I could feel soft, cool hands rubbing my head gently. I turned to look up. I must still have been dreaming, because she was even more devastatingly beautiful than I had ever imagined her to be. When I was a youth, this was exactly as I had wished it to be. I went through the motions just as I had done a hundred times in my dreams. Her modest glances made me more excited than I had ever thought myself capable of. Oh, when did I last see a sidelong glance, a sheer veil covering a face lovelier than the moon itself? Her delicate hands were fragrant with henna. That night I forgot everything.

Every subsequent morning I decided to tell Babuji and Priya all about Lisa and myself, but the three of us were never alone for more than a few seconds. On one such occasion Babuji asked me if Priya and I were happy with each other. I stupidly nodded my head. To make a long story short, I never got over my cowardice, and before I realized it, my week's vacation was over and I was saying goodbye to a number of teary-eyed people. Secretly, I was relieved to leave. I felt privileged that I was allowed to go back to the States to continue my studies. I was supposed to send for Priya, my beautiful bride, as soon as possible.

On my way back, on the plane, I wrote a letter of confession to Babuji and Priya. When the plane landed in Europe for refueling, I mailed the letter. I knew full well that under the circumstances, Babuji would try to reconcile himself with the mistake he had made in not making the situation clear to me in the first place. I also hoped that after an initial period of grieving, Priya would find another path in life. It would be best for me to put the entire episode behind me like a bad dream and get on with my life as if none of this had ever happened.

When I arrived home, the first thing Lisa asked me was how Babuji was doing and if I had told him about my family in the United States. I felt miserable. Her pointed questions annoyed me. I told her that Babuji was so sick that to carry out any serious conversation with him was inviting trouble. "When his condition improves," I told her, "I fully intend to let him know about us."

In the meantime, I expected a letter in a couple of weeks from Babuji, venting his fury. But in fact, to my chagrin, no letter arrived. Lisa also seemed to sense that all was not well, but I had decided not to tell her the truth in her advanced stage of pregnancy. Whatever tensions there may have been between Lisa and me after my arrival from India, a new sweetness and blissfulness entered our lives when our son, Ajit, was born.

Several years passed happily when on one blasted day, my childhood friend Nitin arrived in town and following my trail finally located my house. Lisa was alone in the house when he first called. Lisa jokingly told Nitin that she was the cleaning woman of the house and asked him how my family back home was doing. Nitin then told her that my father-in-law had a heart attack a few weeks after my wedding and had passed away. My Babuji had also passed away two years ago and Priya, my wife, was alone with Satyen, my son.

When I came back home that day, Lisa told me all about Nitin's visit. I tried to convince Lisa how much I loved her and Ajit, but she said that she just could not continue to live with a person who had so completely cheated her and cheated his other family as well. There was also the question of why I had not ended my marriage with Priya during all the past years.

I had never anticipated that Lisa would leave me, but that is exactly what she decided to do, despite all my entreaties. I became violently vindictive. When Lisa had become a partner in the restaurant, she had discontinued her studies. Now I asked the court for my son's custody on the grounds that I was a better provider for his secure future. Lisa fought valiantly, but at last she had to settle for visiting rights only.

Before our divorce, I had not realized that Lisa worked so hard to run the household smoothly. Moreover, Ajit was a frustrated child now, and he manifested his hostility and anger in different ways. Once he almost burned the house down when he left the gas burner on. Another time he somehow set the wiring of the house on fire. To leave Ajit in the house unattended was becoming increasingly impossible. I often thought about my other son, Satyen. Was he also growing up to be a hostile person? Did Priya hate me? What did she tell Satyen about his father? Did Satyen even know that he had a father in the United States?

* * *

Yes, my son Satyen knows very well that he has a father in the United States. Just one week after our marriage the thunderbolt fell. Lalit's letter arrived and his Babuji took upon himself to break the bad tidings to my father, who promptly took to bed and soon left us. To worsen the situation, I was pregnant. Nonetheless, little Satyen's arrival brought a new purpose to our dismal lives. Both Lalit's Babuji and I devoted all our time and energy to bringing up Satyen. My life had not been intolerable up to this point, but things began to get increasingly tough when my father-in-law passed away.

After my father-in-law's demise, Satyen felt quite dejected. Gradually he began to ask me pointed questions about a father he never saw. It was very obvious that he needed a male role model in his life. I tried to fill this gap in Satyen's life by visiting my brother more often. It was then that I received a letter from Lalitji asking us to come and join him in America. He said that he and Lisa were divorced. He promised to do the right thing by Satyen and to give him a proper education and upbringing.

To this day, I have been unable to analyze my feelings and reaction to that letter. I needed help to come to a decision. That evening I took the letter to my brother and Parjaiji. Both of them became very upset. They hated the way Lalitji had renounced his responsibilities and subsequently did not have much faith in his new promises. On the other hand, they wondered if it would be fair to deprive Satyen of the opportunity to reconcile with his father. Finally my brother decided to swallow his pride and write to Lalitji.

Satyen was beside himself with joy when he heard that we were to leave for the United States. I was full of anxiety and resented my fate. When we arrived in the States, Satyen and I were introduced to Ajit, Lalitji's first son. Ajit must have been approximately the same age as Satyen but much different in looks and behavior. In the following weeks things became clearer in regard to why I was needed in my husband's household and what I was supposed to do.

Still not over my jet lag and emotionally quite raw, I needed to learn how to cook and clean. Everything here looked so completely different and intimidating. Even a simple broom looked different. When I was in India, my friends who visited us from the States had told me that life in the United States was very easy. A machine washed your clothes and even dried them. Then there was another machine to wash and dry the dishes. You did not have to painstakingly clean and grind your spices, and there was even a blower to blow the autumn leaves away from your yard. To my naive ears, all that sounded as if in the States one did not have to do a thing!

To make matters worse, Ajit teased me and made fun of Satyen all the time. I did not know how to deal with a child who absolutely detested Satyen's and my presence in what he called "his" house. The hours when both the boys were away at school and Lalitji was at work were the most peaceful for me during my first few days. After breakfast, when everybody had left the house, I watched from the kitchen window as the gusty April showers hit the eaves of the gazebo in the yard. The wind blew the rain inside the platform. I watched the scene quite intensely. The abundant rains, the dark gray sky, and the storm reflected my inner tumult. After a while, somehow, the gazebo appeared to be cleaner. When the tears had finished drenching my face, my heart also felt a little lighter.

I do not know why I was so naive that I did not anticipate a significant event that followed soon after our arrival. I often think about the bewilderment I felt when all this was taking place. I should have expected it, but the event caught me unaware. I was alarmed by a violent tantrum

Ajit threw on the first Friday after we had arrived. When Lalitji came back from work that evening, father and son spent an unusually long time together in Ajit's room.

Next morning Ajit woke up in a sullen mood and stormed through the kitchen to grab something to eat even before breakfast was ready, and then shut himself up in his room. When Lalitji came to know about this he made no effort to cajole Ajit or even to approach him. All this was quite new to me. All of a sudden I heard the sound of a sharp horn near the house followed by a knock on the door. Lalitji opened the door and called out for Ajit to come downstairs immediately. He said to me, "This is the second weekend of the month, and Ajit is supposed to go and stay with his mother for the weekend."

So it was Lisa who was at the door. Lisa, Lisa, Lisa . . . the name that had kept me awake through so many nights. And still, I wanted to see Lisa. My curiosity begged me to give a face to the name. I had always known that somewhere Lisa and I were going to meet each other, but I was completely unprepared when she strolled in quite naturally and gave me a big hug and asked me how I was! She took out a large bar of chocolate from her purse and offered it to Satyen. I absolutely could not sort out my emotions. For so many years I had detested the very thought of Lisa. It seemed quite natural to me that I should hate her. I never questioned the justification of my feelings towards her. Wasn't it natural for Lisa also to hate me and Satyen for breaking up her marriage? Then why this friendly appearance?

Soon she and Ajit left, but the thoughts lingered on in my mind. Later in the day I was surprised to realize that contrary to my expectation, I thought of Lisa in a kindly way. One day I invited her in for some tea. Several casual visits followed after that visit. Gradually these visits led to a close friendship. Thinking of those days, I often wonder why Lisa and I became friends. Before I met Lisa in person, I had ugly, preconceived notions about how we might feel and behave towards each other. When I was in India raising Satyen all by myself, I often thought that if it were not for Lisa, Lalitji would have been mine. At school Satyen's friends would not tease him about having an imaginary father and he would have a normal and healthy family life. Why, in my imaginary world, was it all Lisa's fault?

I have often thought long and hard why Lisa and I became friends. In the end I came to the conclusion that perhaps Lisa and I came together because we were two women who recognized each other's pain. We shared so much. Both of us had a very happy introduction to our respective married lives. Both of us had suffered delusion and disenchantment in marriage. We had both experienced the pangs of separation and disruption in our lives, and above all the two of us recognized the concerns of motherhood. Ironically, we even shared the same man. Or perhaps we bonded together simply because we were women. After a couple of years, inspired by Lisa, I approached Lalit with a proposal to go for higher education. My years in college were the most fulfilling since I had come to the United States.

All the above incidents took place in my life a long time ago. Now I am in my middle age. Lalit did fulfill his promise of providing for Satyen and giving him a good education. Both Ajit and Satyen are grown up. They are now away from home, studying at different universities. Whenever I think back to my early years in the United States, the time swims across the rim of my eyes as if I were watching an old film. A unique film for my eyes only. My aunt was saying something as she got out of her chair and pulled a shawl across her shoulder. I was roused from my reverie. Perhaps the evening was getting to be too chilly for Auntie and she wanted to move indoors. As I began to follow her, I threw another glance at the moon which stood straight in the sky. It looked back at me with a friendly smile. I wondered if it was going to dew tonight.

Litu Kabir

Statement: Cambridge, Massachusetts—Dhaka, Bangladesh. Two cities on two opposing points of the globe: two pasts, two presents, and in ever so many times, two truths. But always, it is one life. One life must touch the two ends, give meaning to the chasm in between, reconcile the irreconcilable. Who amongst us who have left faces, a home, and a land behind have not experienced the anguish of this duality?

A response on one extreme is the acceptance of one or the other society more or less completely and to the exclusion of the other. It is not uncommon. But we also see other paths others follow, such as those who live on the margins of both societies, neither accepting unquestioningly the totality of one nor renouncing in vain hopes the other but striving to be faithful, finally, to the truths of both. It is a harder path. But those of us who remember the early days of our soul-searching as we sought our destinies, indeed began to shape and reshape ourselves by our own truths, will perhaps remember, too, the courage, the joy, and the hope that our haunting questions led to.

Perhaps, therefore, writing for me is shaded, too often it may be, by a remembrance of those times when nothing was given and everything was questioned, of the times we began to understand that knowing little, we still had to know how to live. Is it not true, after all, that one feels most the need to commune when the fabric of this world no longer holds, be that from alienation, one's doubts, or from the thousand other faces of solitude? To borrow Galeano's words, writing for this author is a choice "against our solitude and against the solitude of others." A choice in the end, most certainly, most simply, to share the joys and the sorrows, and be witness to the crimes.

Both "The Return'" by Litu Kabir and "This Thicket" by Boman Desai are reminiscent of narrative-philosophical essays that so often appear throughout South Asian literature, beginning with the classical Sanskrit epic, the *Mahabharata*. The war the protagonist remembers in "The Return" is the 1971 struggle of Bangladesh (then East Pakistan) to win independence from Pakistan. The Mukti Bahini were the Bangladeshi freedom fighters. In this one brief narrative, a South Asian American protagonist interweaves his experiences of politics in Bangladesh with his life in the multicultural society of America. The struggles for freedom and justice of people all over the world become a part of the life and ideals of this protagonist who has lived through a war as a child.

The Return

He hesitated for a second at the door before entering. Seven people sat around the long rectangular table, and their eyes turned towards him.

"Ah! You are right on time."

He smiled back. There was a quietness in the room, as if the odor of fried onions and fish that clung to the air had muffled the hum that flowed outside the door. The dishes were waiting with forks and spoons by each chair, and from a brown wicker basket the ears of rolled up red, black, and white hand towels surfaced. Low beams of evening sunlight filtered through the window panes and shone off the white front of a cupboard behind the dining table. He looked around and his gaze fell longingly on the strips of fish that lay on a large platter; the soft white flesh would melt were a fork to touch it!

"You had no problem finding the place?"

No, it had not been a problem finding the place. What could have been a problem in this wonderful day that brought to his mind the very best memories? He had walked a good distance. Fresh and dense, little plots of garden basked in the sun in front of the houses. Roses swayed under the caresses of invisible hands, and shy tulips beckoned from the shadows of maple and flowering cherries. Snowy winter was a fading memory and the late afternoon was sharp in the full radiance of a spring sun. Spring! In a city twelve thousand miles away, a group of schoolboys are walking under the shadows of overhanging Krisnachura trees whose leaves have burst into red flames. Books under their arms, they are talking passionately: children who discover words as sweet as indulging friendships, friendships as poignant as the mystery of their lives. On this day it was as if that same moment floated down from that other spring day, an autumnal leaf falling through the years to flavor the present with the color of other lives.

"And I lived in that house in Berkeley for the rest of my years in that city. In the backyard there were fig and plum trees and a lemon tree always heavy with golden lemons. Little kids would swarm in the backyard with brown paper bags—for the plums! There was a living room as big as this. Harvey, a housemate who collected books, lined entire walls with his bookshelves."

There was more. Not for a moment did he believe that words could capture the rapture of the existence left behind, yet against that very denial he wanted to speak, carried on by an obscure momentum. He wanted to re-create with words the dizzying warmth of life, the abundance of the sky that endlessly rained its shower of light, the warm laziness on the terraces of cafes, the evenings when the blue on the sky melted in the scarlet glow of the western horizon. He wanted to speak of that low and pretty city that touched the vast Pacific and that was a sister city to a little town far away in El Salvador. He wanted to speak of the bookshops that stayed open all night, of the streets sprayed with graffiti over and over of handwritten inscriptions on old books passed from reader to reader, of the murals on the walls, of the marches of people in the streets who spoke for the brown-skinned versions of themselves who went by slightly different names and dressed slightly differently and lived some miles south of the border.

"It must have been something about the city. Almost everyone I knew was progressive. All my housemates were political or at least had the understanding that things weren't OK. Almost every other weekend there would be a march or a meeting."

Those were the early eighties. Wars were no fewer and poverty no less cruel than other times, and yet, beyond reason, an unmistakable hope had shone on life, a hope questioned, abused, bruised, and mangled, but still vital. It wasn't just that there would be no stadium massacres, no reports of disappeared daughters, no daylong breaking of bricks and stones, labor that was barely enough to feed a child always ill, no, there would not just be a negation of evil but something more, something that was a good yet undefined, something that one experienced today only in fleeting moments but that would become common and more profound. It was something different people expressed in different concepts, all vague, with words such as *equality, solidarity, diversity, love.* Till then, hope endured the many names of horror—Chile, Cambodia, El Salvador. . . .

Not so many years ago in a remote town halfway between the Himalayas and the Bay of Bengal, horror was at the doorstep of a schoolboy who believed that surely the world must stop turning from the enormity of this crime. In the face of murder, do not all who hear the cries cease to be innocent bystanders? And when in a foreign land he joined the chorus of voices pledging support for the people of yet other lands, his eyes went back to the war nights of 1971 when old and young sat in tense passivity in the curfew darkness around a radio. A few events restored the faith that he did not want to lose. By the words that the world at large had not failed to hear, the cries of people in agony, the Resistance, the Mukti Bahini, spoke of the future. But much time passed and he ceased to think of those who went about their lives oblivious to the weight of their existence on other lives and who would not believe that there was this nameless horror stalking humanity from the shadows of history. He did not try to win them over. Instead, there were the few here and there who were different, perhaps in exile from another time, living now in a world of artificial boundaries.

He listened.

"Yes, nobody owns this house. It was bought by a group of people many years ago who passed on the ownership to this cooperative itself. Ever since, it has belonged to whoever the inhabitants happen to be."

A low wave of startling white hair parted from the middle to fall down over her shoulders. Soft wrinkles on an ivory face only accentuated the light smile on her lips and a pride that glowed from deep blue eyes. She was Ruth, the mother of six children, the eldest in the group. Widowed, her children now grown up and living away, her home for many years now had been this household. Was it joy or sorrow hidden by the high note of her laughter?

"I must have seen over twenty people live in this house in the time I have lived here. And many many backgrounds. We had a person from Peru till last year," narrated Richard, the physicist turned teacher. The deep creases on his weathered face were like the furrows of bare mountainsides, but he could not have been much over sixty. Inspired by the Brazilian Paulo Freire, he had roamed over the African continent for a quarter century, teaching and living with nomads, peasants, and street children; had had a family and children; and in the end had come back to live again in this very same household from which he had departed as a young man some thirty years ago.

"He called the other day—the supporter of the Peruvian left now seems to have a wife and a kid," Ruth said with a suppressed laugh.

"Are you saying that anybody who supports a progressive movement must also be an ascetic?"

He who had spoken was named Malcolm. His head was a dense ball of black wiry hairs that curled forever into each other. Frozen like a statue in silence, his dark face left nobody prepared for the laughter that would break out without warning.

Charles wanted to speak. He moved about in his seat and clasped his hands on the table. Tall and energetic, the eagerness of the young student shone through his darting eyes. But his words, heavy with an Australian accent, came out hesitatingly, as if every word and every action had in them unknown powers to harm or heal and needed to be weighed very carefully.

"I would say that there is something about sacrifice. An act is on a higher moral plane when it is concomitant with suffering, and that most people think so is an empirical fact."

Nobody said anything for a few moments. Maria brought her eyebrows together and looked at her glass with concentrated attention. A cascade of black hair over her shoulders underlined the gravity of a brown, oval face. She looked up, and it was her eyes and not her face that spoke.

"Sacrifice has no value in itself."

"All I am saying is that people respect the one who sacrifices over somebody who makes the same contribution to society without similar sacrifices. This is a phenomenon that we have to be conscious of," Charles said with a conciliatory smile.

"People do a lot of other things. It is not moral acts—see?—that our countries need. We just need to do things, the right things."

Alejandro had spoken after waiting for a long time. His anxious eyes carried a passionate intensity, almost as if in pain, as if that gaze that fixed itself repeatedly on others could convey feelings he could not trust speech to convey. Tortured in Chile, his sister long ago in exile somewhere in Europe, he had the easy familiarity of living in this household for years and yet there was an urgency in his speech. There was not enough time for all that must be said and all that must be done!

"Yes, I am no Hegelian," rejoined Malcolm. "The moralist is the same as the idealist who thinks that individual will is what moves history. He wants people to either do everything or do nothing. He would prefer someone to do nothing in his quest for purity over someone who makes a partial contribution of his resources."

Ruth's voice was dry. Was there a tinge of bitterness underneath that tension? "Well, with that line you can justify somebody working in defense research and doing 'charitable work' on the side."

"That's just it. It does not matter where you are or what your profession is. It is the sum of our efforts after the additions and the subtractions that matter," Malcolm said in a tone of adjudication.

Tea had followed dinner and was long since vanished but for the empty cups nursed in a few hands. But the voices had stirred unknown depths, and nobody was yet willing to drift away. It was not clear if the outside world still existed, for it was not mere discussion that was going on: Each was passionately living the moment. Charles leaned forward with a wide smile, as if with the perfect solution.

"But people can better do that good by integrating their day-to-day work with what they believe in," he said. His dissertation work in a university very near this house was on the ways environmental changes were harming the many forms of life.

"So much the better. But should we not give credit for the contribution someone makes instead of condemning him for his failure to do more?" Maria replied with ill-concealed impatience. She was defending somebody or something that perhaps only she knew. Ruth gave her a worried look.

Alejandro spoke again. His measured tones did little to hide his excitement.

"Yes. First see what needs to be done objectively, overall, and then do as much as you want. In the end, after all, it is you who must decide. It is a problem in many places, in Chile, in the North American Left, this sick moralism, not to do good, no, but to be good!"

"How about Bangladesh? Do progressive circles there have the same problems as here?"

He was present, but for a long time he did not know it. He took the glass of water and a wave of joy swept through him. Long ago he had ceased to believe that anything was given in life: first is the void, then the creation. He did not believe that life lived had romance, that there was anything romantic beyond hopes and memories in life, and, yet, what was there in this gathering, something akin to poetry, something at once tragic and joyful that touched his heart and quickened its beat, impossible though it was to define?

Secretly, between silences, he stared long at each in turn, fascinated by the lines on a face, the movement of an eye, and the shape of a glance: Ruth, Maria, Charles, Rosa, Alejandro, Richard, Malcolm. Some who had taken part in the conversation; some who had not. Silent, solitary bubbles, entire universes contained in themselves; each evoked questions as ancient as thought; each mirrored the cosmos in the depth of sorrow, joy, and hope, and this house where these people from four continents and more races had made their home, this house that had seen generations of such wanderers come together, this place with a garden and a backyard, this place that "nobody owned, as nobody owns this planet," was this not a symbol of the world to be past a thousand turmoils to come?

He stepped out of the door and walked past the porch. A persistent drizzle had begun to fall, and the air was damp. A few lone passersby went amid the confusion of shops. There was a wail of a police car in the distance and a rush of cars on the watery streets. The outside world was coming back to life. He was crossing a border that he had not been aware of before, back into time, back into the land of landlords, bargain basements, and TV sets. He fought an atrocious sense of desperation, not at the return to the old world, to alienation and to familiar demons, but with the insidious intimations of an exaltation turning against itself, with the inexorable vanishing of his joy like wisps of smoke in the air.

He opened the door of his apartment, and his hand reached for the light switch. Silence saturated the yellow light that fell on the books, the table, the mattress on the floor. On the wall was a poster, a large black-and-white photograph of a little schoolgirl caught in motion, walking confidently with a smaller boy at her hand, looking at the road beyond. They were walking along a white wall made dirty by bullet holes and scrawled over with graffiti barely decipherable. He looked at the poster, haunted by questions that could not be put into forms that would admit of answers, questions such as those raised by the full summer moon on empty ocean waves, or by the stillness of a blue morning when the perfection of the sunshine and the air is unbearable in this world. And yet, he knew, there was an answer, there was an answer even in this austere room, in this dim light, in the vast indifference of the world that had been drawn in by the silence. He knew it in his heart—he only had never to forget. No, not even that, for this truth would come to comfort him when he needed it the most, as it was doing now. He felt an exultation well within him, serene like a tide. He walked over to the window.

"What a beautiful night!" he said to the darkness outside.

Anuradha Mannar

Statement: I didn't even realize until I started working with *Sanyog* (a literary journal from Duke University) that I had things to write about that came directly from my experience as an Indian in the United States. Once I started writing and reading what other South Asian Americans had written, I was drawn to this literature. I found most of the statements in South Asian American works very poignant and sometimes even humorous. The words of these authors call out to me, and in some way, I think, my words reach them. But the most amazing thing is that my words reach me. That is the reason I write. Putting words on paper helps me explore and enjoy my life as a South Asian American woman living within two cultures.

"You can't give God a granola bar" is part of a series of brief narratives in which a young South Asian American protagonist tries to bridge the traditions and customs of two cultures. Her experiences are sometimes frustrating, sometimes very funny, but always thought provoking.

You can't give God a granola bar

If God believes that the people who stand in the middle of the road get run over, then I am in trouble. I think this as I carry in the Hindu idols, which my mother has carefully given me, to my first apartment. I know some of the rules—enough to want to play, I think, but not enough to know how.

I remember something about taking God first into your home, but the apartment agent takes me in first, and I don't think to walk in with idols and her.

So I do the second best and take them first after she leaves. A compromise, but can you compromise with God?

I think not, but I keep doing it.

So I set the idols up in the kitchen, the true center of the house. And I leave that cabinet door open. Then there is the matter of what to do with these gods, now that I have responsibility for them. I have incense and little cotton wicks. But I hate matches, and I don't like the idea of an open flame, especially since I come and go. So I start off forgoing the small flames and lighting only incense. No matches, certainly not a lighter, but thank goodness I have a gas stove. Turn on the stove, hold the incense to the flame and there you go. Is this bad? After all, if you have devotion to God, shouldn't it be strong enough to overcome a little match? I don't have matches, anyway, I console myself. And, besides, they have gas stoves in India; this choice bit of logic is enough for me to continue my ways.

Then, of course, God must eat. This is an easy one. God eats fruit, I know. And of course, prefers bananas. This I know without a doubt. But what about when I don't have fruit? Vegetables work, surely; products of the earth. Can you give God a granola bar? I'm not sure if the point is to feed God with natural bounty or merely feed God. But what about giving God the best food, such as chocolate chip cookies or almond *burfi*? The *burfi* issue is perplexing. At festivals, it's sweets all the way, but for every day? And logic insists that cookies are as viable as *burfi*. But the granola bar seems wrong, although I decide that raisins pass the test.

It only gets stranger as I wonder what on earth I'm doing. Where did I end in ritual? I believe thought comes first, that details don't matter. The important thing is to seek God and understand the values of all religions. It is better to try to improve the world and not do *puja* than to do *puja* alone. But here I am, worrying about fruits and incense. Just when I decide that thought comes before action for God, I remember that ritual must be carried out in full. It's a bizarre conflict. I believe in the oversoul, all-God, but I can't leave the Ganipathi in my kitchen without fresh food. Is it better to do half a ritual than no ritual? Will I get run over for standing in the middle of the road?

My beliefs lead me to say no, but it seems I have carved a convenient belief that lets me do whatever I want. And that is the opposite of ritual. There should be no exception, no excuses, in ritual. Its value comes from doing it daily out of belief and faith.

To make matters worse, when I step in front of the Krishna picture with incense in my hand, the first movement that comes to my mind is the Catholic cross. Too much television, not enough temple for this. I can't imagine Krishna would mind, but what a combination. The sign of the cross and incense.

Ved Mehta

Statement: Quoted from *Sound-Shadows of the New World:*

The Taxi -driver took a sharp turn.
"Where are we?" I asked.
"On Broadway, " Mrs. di Francesco said.
"Is Broadway a wide road?" I asked.
She laughed. "A very wide avenue—It's the center of the universe."
At home, the center was a circle, but here the center, it seemed,
was a straight line.

The following selection from *Sound-Shadows of the New World* by the well-known writer Ved Mehta is included here to show one of the historical and autobiographical literary works that have influenced many of the works of fiction by South Asian American authors. This selection, Moazzam Sheikh's story "Kissing the Holy Land," and the selection from Bapsi Sidhwa's *An American Brat* give very different views of the first experience South Asians often have with American immigration officials.

Sound-Shadows of the New World

At the airport, I was questioned by an immigration official. "You're blind—totally blind—and they gave you a visa? You say it's for your studies, but studies where?"

"At the Arkansas School for the Blind. It is in Little Rock, in Arkansas."

He shuffled through the pages of a book. Sleep was in my eyes. Drops of sweat were running down my back. My shirt and trousers felt dirty.

"Arkansas School is not on our list of approved schools for foreign students."

"I know," I said. "That is why the immigration officials in Delhi gave me only a visitor's visa. They said that when I got to the school I should tell the authorities to apply to be on your list of approved schools, so that I could get a student visa." I showed him a big manila envelope I was carrying; it contained my chest x-rays, medical reports, and fingerprint charts, which were necessary for a student visa, and which I'd had prepared in advance.

"Why didn't you apply to an approved school in the first place and come here on a proper student visa?" he asked, looking through the material.

My knowledge of English was limited. With difficulty, I explained to him that I had applied to some thirty schools but that, because I had been able to get little formal education in India, the Arkansas School was the only one that would accept me; that I had needed a letter of acceptance from an American school to get dollars sanctioned by the Reserve Bank of India; and that now that I was in America I was sure I could change schools if the Arkansas School was not suitable or did not get the necessary approval.

Muttering to himself, the immigration official looked up at me, down at his book, and up at me again. He finally announced, "I think you'll have to go to Washington and apply to get your visa changed to a student visa before you can go to any school."

I recalled things that Daddyji used to say as we were growing up: "In life, there is only fight or flight. You must always fight," and "America is God's own country. People there are the most hospitable and generous people in the world." I told myself I had nothing to worry about. Then I remembered that Daddyji had mentioned a Mr. and Mrs. Dickens in Washington—they were friends of friends of his—and told me that I could get in touch with them in case of emergency.

"I will do whatever is necessary," I now said to the immigration official. "I will go to Washington."

He hesitated, as if he were thinking something, and then stamped my passport and returned it to me. "We Mehtas carry our luck with us," Daddyji used to say. He is right, I thought.

The immigration official suddenly became helpful, as if he were a friend. "You shouldn't have any trouble with the immigration people in Washington," he said, and asked, "Is anybody meeting you here?"

"Mr. and Mrs. di Francesco," I said.

Mrs. di Francesco was a niece of Manmath Nath Chatterjee, whom Daddyji had known when he himself was a student, in London, in 1920. Daddyji had asked Mr. Chatterjee, who had a Scottish-American wife and was now settled in Yellow Springs, Ohio, if he could suggest anyone with whom I might stay in New York, so that I could get acclimatized to America before proceeding to the Arkansas School, which was not due to open until the eleventh of September. Mr. Chatterjee had written back that, as it happened, his wife's niece was married to John di Francesco, a singer who was totally blind, and that Mr. and Mrs. di Francesco lived in New York, and would be delighted to meet me at the airport and keep me as a paying guest at fifteen dollars a week.

"How greedy of them to ask for money!" I had cried when I learned of the arrangement. "People come and stay with us for months and we never ask for an anna."

Daddyji had said, "In the West, people do not, as a rule, stay with relatives and friends but put up in hotels, or in houses as paying guests. That is the custom there. Mr. and Mrs. di Francesco are probably a young, struggling couple who could do with a little extra money."

The immigration official now came from behind the counter, led me to an open area, and shouted, with increasing volume, "Francisco! . . . Franchesca! . . . De Franco!" I wasn't sure what the correct pronunciation was, but his shouting sounded really disrespectful. I asked him to call for Mr. and Mrs. di Francesco softly. He bellowed, "Di Fransesco!"

No one came. My mouth went dry. Mr. and Mrs. di Francesco had sent me such a warm invitation. I couldn't imagine why they would have let me down or what I should do next.

Then I heard the footsteps of someone running toward us. "Here I am. You must be Ved. I'm Muriel di Francesco. I'm sorry John couldn't come." I noted that the name was pronounced the way it was spelled, and that hers was a Yankee voice—the kind I had heard when I first encountered Americans at home, during the war—but it had the sweetness of the voices of my sisters.

We shook hands; she had a nice firm grip. I had an impulse to call her Auntie Muriel—at home, an older person was always called by an honorific, like "Auntie" or "Uncle"—but I greeted her as Daddyji had told me that Westerners liked to be greeted: "Mrs. di Francesco, I'm delighted to make your acquaintance."

Tara Menon

Statement: My international background helped me adjust when I came to America in 1988. In my first writing workshop, I wrote a story about a mother who ties a black cord around her daughter's neck to mitigate astrological influences. Imagine my surprise when another writer told me that she had thought that the mother was going to strangle her daughter! Differences in culture distort the understanding of characters and their actions. I use my writers' group to ensure that my Indian American characters come across as intended. I want my characters to be true to me and, more importantly, true to the people they represent.

Hosting relatives and friends from South Asia is an important, often annual event for South Asian Americans. The memories of the motherland these visits evoke as well as the attempts to justify, explain, and share one's life in America with the visitors are portrayed with humor and skill in this story.

The Perfect Host

The tension at home escalated with the impending arrival of the cousins. Judy's scissors clicked annoyingly as she trimmed rose stems. She put the vase down on the table with unnecessary force. "Ramu will be too tired to notice the roses."

"I wanted to do things the right way," said Hari.

"I wish we could take guests in our stride like everyone else," she said. Hari shut the door so their daughter, Minnie, wouldn't hear. He'd just lectured her about the Indian tradition of hospitality. He always gave visiting relatives a splendid time and played host as well as guide to Boston. He did much more than anyone else he knew, but the rewards of hearing praise spurred him on each time.

Hari's mother had taught him that reputation was what mattered most. He obeyed and flattered his elders as a child and was rewarded with pats and gifts. His tyrannical aunt often tweaked her son Ramu's ears, but her fingers spared Hari's lobes because he picked flowers for her prayers. Hari was popular among his childhood friends. Following his mother's advice, he bought expensive presents for their birthdays. He invited them to his ancestral bungalow, an imposing structure with two grand staircases and pillars on the porch, where they could play cricket in the yard and swim in the pond.

His mother, proud of Hari until her dying day, departed with blessings of more favor. He maintained his reputation, though it was an effort at times, such as when he married Judy. She was a high school teacher from Newton whom he Indianized in his letters to relatives. He told them she wore a sari, when in reality she'd cut and stitched a sari into a skirt. Her familiarity with the story of the *Ramayana* was transformed into a daily reading of the epic. He boosted her family credentials by citing the absence of divorce in the last three generations.

"So, this is where you live," said Ramu, surveying the neighborhood. He was flanked by his wife, Lekha, and their daughter, Seema. The pristine beauty of the ten-year-old colonial had been revived with a fresh coat of paint. The trimmed lawn and hedges appeared neat and orderly. Hari led the guests inside and gave a tour of the house. Lekha opened a closet and marveled at the lemon scent. She put the tip of her nose to the ceramic potpourri holder.

The suitcases were unlocked. "For you," Seema said, dropping gifts into her hosts' arms. Her low-cut top fell forward, exposing cleavage every time she dipped into a suitcase. She had a streak of orange in her hair and wore three-inch stilettos. Hari had never seen such a modern Indian city girl. Minnie, four years younger at thirteen, wouldn't get out of her jeans and T-shirts but was conservative in comparison. Sometimes he forgot that his daughter was half-American, despite a Boston accent and American mannerisms. She had his curly black hair and full lips. She also had large eyes like his mother's, though they were green like Judy's. Minnie used her looks to advantage during *bharata natyam* lessons. She danced, rolling her irises upward and around to convey ecstasy one minute and despair the next.

Judy explained how things worked in this country. Lights were turned on by flipping the switch up, not down. The shower knob had to be pulled forward. The funny buzz that startled them was only the phone; they rang differently here.

Lekha, listening attentively, asked, "What did she say?"

Her husband snorted. "American accent. No one will understand you in India."

In private Hari told Judy, "You mustn't mind the way he talks. That's his style. He's a senior executive."

The next day sight-seeing began in earnest at Quincy Market. Judy went to teach her ninth graders, but Hari had taken a week off from his engineering job at Polaroid. "Nice of you," said Ramu in appreciation and wrapped an arm around Hari's shoulder. They wandered past vendor carts displaying knickknacks.

Later that evening Seema watched MTV with her heels on the sofa. The adults, stomachs full, discussed life in the United States. "We enjoyed ourselves today. Boston is interesting, but I don't know if I'd like to live here," said Ramu.

"Why not?" asked Judy.

"Everything is artificial here. In the street people smile and ask me how I am, but they won't care if I drop dead in front of them the next minute."

"When I was a new immigrant, I felt accepted by smiling strangers," said Hari. His attachment to his motherland coexisted with a certain amount of loyalty to America.

Lekha joined in. "Life here doesn't seem easy. You enjoy many luxuries, but Judy has to work. I don't have to because Ramu's salary takes care of our needs."

Hari said, "She teaches because she has a talent for it. Last year she was invited to the governor's mansion. Only the best teachers in the state were invited."

Friday was museum day. On Saturday the adults went to Bloomingdale's. Seema stayed behind to watch more MTV. Lekha picked up several bed sheets and nonstick cookware, ignoring attempts to steer her to sale items. At the cashier's line Lekha disappeared, saying that she had to go to the ladies' room. Hari looked for Ramu, but the paunchy figure was at a remote distance admiring crystal vases. He pulled out his MasterCard.

Judy tucked down the corners of her mouth. "You've never taken me shopping here," she said.

"Didn't you see how high the bill was?"

"You don't seem to mind bringing them here and paying for their purchases," said Judy. Some customers turned their heads.

"Are you asking me to make them pay?"

"Yes. For once in your life resist the urge to please." Glimpsing the sari-clad Lekha emerge from the restroom, they became quiet. "They paid," she said when Ramu joined them.

"You shouldn't have. You're the perfect host," he said.

Hari wiped his forehead with a hanky. With ill will from his side and bad luck on theirs, they'd open the packages in India to find discolored sheets and defective pans, he hoped.

That night, turning in bed, Judy said, "I can't stand them. Please don't ask Ramu to extend their visit."

"Don't worry, he has work in D.C. They'll be gone soon."

"I wouldn't be sure. Our last guests overstayed. With you as host, who'd want to leave?" asked Judy. Hari snuggled close to her. "Aren't you glad you're married to me rather than her?"

"Poor Ramu," said Hari. "He's no prize either. They deserve each other."

Hari humored his guests at home, stuffing them with food. Cookie jars emptied and the overstocked fridge looked less crowded. He cooked traditional Kerala dishes, replacing unattainable ingredients with supermarket substitutes. He hunted for an ashtray so that his cousin could smoke inside. Ramu relaxed in the recliner and puffed.

They did more sight-seeing. The Boston Tea Party Ship, the New England Aquarium, and then the John Hancock Tower. As Hari's guests admired the sweeping view of the city, he imagined Ramu praising him. "Hari is a lucky man," Ramu would tell his mother. She'd say, "He's special. Whenever I'd ask you to pick flowers for my prayers, you'd sniff them. Hari brought them unspoiled for worship." And Ramu would continue, "You wouldn't let me go abroad to study. Now look at him. He lives in a big house in great style. He loves Boston and it's a wonderful place."

"Beautiful," said Ramu, looking at the sails against the blue of the Charles River. "Nice city. Glad you're here."

That evening, Seema, dressed in a tight outfit, said that she had a date. Peter, the boy next door, had enticed her with tickets to a Paula Abdul concert. "Come back before Hari Uncle and Judy Aunty go to bed," said Lekha.

But Seema arrived way past midnight, putting Judy on the marital warpath again. "She didn't even apologize."

"Sssh. I bet she slept with Peter," Hari whispered.

"I'm fed up with them. Ramu thinks too much of himself. And Lekha doesn't help clear the table." Judy mimicked Lekha, "We don't waste leftovers in India."

"What can I do?" He held up two fingers. "Two more days."

Morning dawned for Hari with an accusing glare from his wife. She yanked the bed sheet to his feet. "The queen asked for room service. She has a headache. Minnie brought coffee up for her. She wants toast—'two slices with jam and one with butter,'" said Judy, mimicking Lekha again. She opened the bedroom door and rap music drifted from the living room. "I'm going to get a headache too."

Hari took the breakfast tray up. "Thank you," said Ramu. "We did too much sight-seeing and shopping. She isn't used to exertion. We're spoiled by our servants. No exercise."

"I'll run down to the pharmacy and buy Tylenol," said Hari.

On the departure day the sofa, unburdened by Seema, and the re-

cliner, unburdened by Ramu, were reclaimed by Minnie and Hari. The
TV rested. The quiet downstairs contrasted with the bustle upstairs. "Did
you pack my shaving kit?" shouted Ramu from the bathroom.

"You packed it this morning," Lekha shouted back.

Hari hoped they wouldn't contribute to the cardboard box in the basement. It contained miscellaneous items forgotten by relatives—a shirt,
reading glasses, shoes, and a book. One of these days he'd junk the lot,
ending another grievance of Judy's. The departing family proceeded to the
Honda with goodbyes and thanks to Judy and Minnie. "It's your turn to
visit us. We'll give you five-star treatment," promised Ramu.

As Hari eased the car out of the driveway, Ramu adopted a tone of
great closeness. "We had such fun playing cricket when we were young.
You used to hit boundaries off my bowling."

"Remember how you'd get Pitambaran to play with us?"

"He was a good cook. His *payasam* was the best."

The reminiscing continued until Ramu said, "You're a much misun-
derstood man."

"What do you mean?" asked Hari.

"I can't understand how our relatives back home talk unkindly
about you."

Hari turned the wheel to the right to avoid hitting the Trans-Am in
the next lane. "What the hell do you think you're doing?" shouted the
Trans-Am driver.

"What do they say?" asked Hari.

"That you're a show-off. You use every chance to display your success. How can they say that when you're only trying to give them a good
time? I don't blame you if you never forgive them. Renu called you a
hypocrite. She said that though she's your cousin you deceived her about
Judy. She liked Judy, but from your letters she was expecting her to be
different. Mother defended you. She knows you better than they do.
Bina, not my sister Bina but our cousin in Calcutta, said that you try to be
someone you're not. Are you angry, Hari? I'd be. After all you've done
for them. Ungrateful, that's what I call them."

Hari felt a constriction in his throat. He squinted, pretending the
sunlight bothered him. "I don't care," he said. "I can't change their perceptions."

"That's what it is, Hari, perception."

Hari concentrated on the traffic, his brows furrowed, his ears red, his
grip on the wheel firm, and his body inclined forward. Ramu talked
about seeing the White House and the Smithsonian museums. Lekha and
Seema joined in, a trio of voices, unmercifully chattering on.

Returning from the airport, Hari released the mental brake that had
halted the rush of thoughts. He felt sorry for himself. He thought of Judy.

He'd stop by at Bloomingdale's and get her a handbag. The next time there was a potential guest he'd make an excuse. Judy would say, "Gee, Hari. I can't believe you're telling them no." Hari would shrug his shoulders as though he didn't care.

Tahira Naqvi

Statement: Our life in the United States has been, in retrospect, a life that was dichotomized from the day we arrived here and that, twenty-one years later, continues to be complex, pluralistic, and challenging. Coming out of this experience of friction and conflict, my writing, which began with a focus on the immigrant experience, has now branched off into the "Asian experience." It has in turn contributed to an understanding of my Pakistani American/Asian American self. Straddling two cultures has proven to be an impetus rather than a deterrent for me as a writer. I agree with Salman Rushdie when he says that "however ambiguous and shifting this ground may be, it is not an infertile territory for a writer to occupy"(as quoted in Anuradha Dingwaney Needham's "The Politics of Post-Colonial Identity in Salman Rushdie," *Desh-Videsh: South Asian Expatriate Writing and Art,* Special Issue, *The Massachusetts Review* 29, no. 4, pp. 609–624).

In this short story Tahira Naqvi portrays the friction between as well as the blending of two cultures and the tensions that come into play as different generations of Pakistani Americans compromise with one another and with their environment in America. Memories of South Asia as well as the gradual lapses and erosion of such memories and traditions appear as central themes in South Asian American lives and South Asian American fiction.

All Is Not Lost

Fatima should have been shocked when she heard the news. But she wasn't. Instead, she experienced a vague uneasiness, as if she had taken a wrong turn during a rushed drive to town and suddenly found herself in unfamiliar surroundings. When she conveyed the news to Aunt Sakina, who was poised at that moment to pick up the frying pan in which she had prepared the *bhagar* for the *dal,* she reacted in a way that made Fatima feel guilty. The frying pan, small and blackened from overuse and in which the thinly sliced garlic cloves had fried and burnt to dark, crispy half-moons, leapt from Aunt Sakina's hands and landed on the kitchen floor with a muted thud.

Maryam, Cousin Shahid's daughter, was marrying an American. For nearly a year Aunt Sakina had coveted her for her own son, Kamal, who was twenty-five, had just received a master's degree in economics from Baruch College, and was looking for a job. Maryam's silky-white complexion and fine, uncomplicated nose had been in Aunt Sakina's thoughts for a long time; noses and complexions were a major preoccupation with mothers who were scouting for brides for their sons. On the other hand, Kamal, whose own nose tended to be somewhat on the bulbous side and whose complexion was nowhere near fair, had been hedging. Huddled together over tea, mothers and aunts wondered irately about such reticence, while sisters and cousins knew the boys no longer wanted to be passively led into marriage. He wasn't ready, Kamal had told his mother, but Fatima knew that was his way of keeping his mother at bay until sparks flew for him.

"Nowadays boys know nothing about responsibility," Aunt Sakina grumbled, slapping her head with her palm in dismay the last time the subject of arranging a match for Kamal rose in conversation.

Now Maryam was lost. And to make matters worse, an American was to have her. Aunt Sakina was inconsolable. While Fatima carefully mopped up the greasy mess on the floor with kitchen towels, she hunched in her chair nearby and with a morose expression on her small-boned, wrinkled face, muttered on and on.

Aunt Sakina had arrived from Pakistan in May. Now, a month later, she thought she had cause for regret.

"I knew I shouldn't have come. Why did I come? To see this happen?" She sighed, then continued, "I wonder what surprises my son has in store for me."

No doubt she had heard rumors of sparks and the like.

"Don't start worrying about Kamal, Auntie," Fatima hastened to assure her. Of course she was worried, and why not? Sitting down across from her, the crunched-up, oily ball of paper held tightly in her fist, Fatima brushed the perspiration from her forehead and said, "There's enough to worry about already."

"Well, girl, what do you expect? When you send a young girl to work in some faraway shop with no one to keep an eye on her, what do you think will come from that?"

Parveen, Maryam's mother, was an unflaggingly diligent mother. Other cousins whose children were younger watched her with reverence and awe and a hope, voiced openly, that they too could do their job as well as she had done hers. She had taken her daughter to weekend Islamic classes, she made sure the girl fasted and said her prayers regularly, she even went so far as to tell Maryam to carry a plastic glass in her bag so that if she had to use a ladies' bathroom somewhere, she'd not be put out for lack of a container for water. Such pains the woman had taken, and now this. And the weekly Islamic class, in turn, had done all it could to enforce the ideas of a woman's place and the need for her to protect herself against the evil ways of those to whom modesty was just a joke. Parveen had entrusted Maryam to the care of wise, knowing mullahs who had devoted their lives to teaching children. Dapper, sad-looking men with short and long beards, intrepid counselors who uprooted themselves from their native lands to come to America in order to keep children in the fold. And now Maryam had strayed.

Parveen was incoherent on the phone when she called with the distressing news. At first Fatima thought someone had died. "Parveen," she shouted, "for God's sake, what's happened?"

"Maryam wants to marry an American boy," Parveen sobbed hysterically, her voice changing into a prolonged groan. A little later, between sobs and sniffles and complaints about the hard blow fate had dealt them, she said Shahid hadn't left the house in three days. "He's threatening to kill the boy," she whimpered.

Her voice hoarse from crying, she said that Maryam had been reprimanded severely by Shahid, but the girl refused to be intimidated by her father's rage. "She's threatening to run away from home if we don't give our consent."

Fatima was surprised at Maryam's boldness. She had been such a subdued, docile teenager. And she always pleased Parveen's friends with the well-ordered way in which she served them tea, *samosas*, and *gulab jamuns*. "You've trained her so well," everyone told Parveen.

"We're feeling helpless," Parveen said brokenly, not listening to a word Fatima had said about being calm in a crisis.

In her senior year at school, Maryam took up a job as cashier at Morey's supermarket. Now she was a freshman at Rutgers University and she wanted to marry Jerry Noggles, a young man who had risen from the position of stock boy to manager at Morey's. Aunt Sakina made Fatima tell her the entire story twice, chafing her plump hands and slapping her deeply lined forehead alternately as she listened. Finally, she said, "Parents are nothing, they have no control any more, and poor Shahid, he's not going to be able to show his face in the community again." Aunt Sakina began mumbling under her breath. The *channa dal*, her specialty, was forgotten, as was the *bhagar* which she had been preparing so painstakingly. Fatima realized she should have waited until after dinner to tell her, but that was when Ali would be home, and husbands have such little patience with gossip.

Fatima started peeling more garlic.

"Shahid will have to agree to the wedding; that's better than an elopement, Auntie." The garlic cloves, soft under Fatima's fingers, glowed like fat, white almonds.

"An elopement. Yes, that's all we need to have our noses cut." Aunt Sakina tsk-tsked.

"You wait and see," Fatima said, slicing the crescent-shaped clove evenly, "we'll be attending a wedding soon. You should start learning some English, Auntie; you're the only elder here and you'll have to welcome Maryam's American in-laws at the door on the day of the wedding." The taste of garlic drew water in her mouth.

"Don't joke with me, girl," Aunt Sakina said grimly. "I'm not attending any such wedding and that Umreekan 'thoon, thaan' isn't for me. Just think what torment this will be for Shahid's father's soul."

Ah yes, I thought. Old stories, heard in childhood, came up like smoke through a vent, pervasive, soon covering all else. Shahid's father, Uncle Sharafat, my own father, and Aunt Sakina were all first cousins. As teenagers, Aunt Sakina and Uncle Sharafat had made promises to each other in secret, were engaged, and then a family crisis rooted in someone's bad marriage came along and forced them to go their separate ways. What torment, indeed! And such helplessness.

Aunt Sakina rolled her bangles around her wrist and plucked at her *dupatta*. "I'll just have to go to Shahid and Parveen right away. Shahid will need me. If these fools had stayed in their own country," she continued despondently, "none of this would have happened. Why did they leave Pakistan and come to settle in a country where your daughters are not safe from Umreekan boys?"

Fatima turned to increase the speed of the fan on the counter. June in Connecticut this year was no less oppressive than June in Lahore, and they hadn't had much rain. Whatever little had fallen this month had come like some prayer being answered in installments, at an agonizingly slow pace. And to the surprise of all Lahore visitors this year, the Connecticut sun could be as merciless as the Lahore sun. The heat from the stove was not helping matters any either.

The *bhagar* was ready. Fatima turned off the stove. Dark, thin tendrils of smoke arose from the pan and a heavy smell of garlic and burnt cumin seeds filled the kitchen. Picking up the frying pan, she slowly poured the oil and garlic mixture over the dal which had been sitting patiently in the pot all this time. The *bhagar* bubbled furiously and foamed, forming a brown and honey-gold center before subsiding. In the background was a low hum that was Aunt Sakina's lugubrious "Hai, hai."

* * *

Cousin Shahid consented to have the wedding, albeit with extreme reluctance and only when Jerry Noggles agreed to be converted to Islam. According to Parveen, Mr. and Mrs. Noggles stubbornly resisted the idea, insisting they had their own religious affiliations and it wasn't fair that their son be asked to give up the religion of his forefathers. Before long, the argument between the Noggles and the Hussains turned ugly in the Hussain living room in Edison.

In the next room, Aunt Sakina, who had been in New Jersey only a few hours, was pacing as if walking on live coals. If she could have her way, she'd have come out and told the Noggles to keep their church as well as their son. This Fatima received directly from her. Luckily, Maryam, who was with her at the time, prevented her from making any drastic moves she might regret afterward.

"She was acting like one of those old crones in Indian films, Auntie Fatima, those grumpy mothers-in-law," Maryam informed Fatima in a confused, bewildered tone.

Finally, after nearly two hours of heated exchange, Jerry surprised everyone by suddenly jumping up from his chair and proclaiming, "If that's what I have to do to marry her, that's what I'll do!"

"Maryam covered her mouth in excitement," Aunt Sakina said, adding, "I swear that his voice resounded in Shahid's living room like an evocation in a *qazi's* sermon, it was as though Allah had spoken through the boy. A conversion will earn everyone a reward in heaven." Without waiting for Fatima's reaction to all this she continued emphatically, "All is not lost after all."

The name chosen for Shahid's prospective son-in-law was Tariq Hasan. Aunt Sakina advised he be called Sharafat after the girl's grandfather, especially since his soul was bound to be troubled and needed appeasement, but Maryam wouldn't agree.

Aunt Sakina was disappointed. "She said her friends can pronounce Tariq Hasan easily. Can you imagine deciding on a name because your friends can pronounce it easily? Hai, hai, what is the world coming to?"

Dr. Shah, a pediatrician who doubled as *maulavi sahib* when the occasion called for it, performed the conversion ceremony a day before the wedding. By that time Aunt Sakina had learned to say, in a halting tone thick with an accent, "How are you?" "I am well," and "Thank you." Since she'd been warned about not mussing Jerry's hair when she patted him on the head, she patted him on the back instead when he was brought to her to say "Salaamalekum."

On the phone Aunt Sakina said, "He is not so bad-looking, Fatima, and his hair is quite dark; at least he's not bald!" Aunt Sakina spoke with some satisfaction. "But something troubles me," she added, her voice dropping, "and I don't know what it is."

"Too late for that now, Auntie," Fatima clucked. "Kamal will have to marry someone else."

"No, no, girl, it's not that, it's something else." She sounded fretful.

"Well, you've put your head in the mill, why fear the mortars now?"

Fatima used one of her aunt's favorite adages. She was tempted to add, "Who can quarrel with fate?"

In August, soon after a whole week of rains that fell with the ferocity of summer monsoons in Lahore, the wedding reception took place at a place called Three Oaks, a wedding hall, less expensive than a hotel. More private, someone said; we can do what we want and there's no one else to wander into our area and wonder if there's some primitive ritual in progress.

The women—Shahid's cousins, aunts, friends' wives—all sat together. Mingling was a convention they still had not mastered, even though most of them had had the opportunity to learn for over fifteen years. But to Fatima's surprise, Aunt Sakina was intent on moving about, a grande dame of the family, her heavy bulk extended before her like the protective wall of a fortress, a smile that Fatima saw was forced mapped gallantly across her face.

The wedding cake, Jerry's contribution to the reception, was four tiers high. Rows of pink and yellow roses adorned each tier, and on the top, precariously balanced under an arbor of tiny white plastic flowers, were bride and groom dolls that looked suspiciously like Ken and Barbie.

"Tariq insisted we must have a cake. Why not, I said. Where we've done so much, what's the harm with one more thing? Is it not pretty?" Aunt Sakina was explaining the presence of the wedding cake to a group of elderly women who were scrutinizing it as if it were some bizarre object that withstood recognition. But Aunt Sakina couldn't explain away the white of Maryam's wedding gown. "Yesterday, for the *nikah* ceremony she wore a red *gharara* and the jewelry Parveen had set aside for her specially, but today she insisted on . . . on this. There are some customs we don't understand," she said, attempting to illuminate and rationalize. "Everyone knows white is the color of mourning, a bad omen for a bride, but do you think these young people pay any heed to their elders any more?"

"But, Auntie, fashions have changed," interjected Nasreen, a cousin's teenage daughter. She was wearing an off-white organza heavily embroidered in gold, a diaphanous *dupatta* dangling stiffly from her shoulders. "Nowadays the girls don't want to wear bright, gaudy reds at their wedding."

"Such nonsense!" Aunt Sakina retorted. "Tomorrow they will say they want to hold hands with their grooms in public in front of everyone. I say, can't they wait a few hours until they are alone? Such impatience!"

During a lengthy photo session with Jerry's best man and the four bridesmaids, who wore lilac and pink gowns with large bows in the back, Jerry suddenly leaned over and kissed Maryam on the lips. All the women at Fatima's table gasped. Lifting a corner of her blue chiffon *dupatta*, Aunt Sakina covered her eyes with it in dismay, and some of the younger girls, observing her reaction, giggled.

Jerry was nearly as tall as Kamal, who, unruffled by his mother's distress over the kiss or the loss of Maryam to an American, chatted bois-terously with the best man, a fair-haired, chubby boy with a laugh that went spilling across the length of the entire hall and made people sit up and take note. Both Jerry and Kamal had mustaches, but Jerry's sat neatly on his upper lip like fuzz compared to Kamal's, which flapped over his mouth like a crow's wing.

"Shahid warned him to observe our customs for the sake of our guests," Aunt Sakina mumbled. "He agreed and now he is going back on his word." Agitated, she looked around for Shahid. Mercifully, he was nowhere in sight.

"Auntie, don't worry, he's her husband now; the *nikah* took place yesterday. Actually they've been husband and wife for a whole day." Fatima made an attempt to pacify her, but she continued to scowl unhap-pily.

To Fatima's relief, dinner was announced a few minutes later. Aunt Sakina, frowning still, got up from her chair, then sat down. The in-laws were to be served first.

Earlier, when the menu was being planned, one of Shahid's broth-ers had suggested Shaheen Catering be asked to go easy on the red chilies and the *garam masala* in the *korma* and the spinach and beef dish. Aunt Sakina immediately protested: "Everything will taste like hospi-tal food, bland and unpalatable; the community's going to go home feeling nauseated, and the next day everyone will be saying how bad the food was at Shahid's daughter's wedding. Would the boy's family temper their food for us?" No one could answer that with a positive yes.

"Shaheen's been catering in New York and New Jersey and every-where else for a long time," Shahid, exasperated with the argument over food, finally spoke up. "They'll know what to do." And the matter of the red chilies was put to rest.

Weddings. Standing at the table with the aroma of *garam masala* from the *korma* and the fragrance of the saffron in *biryani* wafting into her nose, Fatima remembered the weddings she attended in Lahore as a young girl. Always, there was a run for the largest pieces of chicken floating in the gravy, and later a scramble to get to the cool, sweet, *firni* in the tiny, round ocher-colored earthen plates. Dispensing with spoons, the children used their fingers to lift globs of chilled rice pudding into their mouths, closely scraping the surface of the plate to reach beneath to the last of the sweet, thin, white layer. Sometimes, impatient and adventurous, the youngest among them would venture to go one step further and quickly lick the plate.

When the cutting of the cake was announced, some children, girls in brightly colored, gold-embroidered *shalwar-kamees* suits, ran, shouting, "Cake! Cake!" Another exodus began, this time toward the cake. A voice came over the din, perhaps it was Kamal or one of the other cousins, calling for pictures of the bride and groom with Shahid and Parveen. Fatima and the others pushed them toward their daughter and son-in-law while Aunt Sakina grumbled that this was all unnecessary.

Parveen squirmed and Shahid, a stiff smile frozen on his lips, moved forward awkwardly. Finally Parveen adjusted the *dupatta* on her shoulders and Shahid ran a hand through his hair. There were deep circles under Parveen's eyes and the smile that engaged her lips momentarily, at Kamal's insistence, was tense.

"They should leave now, the bride and groom," Fatima heard Aunt Sakina murmur behind her. "Something might go wrong and then where will we be?"

Given her state of mind, Fatima was beginning to think she might be right. But their guests didn't appear to be ready to leave as yet. The ceremony with the cake had imbued them with lively energy. Suddenly animated, they smiled and made jokes, talking noisily as they were served large, white, fluffy slices of cake. The young bridesmaids, Maryam's college friends, their short, light hair bobbing as they threw back their heads to laugh, flirted openly with the best man. Fatima caught a glimpse of Kamal conversing with one of them, a tall, sprightly girl with an easy smile, and she could see he was taking pictures of her wherever she went. Jerry kept his arm around Maryam and she leaned toward him slightly as if swayed by a strong wind. The sequins on the tiny white florets on the lace of the veil above her forehead glimmered like drops of dew when they caught the light, and her pale skin shone like freshly peeled almonds.

Back in their seats, with cups of tea cradled in their palms and like an enrapt audience glued to a soap opera, Fatima, Parveen's younger sister, Yasmin, Aunt Sakina, and the other ladies in their group watched this drama of unfamiliar exuberance and youthful gaiety unfold. Aunt Sakina was seated next to Fatima. It was past eleven. She was so tired now. She leaned heavily in her chair, ignoring the *dupatta* that had slipped off her head and hung limply from her shoulders. She sighed constantly. Fatima drew her attention to the forgotten cup of tea before her on the table.

"Your tea is getting cold, Auntie," she reminded her.

"Can you think of nothing but tea?" Aunt Sakina snapped at her. "I will not be able to sleep tonight, for many nights maybe."

"But, Auntie," Fatima protested, "everything is all right now. Jerry is Tariq Hasan and the bride and groom are so happy. Just look at them."

Instead of responding to her niece's remark, she rose from her chair suddenly, tipping the chair as she got up so that it fell back with a loud thud, and said, "I wonder where Parveen is, I must find her."

Pushing the *dupatta* back over her head again, she started to walk away from Fatima.

"Auntie, wait, where are you going?" Fatima threw up her hands in despair to the accompaniment of chuckles and head shaking from Yasmin, abandoned her half-finished tea, and sped after her aunt.

The Noggles' guests were lining up to say goodbye to Maryam and her husband. Parveen was nowhere about.

"Auntie Sakina, Parveen is probably taking care of some last-minute chores before she sends Maryam off." Fatima firmly grasped her elbow and propelled her away from the crowd that was rapidly forming around the bride and groom like rain clouds gathering before a storm. The girls were laughing, and Fatima saw Maryam raise her bouquet. Some of Fatima's nieces and their friends also came forward excitedly. "Catch it! Catch it!" With a wicked grin, Yasmin's daughter, Nasreen, whispered in her cousin's ear, "Why don't you catch it?"

"Come with me; there's something I have to tell you." Aunt Sakina's voice crept up on Fatima from behind as she paused to see the tossing of the bride's bouquet.

"What is it, Auntie?" The tone of her voice was alarming, and Fatima decided to forgo participation in the last-minute jollity.

"Girl," she lowered her head and muttered close to her niece's ear. "No one has guessed as yet, but when the truth dawns on people, we won't be able to lift our heads in the community. Ya Allah!" Her eyes welled and in another instant large tears spilled over her leathery cheeks like a river overriding its banks.

Fatima felt goose bumps stir on her skin; her heart pounded in her chest as if she had seen a ghost.

"What is it, Auntie?" she asked hoarsely. Had someone gossiped in her presence, said something about Maryam and Jerry, that they had been sleeping together, perhaps? But she was with her nearly all evening, there had been no such talk, at least none that she knew of. Fatima's heart raced.

Aunt Sakina's face was ashen. "Poor Sharafat's soul—hai, hai, such torment! This wretched girl, why could she not marry my Kamal?"

So that's what it was. Fatima's mind suddenly went blank with relief. Aunt Sakina was indulging in a final regret. Poor Auntie. "Auntie, it's too late for that now; don't get upset. This isn't good for Parveen, you know, to see you like this." Fatima put an arm around her. "There's Parveen over there; let's go and say good-bye to Maryam together."

Parveen and Maryam were hugging. It was a time for solemnity. Giving away a daughter was the hardest thing parents ever did, and it didn't matter where you were and who you were giving her away to. Kamal handed Shahid a copy of the Koran, which would be lifted high so the newly married couple could walk out under it. Parveen began to sob violently while Shahid stood next to her with a stoical expression on his face, the Koran held to his chest tightly as if in an embrace. Jerry had moved to the entrance with his parents and best man. All four of them looked distraught and puzzled.

Aunt Sakina pulled Fatima by the arm. "No, no, Fatima, you don't understand," she whispered fiercely. "It's something else."

"Something else? What?" Fatima brushed tears from her cheek.

"Tell me, girl, what good is a conversion? Saying the *kalima*, saying '*la illaha illalah Muhammadur rasulallah*' is not enough. There are other things a Muslim is required to do." She shook Fatima's arm again and waved a finger ominously in her face.

What other things? Fatima thought wildly. Of course there were other things, but none as important as the conversion. What did she mean?

Fatima looked at her blankly.

"What about circumcision? Do you know we are sending off Shahid's daughter with a man who is not circumcised? What about that, girl?" Aunt Sakina faced her niece squarely and raised a questioning hand.

Circumcision? Fatima stared at her aunt's small, plump hand, then at the heavy, solid gold bracelets that she was saving for Kamal's bride. Circumcision? The constriction in Fatima's throat and the moisture that had gathered in her eyes due to Parveen's sobbing and the sadness of the occasion of a young girl's departure from her parents' home, suddenly seemed quite ridiculous in view of the images Aunt Sakina's query had generated. Foolishly, she looked wide-eyed at Aunt Sakina, whose face at that moment was uncannily like her own mother's countenance.

"But, Auntie," Fatima foundered, "all is not lost, is it?"

Kirin Narayan

Statement: "Hahlf and haylf": saying one word in a British Indian accent, the other with an American twang, this is how my siblings and I have characterized ourselves for many years. We are, after all, partly Indian—our father's ancestors are from Kutch, in Gujarat—and partly American—our mother's mother was from Michigan though married to a Bavarian painter. Increasingly, a neat cultural divide down the middle seems too simple for the tangled, contextually elicited veins of identity shooting through our lives. I, for one, consider myself not just Indian and American but also a woman and a scholar, an anthropologist and folklorist who is also a novelist.

Treading along an increasingly steep academic path, I was anxious not to let my fiction fall by the wayside. I continued to write short stories when I found time in graduate school. As I was writing my dissertation, I wrote a story whose theme was cultural discordances around love and I was intrigued by the characters—Gita, Saroj Aunty, Ajay, Norvin, Zelda. Writing on to find out who these people were and why I was so fond of them, I came to compose *Love, Stars, and All That*. Begun as a story in the spring of 1987, sent out to my agent around New Year's of 1992, the book took form in time snatched away from my demanding years as an assistant professor. I wrote much of the novel on leave in 1990–1991, doing research on women's oral traditions in Kangra, Northwest India. I view my fiction writing and anthropological career as mutually complementary. As I write fiction, I revel in the heady sense of mischief in plotting characters and events. At the same time, in my ethnographic writing, I value the rigor of respecting the words and the circumstances of actual people in today's interconnected world.

On the eve of her departure for the United States, Gita, the protagonist of *Love, Stars, and All That*, is told by an astrologer that her chart shows that a certain month and year are propitious for her finding "Mr. Right." Of course, when the long-awaited time arrives, Gita encounters numerous men with varying degrees of "rightness." The first selection printed in this anthology presents her meeting with two men, a poet (who has been asked to deliver to Gita a present from her aunt) and a professor. The second selection is the interior monologue by Feroze Ganjifrockwala, a Parsi man from India who has been Gita's friend at Berkeley. This chapter occurs later in the novel, when Gita and Feroze meet again after having

gone their separate ways for some years. The two selections are presented here to show the different styles of writing as well as the different levels of discourse, the humor, and the underlying seriousness in this
important first novel.

Love, Stars, and All That (Selection One)

"Holy cow! Not Timothy Stilling." Bet squinted one eye open. She
was soaking in the afternoon sun on the deck in case she was called back
for an audition.

"Who is he?" Gita asked, so excited that the name was recognized
that she forgot to wonder if Bet was making fun of her. She was never
sure whether people in California only said "Holy cow" to Indians. She
was also trying to ignore the expanse of nude flesh before her. Thank
goodness Bet was lying on her stomach; it would have been quite difficult the other way.

"Well, he's sure a Bay Area celebrity. I don't know how well he's
known elsewhere. One of those postmodern Susan Sontag kind of men.
He's in the *Chronicle* sometimes. I read an interview about him once; I
think he writes essays and poetry. You'd better get your little ass right
over to the Telegraph Avenue bookstores to check out his writing. Well! It
looks like that astrologer of yours has something going for him."

"Nothing," said Gita, smiling broadly. She stopped, listening to her
voice. She hadn't used the word that way in months, maybe years. It was
the way girls at the convent had said "Shut up" or "Nonsense." Na-
thing—it seemed to fling away the other person's position even if you
suspected it was right.

"Before you go, remember to pick up, will you? I already told you I
might have some folks stopping by."

"Sure," said Gita. That was the arrangement: if either of them had a
visitor they had to issue advance warning. She put her books in her room,
closed the door, and sped off through streets festive with pink blossoms.

There were two slim volumes of poetry by Timothy Stilling in stock.
The back covers were filled with praise but no picture, alas. Gita turned a
few pages and soon she felt that she was visiting an old, dear friend. The
bookstore bustle disappeared. He was holding up a mirror for her to see
herself. He understood the nuances of what she had never been able to
express. He spoke about places inside her she would like to discover. She
felt herself hugging, hugged by his words, felt herself expanding to
incorporate his mind.

If the books hadn't been hardbacks she would have bought them
both even though they weren't assigned for a class. Instead she checked

them out of the library, reading and rereading them with someone else's marginal notes (yes, he was worthy of a paper, maybe even a dissertation!). She calculated that there was a fourteen-year age difference between them, the right amount of time for someone to grow wise. She stopped dressing up and forcing herself into cafes. It was clear now, she was to be devoted to this man. But being shy, she did not let on to anyone, though it was all she thought about most of the time. Shani Maharaj, with all his weight and presence, and seven gyrating moons, was slowly lumbering ahead.

He was not handsome. Hardly the dark-haired, broad-shouldered prince Gita had always expected. Timothy Stilling was very skinny and quite bald, and the hair hanging low around his scalp was a nondescript brown. His eyes were small under the jutting forehead. His shoulders sloped. If she took him home to Delhi surely everyone would laugh. "Couldn't you have done better, dear?" Kookoo would say in an undertone, leaning forward as she handed back the salad spoons to the uniformed servant standing behind her chair. Dilip would bring out imported whisky and invite Timothy to have a few pegs, then remark later that it was a pity the old chap wasn't much of a drinker, and a terrible shame about cricket and those Yanks. Riding with Timothy on the train to Bombay would be a disaster too; she could already feel the heat of the stares from other passengers. How he would be received by the Shahs wasn't clear yet: after all, they must have liked him if they had forwarded him onward.

As soon as he started introducing his poems, her opinions began to shift. His voice was filled with golden light. His eyes shimmered, blue, wise. His hands were long-fingered and eloquent when he spread them out to make a point. Even the teeth, set so tight and crooked in his mouth, were charming. Yes, Saroj Aunty had picked the right kind of man. Sitting in the back row, Gita became conscious of her breath pumping into her stomach, playing intoxicatingly out over her upper lip. She had felt this way only a few fleeting times before in her life. She remembered the thrill of algorithms taught by the sole male teacher who was not in robes, a nervous young man whom every girl in the convent school longed for but who disappointed them all by getting married over an Easter vacation. She thought of the neighbor's son in Delhi with his short shorts and hairy legs, off with a tennis racket in the early mornings, and how when the parents got together for dinner she had once spent an entire evening in his room wondering what to say as he sucked, scowling, on a cigarette. Before she had pricked up her ears at college for the kinds of things one might talk about with a boy, he had gone off to England on a Rhodes scholarship. It was sad but true that though Gita was so accomplished in other spheres of life, when it came to romance she felt like an ignoramus. Even if Bet was sometimes so awfully condescending, it might not be a bad idea to open up to her in search of advice.

Gita had dressed in Indian clothes for the poetry reading. Before March she had mostly tried to disappear into crowds by wearing jeans and running shoes, hair severely braided down her back. But this day she had loosely anchored her hair in a bamboo hair clip and spent the time before the reading ironing a red-and-black tie-dyed *kurta* to wear over tight-fitting black *churidars*. Saroj Aunty had chosen this outfit from a boutique in Bombay run by two elderly sisters pledged to natural fabrics and vegetable dyes. It bore luck. As Gita waited for the crowds to clear away from Timothy Stilling when he finished his reading, she felt pretty and unique.

Women were fluttering around him, men were shaking his hand, books were thrust before him for a signature. A short Indian (Pakistani? Bangladeshi? Sri Lankan?) girl with a halo of hair around a self-possessed, smiling face went up and extended a hand, accentuating Gita's awkwardness to herself. He was taller than most people, Gita observed. That bald head would be like a white beacon in any crowd, in any situation of the shared story that was rising up with such certainty before them. Finally he was left with just one man.

"I am Gita," she presented herself, conscious of her voice being different, a "charming lilt."

"Gita? Oh yes—" He was puzzled but smiling down at her with all those wonderful crooked teeth.

"Gita!" the other man said. He was short, tanned, with wiry black hair and glasses. "I've seen you around Feeler Hall, haven't I? Aren't you a new graduate student?"

"Yes." It seemed to Gita that she could do nothing but smile as though her cheeks would split.

"Oh no. The present," Timothy Stilling said. "I knew I forgot something. I'm so sorry you had to come all this way. This is terrible. I've been doing this kind of thing lately—there's just too much going on with, you know, the British editions coming out and proofreading for the new book and all the traveling."

"At least you made it here on the right day, Tim," the other man said. "Right month, right time. That's something."

"Oh, cut it out, Norvin," said Timothy. "This is Norvin Weinstein, Gita. He's kidding around because I, umm, wrote down a reading in Cambridge wrong in my calendar. I got there a month early."

Gita was wishing she could disappear. She recognized the name Norvin Weinstein. He was a famous professor, someone her adviser had suggested she take a course with sometime. There was no reason to feel publicly shamed at what wasn't even an obvious assignation, but she did. The professor would surely know that she could have been decoding Foucault's *The History of Sexuality* this evening instead of looking for her March Man. "And then?" she asked, her smile suddenly awkward in its fit.

"Well, nothing. The bookstore folks were stunned. I stayed on to hear the other reading. Then I had to fly back and go out again. The whole experience was like walking into someone else's nightmare. I really am sorry about your package. I even put it near my car keys, but at the last minute the phone rang."

"Look here," said Professor Weinstein, "why don't we all go out for a drink? You can always give her the package later. Gita, I've been wanting to get together with you. I was in India in the Peace Corps. Nasik, Maharashtra. Sixty-six to sixty-eight. I'm sure you know the place. Where did you go to school?"

"Our Lady of Perpetual Succour Convent, Ootacamund," said Gita, wondering why Timothy pressed his lips hard so he wouldn't smile, and the professor let out a whoop.

"Fabulous," said the professor, grinning with what seemed like all thirty-two teeth. "Just fabulous. We've got to talk. And what are you working on?"

What a question! To say she didn't know yet would show her up as a graduate student so young she was still floundering for a Topic. Gita thought rapidly on her feet, bringing an inspirational folklore course she'd been sitting in on into the same frame as Ayah. "The intellectual paradigms underlying colonial folk-narrative collections on the Indian subcontinent," she said.

"Hot stuff!" said the professor. "You can work in intertextuality, imperialism, invented traditions, all the rest of it. Terrific. Well, let's go for a drink. My car's down the street."

By now it was time for Gita to have been studying her daily chapter in the French for Reading Knowledge book. But it was the professor who was insisting. That eased the responsibility.

By the time they had all sat down, she was using their first names. Norvin explained that he and Timothy had been undergraduates together at Harvard. (Harvard! Gita thought—even the convent sisters wouldn't just dismiss this as a nest of long-haired protestors but would associate it with respectable citizens.) They had met the first day, when Timothy was singing a Bob Dylan song with his guitar and Norvin came by from the next dorm room to say the E major chord should really be minor. Norvin, it turned out, was right. It appeared that he went through life being short, dark, handsome, and right. They became friends. When Norvin was in India, Timothy was in Paris. Later they were both in graduate school at Yale. Now they were both stars in their own right. Norvin was known for his contributions to poststructuralist, neo-Marxist literary criticism and Timothy for his postbeat poetry. Gita had heard at some graduate student party that Berkeley had to create a special endowed Doolittle Chair in order to keep Norvin, he was wanted by so many other universities. And neither of them was yet forty!

Norvin was trying to speak to Gita in Marathi. "*Mazha nav* Norvin *ahe*," he said. "*Me* America *la rahatath, Mazha vadhil* lawyer *ahe. Tumcha nav kai?*"

Gita nodded, too awestruck to tell him that she didn't speak Marathi, she wasn't from that part of the country. "*Ho, Ho,*" she assented, remembering that this was how Saroj Aunty's servants said yes. She wished he would stop so Timothy could say something wise. "Walking into someone else's nightmare" had been so poetic. She had no idea what Norvin was talking about except when English words made their way through his Brooklyn accent. She looked nervously around through the clatter and cigarette smoke in the cafe. There was a clutch of Iranian students at the next table, unrolling posters of tortured people. There was a group of girls—probably undergraduates—sharing a jug of beer and laughing loudly at each other's stories. "Give us Bruce Springsteen!" someone shouted at a friend poised by the jukebox. In the midst of this there were people with books open before them, some studying hard and some looking around wistfully. Luckily nobody she could recognize from her classes.

Timothy was drinking herbal tea, which gave her the excuse to order some tea too without looking unsophisticated. As Norvin carried on, Timothy twirled the cup around and around on the table. He began to shred the paper napkins and rearrange the white pieces into different patterns. Then he took a small book out of his breast pocket and wrote something down.

"A poem?" Gita asked hopefully, even though Norvin was midway through some unintelligible narrative. When Timothy took out the pen she felt as if she were stepping into a temple, lamps flickering in the innermost sanctum. She could smell incense and burning ghee and feel the presence of freshly bathed Ayah.

"No, not exactly," said Timothy, fidgeting with the book as he slid it back into his pocket. "Just, umm, a reminder for me to make an international call. I keep forgetting to do these things. Everyone ends up mad at me."

"Well, to cut a long story short," Norvin said, "I managed to convince them that I didn't have to be followed around with a chair, I was quite capable of sitting cross-legged. It took all that! Sorry, Timothy, I really wanted to practice my Marathi. I hardly meet anyone I can talk to anymore. It's important to keep up on all one's languages."

"Very important," Gita ventured.

"I speak six," said Norvin, "twelve if you bring in the reading knowledge. You guys want anything? Sure? I'm going for another beer." As Norvin stood up, Gita noticed that his shirt was textured purple handloom, probably made in India, and just the fashionable amount too big. Timothy's shirt was actually too tight, blue checks that might have been better on a kitchen table, its cut accentuating his bones and angles. And it didn't even have buttons, it had snaps! Thinking that Timothy didn't know current men's fashions made her feel protective.

"People should understand that you're busy," Gita said, leaning forward and looking into Timothy's long harlequin face. "I mean, being creative and all is hard work."

"It's not the creativity," Timothy said, "it's the being on display. All the expectations and demands. You know how that is?"

"Oh, *yes*," said Gita, flattered that he thought she might. She had to force herself not to flinch as his eyes connected with hers.

"At this point in my life I just want to have enough time alone to keep writing, but that's not what anyone else seems to understand. I mean, fulfill expectations and time becomes this leaky faucet, drip, drip, unrelenting drip."

"Oh, I know *exactly* how it is," Gita said. "Here in America it's something that you have to always be rationing."

"Ration," said Timothy. "Great word." He took out his notebook again and wrote it down. Wrote her word down! What else could she say?

"There's a famine on time here," Gita said carefully. "Everyone works but is hungry inside." She waited for him to write this down too. He didn't, and the pole of attention went back from her point of view to his. "You must look after yourself," she said. "Can't you get a secretary to make those calls and all so you can write?" She paused, then said in a rush, "Your poetry is lovely. You must give yourself maximum time."

Her ears began to burn as soon as she said this. She looked into the dregs of her rosehip tea. Lovely was such a tame word, and really what she meant was: you need a wife.

"Thank you," said Timothy. "I'm glad you like my work." He had the kindest smile that pierced blue-eyed through her heart right to the other side.

Love, Stars, and All That (Selection Two)

Why is it that some of us go back to live in India and some of us stay on in the U.S.? I'm sitting in the Frankfurt airport in a haze of exhaustion and displacement, my carry-on bag tucked between my ankles. What the hell am I doing returning to New York? The question hasn't stopped bugging me ever since I turned away from my parents and went into security at Bombay's Sahar airport. As we embraced, I noticed how tired my father looks, his skin hanging so loosely on his face that his eyes seem bloodshot and huge. And my mother seems to have shrunk, her head bent forward, shoulders hunched. One arm was still in a cast from when she slipped at the end of the monsoon. But with the other arm she held me tightly, whispering blessings in my ear.

There is a constant stream of people in this airport, rivulets from many sources coming together to flow out in new combinations through different gates. There are Arab gentlemen gliding along in long white robes, immaculate Swiss couples speaking to each other in brisk, flat tones, several African children clambering over their sleeping mother, two women who looked like they might be of Indian origin (Ugandan? Canadian?) and both in pantsuits with artificial pearls, bent toward each other in conversation. An Indonesian delegation of short men in batik shirts has just gone by; a troop of healthy-looking hostesses, perhaps German, wheel their suitcases past; and some American college kids with backpacks arrive with raised chins to study the schedule. With a patter of shutters, the flight arrivals and departures are switched on the board overhead. What am I doing in this place? If I had not got on the plane, it would now be time for an afternoon nap, the fan in my room rattling.

There was this prof chap I once landed up in a seminar with in those days when I was wandering across departments at Berkeley. He'd been a campus hero from the faculty side during the sixties, but now he seemed sort of tired. Pale, lined face, gravelly voice, faded jeans jacket—I can still picture him exactly. He used to say that there are two kinds of social theorists: those who view life as spectacle, and those who see it as predicament. I understood at once that Marxist scholars clearly belong in the second camp, and actually, most feminists do too. You look at things and see their imperfection, and then you try to figure out a way it could all be changed. What was intriguing about this fellow was that from his writings it was clear that he saw us all as landed in a bloody horrible predicament: capitalism, racism, sexism, nuclear arms, environmental crisis, all the rest of it. But then if you went to see him in office hours or anything, he would hold forth with funny stories, spectacles of the first order. Crazy stories, like how some Indian students who'd been Naxalites before coming to grad school had once left their elite college and gone off in theatrically rumpled white kurta-pajamas to a village to raise everyone's consciousness. They got a grand reception, lots of tea and pakoras and marigold garlands and rope cots pulled out for them to sit on. By the end of the day, just when they thought they were making good progress on uniting the masses against oppression, they learned that actually the rumor had gone out that they were here to view marriageable girls. Every house where they'd been received had daughters who'd served the snacks. Apparently, the villagers were pretty much just humoring these potential sons-in-law. They listened to the speeches and smiled.

Anyway, telling stories like this, it seemed like this prof chap had a vision of the world in which, within the huge predicament, most human interactions were a bloody absurd spectacle. I still wonder whether his stories meant that he'd given up, or whether he'd just accepted that there are some things too enormous to always keep in your mind or to tackle directly. I can see that teaching could be a form of political activity if you change the perspectives of your students. Choosing teaching and letting other fronts of action slide, maybe he had just accepted his own limitations.

Learning limitations is tough enough, but living with them is a constant struggle. I keep wondering if I should have tried to stick it out in India. Not just now, in the airport, but also when I'm in New York. The thought keeps pestering me: in the office when I talk to people who've been forced to leave their countries, on the subways when I see old people, in my empty apartment that registers flushing toilets, squeaking bedsprings, keening kettles, and unhappy babies from all the apartments around. My parents aren't exactly in the prime of their lives. I was born to them late, when they'd given up hope of ever having kids, and my mother dismissed what was to be me as menopause. If I were a good son I'd be living with them now. But just from the few months I was there after I'd graduated from Berkeley, I knew that I couldn't stand to be cooped up in that apartment. The Malabar Hill mansion has long since been torn down: The only tokens of it are in the huge urns on the gateway and the banyan tree at the back of the property. Otherwise we're boxed in among thirty-two floors looking out toward Marine Drive. It can be a peaceful place, too high for the city's noise, too high even for crows, with strong breezes and a beautiful view of the sea. Comfortable living too, meals appearing at the right time, and clothes left in the laundry basket reappearing freshly ironed from the dhobi. But I couldn't stand it. I couldn't take being reduced to a child. The old servants who smell of strong beedi tobacco always call me Baba. My father waits up for me to come home at night before lumbering off to sleep himself. My mother flits in and out of my room to tidy up my drawers and check on whether I am happy. Then too, the bloody phone, right in the living room, and the way both parents like to contribute to any conversation. "Who is it? Kaun? Why is she calling now? Tell her that we hope . . ." And the old beaked aunties who chuck me under the chin and declare me ketlo sweet, but when will I have a real job, isn't it time? I just couldn't and still can't handle it.

What I really wanted to do when I finished my degree was activist work. But those bloody amoebas just about wiped me out. You can't have a stomach raised on boiled water and expect to mingle easily with the proletariat. Not that I could mingle easily anyway—there were days when I just felt like getting some pigmentation injected into my skin. Currently there are these racist contact lenses available to make brown eyes blue or green, but I frankly wouldn't have minded some contacts that would have made my light brown eyes a penetrating black. Well, there are other Indians as fair as me: Kashmiris, or Saraswat Brahmans; I still can't put my finger on why everyone treated me so much like a foreigner. I took off my Reeboks and got Bata Keds instead; I left my best North Face backpack at home. I only wore clothes of the roughest homespun khadi. But all the same, I never really mingled. I know, I know, it might have been more appropriate to wear polyester safari suits if I really wanted to look like a modern Indian.

For example, on the train into central Maharashtra, where I was going to work with tribals being harassed by forest contractors, a ticket collector in his black-and-white uniform sat down at the end of my seat and stared through his black spectacles. Finally he asked, "What is your good country, sir?"

"India," I said.

He laughed, as though I'd said something witty. "That you might choose, and we will be very happy if you say so. But your native place? Originally?"

My native place? What was I to tell him? That originally, hundreds of years ago, some people bearing the eggs and sperm that would travel down in twists of DNA all the way to me had come as refugees from Persia? Or that one of my grandmothers was French? "Look, I'm from Bombay," I told the man.

"Ha ha ha," was his comment. "So how you are enjoying this country? Visited our Taj Mahal as yet?"

I went to all that trouble to learn Hindi in Berkeley, but for my political work Marathi would have been better. Maybe I should have tried to take a reading course with that professor who was always carrying on in Marathi. Then too, even when I spoke Hindi, my accent was never quite right, my ds and ts always ended up being harder than they ought. Whatever I did in villages, people kept calling me Saheb. Just when I was beginning to get more comfortable, beginning to blend in, beginning to operate through my anger over the hopeless exploitation; just when it was all falling into some sort of productive rhythm, then wham, I'd bloody get sick. Jaundice. Malaria. Cycle after cycle of what my father calls Amoe-Baba and the Forty Pills.

I used to look down on people who'd come from the Third World to be educated in America and Europe and who then would just stay. I thought they were selfish, that it was their duty to go back. Like Gita: she never ever spoke of returning. I couldn't understand it, a smart woman like her and all she could do in India. Now I see that there were things about her background that she was escaping, that dreadful mother and who knows what else. I see that for each and every one of us, it ends up being not a matter of principles but of situations. Take Najma and Ravindran: they have families they can stand, situations they can live with. Sure, they don't have hot water available twenty-four hours a day, and they can't afford all the books they want to read. But they have some sense of home that makes them happy.

I'm too tired to listen closely to the announcements over the intercom, but I should start moving toward the gate. Got to stop at a water fountain so I don't get too dehydrated. Was I being a coward when I came back to the U.S. by the end of the year and went to law school instead? I can make all these rationalizations for how political action shouldn't take a nationalist cast so that caring for people like ourselves is all that counts. But I know this isn't the real reason I returned. Sure, it's the usual thing for political activists to confuse the boundaries of social responsibility with nationality. When I'm in India some activist fellows pick on me for living in New York rather than some village in the hinterlands. I always have to take a few deep breaths so I don't get into a big fight or become apologetic. I now tell them, "Look, yaar, we all have to work with who we are. I'm not getting on your case for drinking beer rather than toddy brewed in the village. I don't know what your situation is, but for me it's easier to do something constructive elsewhere." The work I'm doing with refugees who are too powerless even to document that they've been politically persecuted turns out to be for no country at all but for very specific people. In a way, you could say that my work is to chisel holes in the borders between nationstates, to blur the meaning of "citizen."

Hell, this bag is too heavy, I shouldn't have packed in all those pamphlets. My feet have swelled in their shoes. It will be nice to pull out a blanket on the plane and wedge a pillow against the plastic window frame. All this is too complicated to sort out now—I can think it through later. Wasn't it Gita who once quoted that Rilke chap to me, something

Usha Nilsson

Statement: The legacy I received from my family was not money, not
materialistic values, but a deep love for India; a belief in equality, gen-
erosity, and helpfulness; and a love of books. My language in my writing
is moving toward stark simplicity and has developed an inner rhythm. I
have reached a point where my first version is the last version. I am concerned about presenting in my stories fractured interpersonal relationships, alienation, and emptiness. The complex lives of women and the
ways they are treated by their society (in India and in America) have
been the focus of my writing from the very beginning. I am at present
writing a novel in English. For fun. Away from formulas for success. I
suppose one day I will wake up and start rewriting it in Hindi. Writing
in English is work. Writing in Hindi is a pleasure.

Usha Nilsson is a prolific writer and has published numerous short stories, novels, and scholarly essays, but because she writes mainly in
Hindi, her work rarely appears in collections of South Asian American
or Asian American writings. She has translated some of her works, such
as the story that appears in this anthology. It is interesting because it presents the dilemma and the quiet grief of a married woman who is in love
with another man. Although stories such as Neila Seshachari's "The
Bride Comes Home" and Naseem Hines's "The Dew and the Moon"
portray South Asian men in love with women other than the wives chosen for them by their families, the reverse situation shown in Usha
Nilsson's "What a Big Lie" does not appear very often in South Asian
American literature.

What a Big Lie

She got up very early in the morning and, opening the back door, sat
on the steps. It was cold, and she shivered. She found she liked the cool
freshness of the morning air.

In the back of the building there was a large empty field where the
kids played soccer on weekends. Nearby spread the community gardens, and in the neighbor's lot she could see a large sunflower still
blooming. It really faced the sun.

Kiran wrapped her sari tightly around her back and her arms. She wanted to cry out like a new widow, but she clamped her teeth on her lips and kept staring at the trees, flowers, and the grass. Everything seemed to blur.

Yesterday Kiran had returned from her ten-week trip to India. Fresh and happy. For the past two weeks she had often found herself thinking about coming home. And by "home" she knew that she did not mean the walls of the house or the furniture. She had worked out the details in her mind. She would arrive in the afternoon. Her husband was planning to drive to the camp to pick up their daughters. The house would be empty. She would call Max right away. It happened just that way. She crumpled the note her husband had left for her and threw it in the wastebasket. She went to the phone, and as she dialed the number, she noticed the layer of dust. Her heart jumped as she heard the phone ringing at the other end of the line.

The receiver was lifted at the third ring, and a girl's childish voice answered, "Mrs. Boswell."

Kiran was taken aback. "Who?" she blurted out.

"Oh, it's you, Kiran." Laughter flowed toward her. "I'm Barbara— Max and I've been married. When did you get back?"

Kiran said, "Barbara! I'll talk to you later. The kids want a snack." Then she added, "Congratulate Max for me. Will you?"

She did not know right away how she was really feeling. Her immediate reaction was of deep disappointment at being deprived of Max's physical touch. During the long journey she had felt as if her body were on fire. She had thought of nothing but being with Max, and her lips had tried to conceal her secret smile of anticipated pleasure.

Kiran found herself trembling. She lay down on the sofa. Thoughts rushed into her mind, and she suppressed them. She remembered the color of Max's eyes; how clear they seemed when he was contented. She would never ever touch Max again. She dwelt a long time on the fact that Barbara must be a good ten years younger than herself. Kiran's eyes filled with tears. What could an Indian woman do? She could not go and pull out Barbara's hair by the roots, nor could she hurl abuses, or kick or strike Max. Max had written her only two letters. They contained no news of any kind; they were filled with chit-chat. "Kiran must be fine; she must be enjoying her trip; everyone was fine around here." And then there was a long silence. She should have known. But how could she? She trusted Max.

The front door opened and Neeta and Leena rushed in. Leena, the little one, still clung to her mother; Neeta stood apart, smiling, waiting for her mother to come to her. Kiran patted her on the head and asked, "How was the camp? Did you learn to swim? You didn't bother Papa, did you? Did Leena quarrel with you?"

Neeta just smiled; Leena asked, "What have you brought for me, Mummy?"

"It's on your bed. And there's something for you too, Neeta." The girls ran to their rooms, and Kiran found herself alone with her husband. He gently took her in his arms, and Kiran silently rested her head on his shoulder. A tear fought to come out, but Kiran suppressed it. She moved away and said, "I've got a present for you also." Vishwa smiled; Kiran always bought duty-free cognac for him. Vishwa was a man of very few wants.

He looked at Kiran's peaked face and said, "You must be tired. We'll go out to eat. No need to do any cooking."

Kiran sat with him. The windows definitely needed new curtains. The carpet had become very dirty, and the house plants stood wilting in their pots. The cleaning woman had probably forgotten to water them.

Kiran got up and went to her room. She lay on the bed and put her arm over her eyes. Let the plants die, she thought. I'm not going to cry. After all, it was my choice, Vishwa, Navaneetu, and Devaleena . . .

"Mummy, can I have some ice cream?"

"Papa's taking us out. If you have ice cream now, you won't be hungry," she replied.

"Just a little—just a spoonful?"

"OK, but just a little."

Vishwa stood rummaging through his shelf. "I forgot to pick up the shirts from the cleaners. Now I'm all out of clean shirts . . ." he said.

"You go and take your shower; I'll get you a shirt," she answered getting up. She opened the closet, took out a clean shirt, and handed it to Vishwa. She always kept some clothes in her closet for just such an emergency.

She went back to bed.

"Don't you feel well? Do you have a headache? Aren't you going to change?" he asked.

"This is a Hong Kong sari; it doesn't get crumpled." Kiran turned her back to the door. Soon after Neeta came with a glass of water and the bottle of Anacin.

"Mummy, Papa says that you've got a headache and I must give you some pills."

Kiran swallowed two pills. "Thank you, Neeta." Neeta kept standing there.

"What is it?"

"What sari are you going to wear?"

"The one I'm wearing. Isn't it all right?"

"It's all right," Neeta looked at her thoughtfully, "but if you change, you'll feel fresh."

"OK, I'll wear another sari. Just go and see if Leena's eating too much ice cream."

Kiran wore a white lace sari. She went and sat in front of the mirror. Yes, I'm not young anymore, she thought as she poured some moisturizer on her palm. She put it carefully on her face, smoothing it down to her throat. She applied the foundation and the blusher and put the eyeliner on her lids and smoothed her brow. She dabbed perfume on her earlobes. Carefully she did her hair and rolled it in a bun. She put on earrings and selected white glass bangles and arranged them with gold ones. She got out white sandals. She usually didn't bother, but the ritual seemed very important to her this day.

Vishwa watched her getting ready. Kiran was aware of the pride in his eyes—the pride of possession, of having an attractive wife.

"Will I always be on the periphery of your life?" Max asked. It was a fall afternoon, warm, bright, colorful. They had met after a long interval and were lying close to each other, happy and content.

Kiran said, "You're not on the periphery. I was given to Vishwa." She fell silent. She saw Max day after day as Vishwa's friend and felt his attraction. Many months and years went by, and one day the moment came; she gave herself to Max. It seemed like a natural expression of her inner being. They met whenever they could find time. Max began to talk of taking up another job, of moving to another part of the country with her. People would understand. It had been done before. She shook her head; it could be taken for both "yes" and "no."

"I'm almost ready." She found Vishwa staring at her.

"There's no hurry," Vishwa said. Torn, Kiran stood near the phone. After Vishwa went out of the room, she hurriedly dialed Max's number but Barbara answered. Kiran put the receiver down and left the room.

Neeta and Leena were ready and waiting for her. "Is this a new sari, Mummy?" Leena asked.

"Don't you remember? Papa brought it from New York last time," Neeta said, assuming a grown-up air. "Mummy, when it gets torn will you make a small sari for me?"

"Mummy's saris never get torn," Leena said. They locked the front door and went to the car. After her return she always felt strange. Everything seemed dull, dusty, and without any charm.

"Shall we go to the Agra?" Vishwa asked. Neeta and Leena seemed delighted. The Agra had good sweets, *sandesh, rasgullā!**

---

*sandesh: a type of cheese-based fudge; *rasgullā:* cheese puffs in rosewater-scented syrup.

"Yes," Kiran replied.

Agra's owner knew them. "*Bhābhījī*, welcome back.* How was your trip? What can we do to celebrate your return?" Then he called out, "Sitaram! Bring the menu." Agra's walls had acquired bright red wallpaper; cheap chandeliers hung from the ceiling; there were new carved-wood Kashmir partitions.

"You've made quite a few changes," Kiran said to the owner.

"It's all your blessings, *bhābhī*"; he beamed with pleasure. "My young brother and his wife have also come. My brother keeps the accounts. Ravi, come and meet Professor Sahab."

Ravi left the counter; introductions were made and he chatted a bit before going back. Vishwa knew who liked what. The children would have kabobs; he, his favorite lamb curry. Kiran always had the same things: *khoyā matar, dahī bare*, also *parāthā*.† She rarely varied the order, and even then, very little. She might order *nān*‡ instead of *parāthā* or another dish of grams. She held the slightly soiled menu in tired hands. She ran her eyes over printed words. "The usual," she said.

The tablecloth had a few spots. The tape recorder played an old song of Saigal. A new Indian family sat at a nearby table. Kiran had not seen them before. The woman wore a blue Aurangabad sari; looking ill-at-ease, she stared at Kiran. Vishwa appeared satisfied. After eating at the Agra he usually looked like that. "I ate a lot," he said.

Neeta and Leena were concentrating on their desserts. The vermicelli in their bowls was disappearing fast. Leena scraped every bit with her spoon and said, "A-a-a-h!"

"What a pig!" Neeta said to Kiran.

"Honey, would you like to have anything else?" Vishwa asked Leena.

Leena looked at her mother, then at her sister. She nodded her head and said, "Yea! Some ice cream." Neeta burst into derisive laughter.

Leena was crushed. "No, nothing more," she said. Tears came to her eyes.

Kiran put her left arm around Leena and said to her husband, "Do order *kulfī*.§ We'll all have some. Neeta too."

They had to wait for *kulfī*. A newer song played. People came in large numbers, and the many-colored lights began to twinkle. Kiran

---

*bhābhī: literally, "sister-in-law," brother's wife; a respectful term to a married woman; -jī: a suffix denoting respect.
†khoyā matar: peas cooked in thickened milk; dahī bare: lentil dumplings in yogurt sauce; parāthā: griddle-fried whole-wheat bread.
‡nān: a thick, oven-cooked bread.
§kulfī: Indian ice cream.

traced imaginary lines with her right finger on the table cloth. How old was Barbara? Not more than twenty-three? Maybe twenty-four. It was Barbara who had come and stood in front of her. She was short and slender, and had something artificial about her. She had been Max's research assistant for the past two years.

"So! Leena! Here's your kulfī. Eat it carefully," Kiran said to her. Leena began to smile. What bright beautiful eyes the child has, Kiran thought.

"Is it good?" Vishwa asked.

Kiran took a little in a spoon and tasted it; "Yes, it's good," and she put almost all of it on Leena's plate.

It was now quiet. Leena and Neeta had changed into their night clothes, watched their favorite TV show, and gone to their rooms. Vishwa shut the TV off and opened the cognac. Kiran washed up a few dishes in the kitchen. She dried her hands and came back to the room still rubbing in the hand lotion. Vishwa poured the cognac carefully into two glasses; then handing a glass to her, he said, "Welcome back, Rani!"

"Thank you, darling," she said in English.

They sat close together in silence and sipped from their glasses. They seemed like an ideal husband and wife, contented and happy with each other. Then Kiran broke the silence, "I've heard that Max has married Barbara!"

"Yes," Vishwa replied. "The department gave them a party. I think they're still honeymooning in Mexico." He emptied his pipe in an ashtray.

Kiran said, "The cold weather seems to have come early this year."

"Yes. A little more?" Vishwa took her glass.

"No," she said. She sat looking at Vishwa for a long time. Then she got up and took Vishwa's hand in hers. She said, in an almost inaudible voice, "Come, let's go to bed."

Rajesh C. Oza

Statement: Like the variegated, adventurous youth in Joseph Conrad's *Heart of Darkness*, my life is a patchwork quilt based on eclectic interests and experiences. But there is a thread that runs through it—continuity and change. Writing in America provides me with a dynamic opportunity to reflect on traditional values in tumultuous times. I am always looking for an answer to this unanswerable question: How does the endearing civilization of my ancestors endure in the multiple futures of my descendants?

As this anthology shows, South Asian American writers, like writers from any time and any place, exercise their rights to write about experiences, characters, and emotions that interest them as writers. Some South Asian American authors write about South Asian and South Asian American communities, others about the lives of South Asian American characters as part of the larger, many-cultured life of America, and still others simply about life in America without any specific reference to South Asian Americans. "Dr. Mango and Johnny Fish" presents the age-old, universal tensions between generations and the difficulty of choosing a career. It also brings in the underlying historical connections and possible shared interests between the people who come from South Asia (the India Columbus was supposedly trying to reach) and the indigenous people of the Americas.

Dr. Mango and Johnny Fish

Amid six wannabe physicians, I uneasily sit in the University of Illinois Medical School Admissions Office. To get here, I took an elevated train. A part of me is still floating above ground level. I can't believe I've actually come here. Along the way from the train station to this mirror-like glass building, I had gingerly stepped around a flower vendor and a wino territorially jousting over their few square yards of sidewalk. They had staked claim to the cracked and uneven concrete with old paint buckets full of roses and opaque, paper bags shaped like whiskey bottles. Trying to avoid the bloodshot stare of the consumer of the bottle piñatas, I had stepped on an old syringe. Now, on the plush carpet of the medical school, shielded by my briefcase, I surreptitiously deposit the glass and metal debris from my shoe's scarred heel.

While digging out the remnants of the syringe from the bottom of my polished wing-tips, I think of my two fathers halfway across the continent, a world away from me and from each other. I know Dr. Mango wants me to ace this test; he calls the admissions interviews "the final exam before the payoff." Johnny Fish has hinted strongly that a lot rests on my shoulders; he's expecting "a return on the investment."

Dr. Mango is floating along with me. His real name is Mangilal Vyas, Ph.D. At least that's what I've seen on all the stationery from our California landscaping nursery, Golden Gate Growers. Though he usually introduces himself with the doctorate appended, I've never heard anyone address my father this way. My mother calls him by the same nameless syllable that he uses for her: *Oh* (followed by a gentle upward nod). His friends—a fraternity of professional Indian Americans—call him *Bhaisahab* or, if they're sharing a joke, *Yaar*. His customers—mostly the managers of the local hardware-cum-gardening stores—call him Dr. Vyas. Almost all of them mispronounce "vee-yaas" as "why-as." Behind his back they call him *Wise-ass* for his reputation as a no-nonsense negotiator. I call him Papaji.

Johnny Fish might have been the drunk on the street. He could just as easily be one of the interviewers. No one knows his real name, not even himself. He thinks that his mother died on an Indian reservation at his birth and his father a few months later of an "over-liquored liver." He knows his off-reservation foster parents gave him the name that is on his postdated birth certificate: John Thomas Benson. At my undergraduate school, he was known in the class schedule as *A16: Intro to Biology. Paiute.* The students called him Professor *Peyote* for his involvement in a demonstration to legalize the use of sacred hallucinogens in ritual ceremonies. The administration classified him as *John Paiute: Problem-high, Priority-low.* On campus, he pontificated more than he published. Yet he didn't perish, at least not at the hands of the tenure committee. Instead he drifted away from academia. What started as a sabbatical at the Pyramid Lake Indian reservation, gradually evolved into a lifestyle change. The Indians at this Nevada reservation—the Paiute tribe from whom he co-opted his last name—call him *Pro*, short for Professor, and differentiated from the *Bro* the men use for each other. At Pyramid Lake, my home away from home, he is my BabaJohn.

Both Papaji and BabaJohn had a big hand in my getting to the interview stage of the application process. To take advantage of the minority quota for Native Americans, they had me change my name to Rojas Paiute and list Pyramid Lake as my home.

"Look, Raja, every advantage counts," Papaji counseled, "and I'm telling you that with your grades and test scores, being an American Indian will guarantee admission. You're always telling me that you need something unique on your application. That was your excuse for living on that reservation every summer, nah? Well listen to me just once. There are so many of our Indian doctors that the whites are applying reverse discrimination. You could turn the tables on them."

"Screw 'em, Raj," BabaJohn encouraged me. "You've spent more time on the reservation than most Paiute kids do. You know more about our culture than some of these elders looking at the past through a bottle. And anyway, you and I have a deal, right? You're coming back here after you finish your residency! I'll mention your Paiute life on the recommendation letter."

I wasn't crazy about the name change, but I did practice signing my name a few hundred times before appending it to the application. I was even less crazy about the paternal lectures on the value of a medical education, but I listened with a mix of filial piety and stoicism.

When I received a notice from the University of Illinois inviting me in for interviews, I immediately called BabaJohn and Papaji. For me, the letter was reward enough for the academic work that I had a flair for but did not particularly enjoy. It was as if the medical community had accepted me, and there was no need for the next steps; I could reverse directions and go back to my passion for anthropology. After all, I had no desire to practice medicine and thought that the letter sufficiently fulfilled my fathers' expectations of me. I had called them hoping to be released from my implicit contracts, hoping to be returned to cross-cultural socialization fieldwork. But for once, my two fathers agreed with each other in their violent disagreement with me.

BabaJohn said exactly five words: "No! Wait for my letter." His letter was a bit more verbose, but equally to the point:

Dear Raj,

    No! No! No! If not for me, then for Nokomis. If you've forgotten your Longfellow, allow me to jog your memory . . .

        By the shores of Gitche Gumee,
        By the shining Big-Sea-Water,
        Stood the wigwam of Nokomis.

    Perhaps now you remember not only Hiawatha, but also why they call me Johnny Fish. Pyramid Lake is ours; our wigwams are on its shores. I gave up one life to keep the water rights in Indian hands. The uselessness of the white paper on which the federal government gave the Paiutes ownership to the land, BUT NOT THE WATER, has obsessed me. We need the basic resources to live our own lives.

That's why I need an Indian doctor here to control our destiny.

At first I came here to test my hatchery theories in the field. Over the years, I've come to care more for the human aspects of the ecosystem. With the lake drying up, the fish would not spawn. Without the fish, the Paiute way of life would have dried up faster than the lake. Including some misguided Indians, more and more parties involved in the debate over water rights were beginning to say that the lake was useful only to the nearby, white irrigation farmers. By artificially spawning the fish in the pools and releasing them into the open, the hatchery was able to make the Paiute care about Pyramid Lake. At the same time, I took on the government lawyers and obtained more tribal control over the water. My work saved the lake, the fish, and thus the people. The Indians here heralded me as Professor Fish.

All of this PR you should already know. Allow me to further refresh your memory of some things you won't read in the papers.

I was literally drunk with my initial successes in the law courts and the spawning pools. At last I had a place I could call home. But in trying too hard to be a Paiute, I developed a serious drinking problem. I still haven't overcome my alcoholism. In many ways it became debilitating. I had no desire to go back to the university. And at the same time I had lost my willpower to fight the white man. The farmers knew they could buy me off with a bottle and, with derision in their voice, began calling me Johnny Fish. You know, "Johnny, the Indian, can drink like a fish."

There the wrinkled old Nokomis
Nursed the little Hiawatha . . .
Many things Nokomis taught him
Of the stars that shine in heaven . . .
Showed the Death-Dance of the spirits . . .

Just a few weeks after I got out of de-tox, you showed up at Pyramid Lake. It was Spring Quarter of your confusing freshman year. All these summers that you've been coming back, you've always thought that I did all the teaching and you the learning. But in teaching you, I've learned about myself and my ancestors. Too much has been lost or stolen. We need you here to perform the Ghost Dance and chase away the white man. I only want you to come if your vocation brings you. That will keep you here. Your desire to study our ethnology does us little good. It's a nice diversion for the blue bloods that have everything. My people need the strongest medicine you can offer.

I have spoken . . . BabaJohn

Papaji said the same thing over the phone. After I informed him of my intention not to proceed with the interviews, my role in the conversation was limited to mild protests and signals that I was still on the line.

"Look Raja, I didn't bring you, your sister, and your mother to this country to have you throw everything away. I know how you must be feeling, okay? I was young once you know. My dissertation on *The Green Revolution's High-Yield Varieties* was published here and in India. Wah! Maybe a lot of people benefited from the work. But really what good did it do, huh? My seminars and field studies took me away from the family. I wasn't even home when you came into this world. Your mother has been a saint all these years."

"But Papaji, what's that got to do with me?"

"We'll come to that. We'll come to that. Try to be more like your mother and have patience. So, I sacrificed my personal life for the starving masses. We even moved back to India. Gandhiji would have been proud, nah? I'm telling you Raja, nobody but your family appreciates you. It's like the *Gau Mata*. People elevate her to a goddess, but then they milk her until she can't feed her own calf. Are you still with me?"

I grunted a soft, "Hunh."

"Okay. So I gave up all my idealism a long time ago. This was about the time we returned to America. This time, side-by-side with the university job, your mother and I started the nursery. I was growing plants with my hands, the same way your *Dadaji*—my beloved father—managed his farm in Rajasthan. I had to fight with the *salas* in Immigration for my green card. But the minute I got it, I put all of my time into Golden Gate Growers. I did it so I could be home to raise you and your sister as Indian success stories. Remember what I used to say about raising you children?"

"Hunh."

"Then, tell me."

"I don't know, Papaji. Something about roots."

"Right! A child is like a seed. You can put it in any soil, and, if it has the right genetic makeup, it will become a seedling. But in the early years, strong roots and a strong trunk are needed, nah? You have to support it with discipline. Then only will it remain standing when the wind blows."

"Studying anthropology isn't going to blow me down, you know."

"Do you know why I have the name Dr. Mango?"

"Because the farm workers could never pronounce Mangilal or Vyas properly."

"*Nah re*. That's just what I tell everyone to make them laugh. You don't know it, but a long time ago I grew a mango tree in our greenhouse. All the botany books said it couldn't be done with the cool

California nights, but I did it. Of course I had to remove it when it reached the ceiling, nah?"

"So do you want to cut me off at the neck or the legs?" I countered, while imagining my father hacking away at my shins with his pruning knife.

"The point is I did it. The mango: native to India; grown in America. Anyway, the *junglee* workers began calling me Dr. Mango to my face, while at the same time, behind my back, eating all the fruit."

"You should hear all the other things they call you behind your back."

"Be quiet. You are my prize fruit. I will not allow you to spoil your future. You will find a suitable girl and then settle down, nah? Then only you will know that your anthropology-panthropology is no life. Certainly not for a family man. Right now you are still young. That's okay. But there's so much you have to go through."

"Papaji, isn't it about time for a change?" I pleaded.

"Help me, Raja," my father demanded. "I'm old, but I'm happy. Don't take that away from me or your mother. Now, let's end this conversation in agreement and in prayer to *Krishna Bhagwan*, the same way we used to just before sleeping. Okay?"

I surrendered to nostalgia, "Okay, Papaji. Just like we used to."

> *Tvameva mata* / You are my mother,
> *Ca pita tvameva* / Indeed you are my father.
> *Tvameva bandhu* / You are my friend,
> *Ca sakha tvameva* / Indeed my friend from childhood.
> *Tvameva vidya* / You are my wisdom,
> *Dravinam tvameva* / My health and wealth.
> *Tvameva sarva* / Indeed you are my everything,
> *Ma ma deva deva* / I bow to you, God Almighty.

It seems that a couple of hours have gone by, and yet I have not been called by the receptionist. The room full of anxious premedical students has thinned out. It's just me and a somewhat overage and underdressed candidate. I ask him, "Say, has your name been called?"

"Called? Called for what?" he replies.

"Aren't you here for the medical school interviews?" I probe.

He screws up his face and shakes his head vigorously, "No way, bud. You think anyone would interview without a tie? Anyway, I gave up on this scene a long time ago. I'm picking up my old man to take him to the opening of my exhibit. By the way, he happens to be the chairman of the admissions committee. You want me to put in a good word?"

Ignoring the offer, I quickly move to the receptionist's richly stained, oak desk. I knock on the desktop to attract her attention: "Excuse me, are we running late with the interviews?"

Absorbed in a filing cabinet, with her back to me, the receptionist waves a lacquered fingernail in my direction and chides me, "I don't know about *we*, but you're way behind schedule. I called in all the candidates almost two hours ago. You must be Rojas Petty. I called your name several times you know."

I half correct her, "Uh, no, I'm Rajendra Vy . . ." But then I realize the mistake is mine. She is referring to the name on my application: Rojas Paiute. I've only heard it pronounced correctly a few times. In a moment of inspiration, Papaji borrowed the first name, "ro-has" with a rolling *r* and a silent *j*, from one of the nursery's soil tillers. He thought that a Mexican sounding name with a Native American background would provide double advantage. Years earlier, BabaJohn had taught me to pronounce my adopted last name as "pie-ute."

I find myself at a loss for words. My pounding temples find some solace from my thumb and fingers. I'm desperately seeking an explanation for this bizarre goof. Maybe the receptionist's bastardized "ro-jus pet-tee" is so far from reality that I couldn't recognize it as my nom de guerre. But there have been more creative transformations that I've responded to; for an entire year in high school a teacher called me *Rosendro Villa*. Today, of all days, how could this happen?

There is perhaps a more simple answer: I have not given up being Rajendra Vyas.

As I'm about to implore the secretary to reschedule the interviews, she stops ignoring me for a moment, does a full pirouette, and smiles sympathetically. She points to a group that looks like the interview team and declares, "See those guys. They knew you had to be Petty, but they told me not to bother asking you directly. The chairman said that if you were daydreaming on your most important day, you would probably fall asleep in the ER. As for me, I'm sorry. I really am. I do hope that you applied elsewhere."

In picking up my briefcase off the carpet, I see the mess I had made earlier. I carefully gather the shards of glass and the bent needle and deposit the recycled syringe on the receptionist's desk. I glare at her and shout, "Here, take this into your friends and tell them to stick it!"

I rush past the smirking son of the chairman and race an incoming train to the station. I hop on board—disoriented and out of breath, but certain that I'm on the right tracks.

Uma Parameswaran

Statement: My personal life has been on an even keel, and since writing needs an intense tension at its creative core, I have located it in spaces of morals and morales, such as immigrant sensibility, women's psyches, and the transplanted ethos. Having entered academia, I got preoccupied with academic pursuits for years and turned only recently to the polishing and pruning of cartonloads of poetry and fiction.

"Darkest Before Dawn" is part of a novel in progress. In this work, Uma Parameswaran presents the role of memory in the lives of Americans of South Asian descent who arrived in North America as children. This excerpt sketches the memories of India in the lives of the two protagonists, who define their lives in Canada through their memories of relationships and traditions as they are defined in India. The bond between a child and the grandmother and between a sister and brother has always been viewed as nearly sacred in most South Asian communities. When the editor of this anthology was leading a workshop at Duke University in 1991 on the importance and techniques of pursuing oral histories in the South Asian community, she asked a group of nearly thirty South Asian American students (undergraduate and graduate) as to the relative (known or unknown to them) with whom they would want to spend time. With the exception of four members of the group, the answer was "my grandmother." When asked which family member was the most important in their lives, the answers were divided between the mother and a sister/brother. The bond between the sister and brother in "Darkest Before Dawn" is depicted not only in the episodes that take place in the present but also in the brother's vivid memory of the role of the bride's brother in the ancient marriage rituals celebrated in his community in India. As he remembers these rituals, he sees himself transporting, transforming, and playing his role as an Indian brother in Canada with a non–South Asian brother-in-law.

Darkest Before Dawn

Jayant put away his violin. He couldn't get the right note. He wasn't surprised. Everything he touched turned to dust and ashes. Treachery

had been his companion as far back as he could remember. Everyone to
whom he felt close ended up betraying him. He should be used to it by
now; yet each time he was caught unprepared; each time it was a sudden
rapier thrust. No, that was too dramatic, too romantic an image; only
Romeos and Caesars got hit that way. There was this commercial fish-
hook, a fail-proof hook that twisted itself ninety degrees into the fish,
and the fish died a long, slow death.

His sister's eyes had twisted the hook into him. It had started off
with her trying to tell him how much they'd miss him, but all too soon it
reached a point when she coldly said, "I am glad you are pitching out
because that is the only way you'll get into that thick skull of yours that
we are different, and no matter what we do, we are never going to fit in
here. Take to the road, get high, sleep around, but still and all, we'll
never belong except in our own homes."

"Fuck off, Jyo, you'll see."

"All those expletives, all the in jargon, but you are never going to be
one of the boys. Not that I see why anyone would want to fit into this
mold."

"Don't you come at me with all that crap about morals and Hindu
values. I've had an earful from Dad nineteen fucking years. He and his
pipe dreams about India. Why the hell didn't he stay there? A nuclear
scientist, Trombay, the whole bit. He'd have been somebody by now.
Instead he quits the place to be and rots here selling houses." Jayant
picked up a Ping-Pong ball and squeezed it in the palm of his left hand.
As he raised his hand to run it through his hair, a habit he had, a faint
smell of camphor from the ball wafted up, arousing deep, nebulous
memories of another place, another time.

Jyoti said, "It couldn't have been easy for him to pack up everything
and move out at thirty-five, and it is no bed of roses here, mowing the
lawn and painting the house and a hundred menial chores which were
done by servants in the luxury of his ancestral home."

"Some house that, a sprawling shambles handed down untouched
from the time of the Peshwas where you have to walk half a mile to get
to the shithouse, Jeesus. And the irony is that all that crap about giving
his kids a better future was just a way of rationalizing his failure."

"Stop that, Jay, stop it."

"And you know what your trouble is, kid? You are on the moon with
that Pierre of yours, holding hands and singing moonshine into his
blonde hair. If you'd get laid a couple of times you'd come off all those
preachy echoes of Dad's slogans."

He looked at her, and there was something in her eyes that drew him
sharply against the wall of recognition. In a whisper he said, "You
haven't, sis, you haven't." It was clear Jyoti had. Jayant grabbed the darts

from the Ping-Pong table and zinged them at the board in lightning sequence. All three lodged in the inner circle, one dead centre.

Jyoti had slung her denim jacket over her shoulder, and gone to the stairs, leaving Jayant amid his open suitcase and stacked T-shirts.

* * *

Jyoti went to her room, and her fingers trembled as she tried in vain to shut the door on her memory.

They were in India still at the time. She was about ten. Jayant's school, even though run by the same Roman Catholic Mission as hers, had a longer December vacation, and he was visiting cousins in Delhi. In the interclass Recitation competition, Jyoti had been chosen to represent her section. She was already known for her talent for memorizing poems overnight, and this was not the first time she had competed. That evening, as she memorized the selected poem, the import of the lines hit her:

Oh call my brother back to me!
I cannot play alone:
The summer comes with flowers and bee,
Where is my brother gone?

She burst into tears. The scenes were so clear—Jayant run over by a lorry; Jayant on the Yamuna, his usually curly hair straightened out and streaming behind him as he floated feet first; Jayant tripping on the railway track and being scooped up and flung away by the engine's cowcatcher. Jyoti cried herself to sleep, sure Jayant was dead. She went to school next day, her stomach knotted with cramps. But she couldn't withdraw, for that would be letting down her team. And so she singsonged her way—ti dum ti dum ti dum ti da—that way the meaning didn't matter.

* * *

Jayant picked up the violin and ran his bow lightly across the strings. He tried an old melody, the very first he had learned. And he remembered.

He remembered his grandmother, seated in the courtyard of their ancestral house on the familiar, thick, woven mat of silk straw. The courtyard was large and rectangular and seemed cut in two halves. The farther half had trees, a *bakul* tree that spread its branches over the far right wall, and there were flowering bushes of jasmine and *raat-ki-rani*, and a clump of banana trees. Along the far left wall was the vegetable patch from which the gardener brought in coriander leaves or mint and fresh okra or long beans every morning. In the middle of the far wall was a door beyond which were latrines and, still farther, the servants' quarters. The nearer half of the courtyard was flanked by the house on one side, by storerooms and bathrooms on another, and by the kitchen and dining room on the third. Here the ground had been plastered smooth with years of daily sprinkling of cow-dung water so that it was an even, mellow yellow, hard as a tennis court. At the centre was a planter of whitewashed brick for the *tulsi* plant, complete with little niches where the clay lamps and incense sticks could burn despite rain. And near it, under the shade of a *parijata* tree, sat his grandmother with her violin.

It was a scene etched in Jayant's memory, a scene to which his spirit returned in quiet moments, a scene he sought out when storms came up. A scene where everything was in place, exactly in place; Aji playing her violin every day just after her three o'clock tea.

At the time of his first visit back to his grandparents, from Canada, Jayant had been fourteen, not young enough to admit openly that he wanted to sit by his grandmother, not old enough to take the initiative and speak to her. He was self-conscious of his Marathi; it had rusted in the last four years away from India. Even though his parents spoke Marathi at home, he and Jyoti had switched to English and his kid brother, Krish, could not even understand Marathi. Jayant could not bring himself to enunciate once familiar words lest he make a fool of himself. So he lingered every afternoon, on the *charpai*, the string bed, or the swing, a book in hand, close enough to smell the potpourri that gave all the contents of her mahogany chest of drawers a subtle jasmine fragrance, but not letting on that he was listening. Sometimes Aji sang as she played; she had a well-trained voice; even his untrained ears discerned the felicity with which her voice moved like rippling water through the notes, the way she manoeuvered her voice in the *alapanas* like water falling over rocks in shallow rapids.

One day, as he sat on the swing biting into a green guava and pretending to read, she stopped playing after just a few minutes. He waited without turning his head, disappointed.

"Jayant."

"Yes, Aji."

"Come here. I've never heard you sing, *baba*."

He came over, lay on his stomach, and raised himself, his elbows just inside the edge of her mat, cupping his face in his hands. "Aji, I don't know any good songs."

"Come, come, you know many English songs, right?"

"Oh, I'll never sing those; they sound so awful compared to yours."

He laughed, embarrassed.

"When some say that, I know they just need some persuasion; but when others say it, I know they mean it."

"And which am I, Aji?" he said teasingly, holding out two fingers. She clasped both and then took his hands between hers. "Why, Jai *baba*, your palms are calloused. What have you been doing in Canada? Are you a woodcutter there?" She too knew how to tease.

"Aji, even woodcutters there have Palmolive soft hands," he hummed the TV commercial tune. "We have machinery for everything." He imitated the sound and action of a chain saw and then proudly said, "I got all these here from chopping wood. Ask Chhotu."

Chhotu was an old retainer, well over sixty and still straight backed and steady armed. He chopped wood for the wood stove on which bathwater was warmed for the whole family. Chhotu had gone into a tizzy when the *vialyati baba* (the boy from foreign lands) had first wanted to chop wood, but Jayant had cajoled him into yielding. Chhotu had taught him how, but only after absolving himself of responsibility by calling on all the gods to bear witness to the stubbornness of the young master. Some of the callouses were due to tree-climbing, an old pastime that Jayant had picked up with alacrity within days of coming to Pune.

"Do you know where I would like your callouses to be? Here, and here and here," she touched the inner tips of the fingers of his left hand, "like mine." She ran his fingers over hers, and he could feel them just under the fine, pale brown skin.

"When Savitri wrote to me years ago that you were taking piano lessons, I told myself I would teach you to play the violin and leave my violin for you."

Jayant's eyes smiled brilliantly as he leaned forward. "Would you, really?" and then because he had meant the bequest, he added quickly, "Teach me, I mean?"

Aji laughed, her small white teeth circled by the red tinge of *chunam* that spiced the betel-leaf roll she ate after lunch. "It is quite all right to mean both, *baba*, and I really would love to do both, teach you now and leave the violin for you when it is time for me to go. Can you believe that no one in our family—little Anu is my forty-eighth descendant your uncle Balwant tells me—not one has taken to the violin? We have vocalists, dancers, tabla and sitar players but no violinists. Not one."

"You have one now," Jayant said, and in the next three months he had picked up the rudiments of classical music on the violin.

Aji died two years later. Had she left him her violin? Perhaps he would know only when his grandfather died.

His inheritance. Just outside old Pune, in the shadow of Shanwar Wada, the stronghold of the Peshwas, within sight of the Hill of Lakshmi, whose slopes housed their family deity Vithoba. His inheritance: of trees that had stood there since the time a patriot had climbed the sheer face of the Moghul fortress with a rope tied to the tail of a giant lizard and earned for himself the name of Ghorpade; of fields and villages that had increased gradually since the time Ram Shastri, to whom the family traced their lineage, had left Pune vowing never to return until the murder of Narayan Rao had been atoned with the ascension of Madhav Rao. Jayant remembered every detail of the proud family history that had been passed on to him through bedtime stories.

His inheritance. Foreclosed by his father.

How impatient his father had been to leave India! Jayant remembered the trips from Bombay to Delhi for their immigration formalities, the numerous trips to Pune to fill out forms for which only the family lawyer and *munshi* knew the details: What property had he inherited? What had he added? Moveable, immoveable? Income tax? Arrears? Did he have proof there were no arrears? Had he resigned his job? Had he proof his resignation had been accepted? Did he owe his employers money? Did he have proof he didn't? Would he repatriate the money he'd spend on airline tickets?

Forms, legal advice, bribes just to get people to do what it was their job to do. In order to expedite the paperwork, his father had legally renounced all claim to ancestral and paternal property.

And now he was a real estate broker.

Betrayal, his lifelong companion.

* * *

Jyoti parked her car near the Khoslas' driveway, even though it was the no-parking side. Picking up her cousin Priti would take only a minute, she thought. Kamla, who was eight years old, same as Priti, opened the door after fumbling with the latch and key; she pushed the stool away as Jyoti entered, and Jyoti knew she was alone and had looked through the peephole before opening the door.

"Come in, *didi*. Mom just went out to pick up Dad. She'll be back in a minute."

"Everything is so quiet here. Where is Priti?"

"She never came, didn't you know? Aunty Veejala phoned to say Priti couldn't come today, but she promised she could sleep over the weekend. It's going to be so much fun." Kamla went on to tell Jyoti of the plans she had for the weekend.

So like Aunt Vee to have changed her plans and to forget to inform Jyoti.

"Please do stay, *didi*, and see my science project." Jyoti obligingly took off her boots and was about to follow the girl to her room when the doorbell rang. Both went to answer it. "First check through the peep-hole," Kamla repeated the injunction that no doubt had been given to her a dozen times before her mother had left.

Jyoti opened the door. "Collecting," said one of the two boys at the door, ready to tear the yellow tab for the newspaper subscription.

"Nobody's home," Kamla said, "you'll have to come later."

"Nobody's home," the boy mimicked to his companion. "What you see ain't people but ghosts," and both laughed far more loudly than the joke warranted. Jyoti closed the storm door and was about to close the inner door when she heard the boys shout, "Paki, Paki house, dirty dirty."

A shiver went down her spine. She wondered if she'd heard right. "What did they say?" she asked. Kamla nodded mutely. "Did he say Paki?" Kamla nodded again.

Jyoti opened the door and walked out in her stockings. One of the boys had just thrown a snowball at the window, and the other was about to follow suit but stopped at seeing Jyoti and pretended to clean his gloves with the snow. Jyoti caught the newspaper boy by his coat collar and dragged him into the house.

"Did you say something?"

"Nothin'. I did say nothin'," he mumbled sullenly.

"I heard someone shout 'Paki.' It couldn't have been you, could it?"

"Wasn't us."

"Now, who could it have been, do you think? Eh?" He struggled to shake himself free. She unzipped his parka with her left hand so she could get a better hold of him. The other boy stood on the steps, won-dering what to do. Jyoti shut the door, stood with her back to it, and turned the boy with both her hands so he had to face her. Then she let go of him.

"You want to grow up a barbarian, eh? This is a great country but snot-faced kids like you are stinking it up." She chucked him under his chin so he had to look at her. "We are getting a little tired of obnoxious pigs like you, and our older boys have formed a clean-up brigade. Did you know I have only to make a phone call to get them to take care of you? They might not move in today or tomorrow, but you can bet on it they will move in on you when you are not looking; and when they are done with you, even your mothers won't recognize you, eh? And they'll throw what remains of you in the garbage can in your back lane. You wouldn't like that, would you?"

The boy stood as though she were still holding him.

She whipped out a colour clipping of a California quartet with trendy spiked hair and jackets. The picture had happened to be on the back of a newspaper item she had cut out for her sociology term paper, but she knew the quartet were just right for what she wanted now. She waved it in front of him. "Just to give you fair warning, this is them. How come you haven't heard of them, eh?"

"Can I go now?" he tried to sound nonchalant and failed.

"There's something you have to say, remember? Starts with an *s* and it is not your favourite four-letter word."

"I'm sorry," he said.

"Be sure to tell your friend and anyone else you care to tell. And don't forget the garbage can. I should tell them the BFIs are easier, that's an idea." She pushed him out, closed the door, and watched him through the window. She was trembling inside with a deep sense of power that frightened her.

Kamla was looking at her with her round eyes now rounder with admiration. "Oh, *didi*, did you look at his face? He was so scared he'd have peed in his pants if you'd let go."

Jyoti ran her fingers through the girl's hair absently. Kamla wore her hair like most everyone her age, parted at the middle, feathered at the sides; she looked like every other eight-year-old, in blue jeans with an open-laced shoe on the hip pocket, a plaid shirt exactly like everyone her age, born here and unaware of any other place, leave alone any other country.

"Have you ever peed in your pants?" she asked.

Kamla laughed. "I've sometimes felt like it, but of course never really done it, oh no."

"When have you felt like that?"

"You know"—how like her kid brother Krish she used that phrase with the stress on "you," Jyoti thought—"these junior highs who hang out at the 7-11; they make swear signs," she giggled with embarrassment.

"Do they call you Paki?"

"Not when I'm with Sandy and the rest. We always walk home together."

Jyoti felt nauseous. Her outburst had worked. It was frightening that Vithal, Priti's brother, who was in the angry-young-man phase, should be right. Oh God, she had acted exactly as her cousin would have them act, and it had worked. Or had it? Had she only jeopardized the poor girl's walks home?

Jyoti's stomach was all knotted up. It was her first encounter with racism. Oh, she had heard of incidents all right; with Vithal as cousin, there was no way she could have stayed ignorant, though she had thought he exaggerated everything. But now she had felt it for herself, the sudden uncontrollable spasm of fear and shock at hearing the word "Paki" flung at her.

It was just a matter of time, she told herself, before the problem resolved itself. Just wait a couple of generations and there'd be a lot more interracial kids. Her own, for example. They would be beautiful; they always were, these children of two races. One just had to wait. Jyoti caught herself short as other thoughts spilled over. Pierre, was he the man? But how could she doubt it, why this nagging fear? One thing at a time, she told herself, and the thing right now was to get her term papers and exams out of the way. She would not think of anything but the exams. Not about Vithal, not about Pierre. But how could she clear her mind of them, of those junior high boys she had never seen who made obscene and intimidating gestures to eight-year-old girls? What about Priti? Jyoti broke into a cold sweat. And what about Pierre? Was he the man? Would he ever understand what and how one feels to have the word "Paki" flung at one?

* * *

Jyoti's words had twisted the hook into him. Jayant felt he would gladly run his sword through Jyoti's boyfriend, Pierre. That guy was slimy. There was something altogether suspect about his appearance; something phony about his symmetrical face that looked like a plastic surgeon's cast of Adonis; his hair a perpetual Dresdan commercial, greaseless, blow dried, each hair bouncing back into place separately; his clothes that seemed taken out of glossy magazines; he earned good money though he was a college dropout, and he drove a Porsche. Except that he hadn't been driving lately. Jayant knew that his license had been suspended for three months but didn't know just why; did Jyoti know? Three months ago he would have asked Pierre the most personal questions without hesitation, but now he hated the guy so much he couldn't get past even the formalities of greeting. And at this moment he knew why—his instinct had alerted him to what Jyoti had just told him.

Betrayal. His life was haunted by shadows. Pierre whom he had loved was a guttersnipe.

Betrayal had been by his side always. Jayant strummed listlessly on the violin with his fingers. Yes, of course he was jealous of Pierre. Not jealous in the narrow textbook way that reduced everything to the physical and to complexes neatly pigeonholed with pretentious pseudoscientific names. Jyoti was an extension of himself. It was a sacred, inviolable bond that could be expressed only in symbols. Like the *rakhi* that girls tied round their brothers' wrists on Rakshabandhan day; like the Rajput wedding rite where the bride's brother stood at the gate of the house and challenged the coming bridegroom to a symbolic duel, after which they embraced and went in together to the bride, who waited with roses to garland the groom.

Jayant sipped at the pop that had gone flat. Some part of him was still resisting. Hogwash, it said, all this hype about rituals; but another part knew it was not rituals he was talking about.

He had loved Pierre once, and not without cause, and therefore could love him again. Jyoti loved Pierre; and if she was not as radiant as she should be, it was because of them—he and Dad and Ma—their instinctive resistance to this alien seducer who had pulled away one of their own. They were taut, like high-tension wires that vibrate almost unseen to sounds almost unheard.

The shadows around him, undefined but familiar, moved to some inaudible theme song of the collective unconscious of all their lives. Jayant placed the violin carefully beside him.

Like the headlights of cars that paused at the stop sign on the bay across the street and cast on the living room wall distinct shadows of the leaves and fruit and branches of the ornamental crabapple tree below the large window, his memory—or need—from time to time shone on silent shadows within, defining one or two with recognizable outlines whereby they came alive with a face and a name. Ajoba's library, Aji's jasmine-scented saris, the stop sign across the street, Jyoti's denim jacket, the smell of camphor in the niche of the tulsi tree, the ridiculous over-sized billboards on Pembina Highway advertising Stanfield briefs and Cougar boots, all came together in an epiphany of vibrations.

He would do with due grace and honour what he had no doubt done with due grace and honour in a hundred past lives; when Pierre came on his white mare and in his plumed silk turban tasseled with red and white flowers, he would meet him with drawn sword, sheathing which he would anoint him with sacred vermilion and turmeric and embrace him, with stars and moon and assembled guests as witness.

The dark night of the body was over.

Javaid Qazi

Statement: Writing fiction in English has always been a struggle for me. In the initial stages the struggle centered on learning how to use the English language effectively; then came the struggle to learn the art of story-telling, followed by the struggle to get published, gain a portion of the mind-share of the reading public, attain a toehold on the slippery slopes of literary fame. But after all is said and done, and the captains and the kings depart, and the brouhaha has quieted down, the only truly reward-ing part of being a fiction writer is hearing someone say: "Hey, I read that story you wrote. I liked it."

"The Laid-off Man" addresses an important issue of life in America today. The narrator is faced with the very real concern of losing his job and the terrifying solution, violence, used by so many Americans. Javaid Qazi places this very American situation within the context of the protagonist's South Asian background. Neither the protagonist nor his wife has ever known of loyal and long-standing workers' being fired from their jobs in India. Neither of them could even envision turn-ing to violence as an answer. He tries to look for a fault within himself for being turned into a laid-off man. The story unfolds to show the sor-rows and the pain involved in becoming a part of the darker side of American life, of working in America, of losing friends who play out the Rambo role in real life. And yet the author also shows the gentle transformation of the protagonist's loss into his discovery of painting, which he uses not only to make some money but also to portray his life for his niece in India.

The Laid-off Man

Dev woke with a start and squinted bleary-eyed at the digital clock-radio on the bedside table. In the early morning dark, glowing red num-bers announced the time with pitiless precision: 5:55. As always, he'd woken up exactly five minutes ahead of the alarm. Beside him on the double bed, Rushmi still slept soundly.

Then it occurred to him—he didn't have to worry about the alarm going off. He hadn't set it the night before. He was a laid-off man. He didn't have to get up early anymore. A laid-off person has no job to go to, no need to get up, get dressed, swallow soggy cornflakes, and rush off to work.

He shut his eyes tightly, grimly determined not to think about being unemployed. If he could only sleep a little longer. . . . But he couldn't. His heart had started to thump like a runaway drum solo, and his brain was replaying every painful moment of his last day at Techware Solutions.

Techware hadn't been doing well for a long time. This much, everyone knew. In fact, all the local newspapers had been running stories for months on the "meteoric" rise and slow decline of Techware. The editors who tracked high-tech companies were quick to assign blame. Some said it was the fault of the management, others the weak economy. Still others felt that Techware's products were out-of-date and lacked the nifty features offered by competitors for much less money. And then there were those who blamed Japan. In fact, blaming the Japanese had become very popular all over the country even as jobs vanished and the lines of the unemployed got longer and longer.

For over six months, Dev had been hearing rumors about a massive layoff. But he didn't think Techware would fire him. Hell, he had seniority; he'd been with the company for over five years. Moreover, he'd been working on a high-priority project for nearly eighteen months, and he knew that he alone could bring it to completion. This awareness gave him a sense of security.

But then everything changed one sunny day. Techware started chopping off heads, and Dev found himself among the casualties. Dozens of other employees also were forced to clean out their desks and evacuate their cubicles. There were quick, embarrassed handshakes and farewell hugs on every floor. Tears in the parking lot. Promises were made to stay in touch. Some left stoically silent. Others bitched about "unfair tactics," "capitalism in action," even "blatant racism." Before all the bloodletting came to a halt, engineers who'd been with the company for over ten years found themselves pink-slipped and put out to pasture.

Dev blamed himself for this sudden reversal in his fortunes. Feeling guilty came naturally to him. His ethnic background and family influences had molded him to always consider his own deficiencies when faced with failure. He must have some inherent flaw or shortcoming in his character, he reasoned. He must have done something wrong or displeased his managers in some way. He must not have performed to the high standards that Techware espoused as a company. He must not have worked hard enough or fast enough. Perhaps he hadn't put in extra time at his computer. Or (and this charge hurt most of all) he simply didn't have the smarts to be a Techware employee.

However, Bob Wilson refused to take the blame for Techware's decline.

"Look, man, we got lousy leadership," Bob told Dev on the phone. "We did exactly what they told us to do, but they never came up with a good strategy. Shortsighted planning and plain old greed, that's what got us into trouble. Instead of taking some of those earnings—all the bucks they made in the early years—and ploughing them into research and development, the top managers simply skimmed the profits and made themselves rich."

"Oh, well," Dev sighed. "Maybe we didn't work hard enough."

"Shit, I gained one hundred pounds from sitting at the computer for all those hours," Bob said. "Don't tell me I didn't work hard enough."

"I know. I know you did," Dev responded.

"Techware was robbed from the inside, my man," Bob said. "Plundered and mismanaged."

"Well, I suppose you're right," Dev murmured. "But what can one do? We're just cogs in a bigger machine."

"The hell we are," Bob said with real energy. "I'm not taking this lying down."

"But . . ."

"I'm going to get even with these bastards. They can't use me and throw me aside like, like I'm some kind of garbage."

"Take it easy, Bob," Dev advised. "Calm down. You'll find another job. Surely."

Bob did have a point. Several of the top people had transformed themselves from ordinary, middle-class types into multimillionaires in just a few years. But even as this gang of four or five got rich, Techware, as a company, dwindled and declined and slowly melted away like a Popsicle on a hot sidewalk.

* * *

Growing weary of tossing and turning and afraid of waking up his wife, Dev got up and headed for the kitchen. Rushmi needed her sleep. She worked long hours as a clerk at a nearby grocery store. They'd been married for a little over two years and only recently had she begun to feel secure enough to start talking about having a baby. He got along well with her, even though he hadn't known her before they'd tied the knot. Theirs had been an arranged marriage. Dev's parents had selected Rushmi and planned everything according to the customs of the Brahmin families of Rameshwaram, the little South Indian village where he'd grown up.

* * *

Dev made a pot of tea, another cultural habit he had not been able to let go, and started looking over the morning paper. There might be an opening somewhere. Another company might be looking for a software engineer. Even though jobs had been few and far between lately, like a trained rat, he went through the ritual of looking every single day.

Suddenly, the name of his old company caught his eye. "Disturbance at Techware," read the headline, and the subhead gave a few more details: "Disgruntled Ex-Employee Terrorizes Workers."

Dev put down his cup and quickly scanned the story. "A disgruntled ex-employee created a major disturbance at Techware Solutions on Friday afternoon. The company, which develops software, found itself under a virtual siege as the man roamed the corridors of the building, shouting insults and making threatening gestures. Responding to a 911 call, a SWAT team evacuated the building and arrested the man. The intruder, one Bob Wilson, apparently upset over being laid off, decided to vent his frustration in a public display of anger. He was unarmed but appeared to be intoxicated. 'We're seeing lots of similar incidents lately,' Detective Sergeant Butkus told our reporter. 'With the downturn in the computer industry and all the layoffs, people are under a lot of strain. Some of 'em just can't take it anymore.'"

Dev put the paper down. His hands were shaking.

He could hardly believe his eyes. The Bob Wilson he remembered was a decent fellow, so bright, so witty, so cool-headed. He was a computer science graduate from MIT, for god's sake, not some wacked-out psycho.

Dev raced to the phone and started punching numbers feverishly. After a couple of calls, he managed to confirm the newspaper account. The most reliable source of information proved to be Janet, Bob's current girlfriend. She sounded relatively calm for someone whose boyfriend was in jail.

His parents are bailing him out, she said. The cops had charged him with disturbing the peace, unlawful trespass, resisting arrest, and being in possession of a contraband substance. They'd found some cocaine on him, she told Dev.

"I can't believe this," Dev murmured. "I never knew Bob took drugs."

"Oh, well," Janet said, "he's not an addict or anything. I mean, who doesn't like to get high once in a while? Nothing wrong with that."

"Oh?" said Dev.

* * *

When Rushmi woke up, he showed her the Bob Wilson story. "The guy's gone crazy," said Dev. "I can't believe it. His cubicle used to be right next to mine."

"I'm worried about you," said Rushmi. "Bob has a family here. They'll take care of him. You are alone. What are you planning on doing?

We can manage on my salary for a while, but we'll have to sell the new car and cut back on extra expenses."

"I guess we don't need a second car since I'm not working," Dev murmured. "I'll put an ad in the paper. We'll lose a ton of money since we've only owned it for a year, but at least we won't have this expense hanging over our heads every month."

Rushmi nodded in agreement.

"I really don't understand this layoff business," she said. "My father worked all his life for the Indian Railway. We weren't rich, but I don't think Daddy-ji ever worried about waking up some day and being without a job."

"Nor did my father," said Dev. "Our family has been in the silk and coffee business for generations. Daddy didn't even know the meaning of not working."

"I just don't understand this system," Rushmi said. "But I'm sure you'll find another job. However, when you do find work, I'm not going to let you rush out and buy a new car."

Dev grinned sheepishly.

* * *

After Rushmi left for work, Dev moved around the small apartment like a nervous gerbil. The TV blared loudly with giggles and laughter and on-camera psychotherapy sessions. Under the probing scrutiny of cameras, people seemed eager to reveal all sorts of amazing secrets about their private lives. Talk shows had turned the sacred rite of Confession into a public show. Voyeurism had become respectable.

Seeking relief from the idiocy on TV, he went into the guest bedroom, turned on his computer, and wrote a letter to his father. He made some general comments about being in good health and spirits, but he didn't mention the layoff. His parents wouldn't understand anyway. People in India looked upon the United States as some kind of magical Wonderland or El Dorado, where everyone had money and nothing to worry about. Besides, the exchange rate between the dollar and the Indian rupee was so lopsided in favor of the dollar that his folks couldn't really help him moneywise.

Next he fiddled with his resume, updating it, adding information, formatting and reformatting. Then, just for fun, he decided to write a letter to Meena, his little niece. He hadn't seen her since her kindergarten days, but she'd grown up fast and turned into an articulate young person. Dev found that communicating with her was like establishing a link with his own lost childhood. She attended an Irish Catholic convent school near Rameshwaram, where the nuns were teaching her English. She had developed into a pretty good letter writer and got a big thrill out of hearing from her "American" uncle.

But when he saw the letter he'd written, he grimaced. It looked so dull. The contents were cheerful enough, but the printed words were boring. Wouldn't it be nice if I could actually paint the scene, he thought, really capture the clouds, the ocean, the green grass, and the tall white lighthouse in the background?

On a whim, he decided to drive over to a nearby art supply store and get some watercolors and brushes. He would decorate the letter with splashes of color. He wasn't an artist by any stretch, but Meena would enjoy getting a letter filled with colorful illustrations instead of the usual solid blocks of print he sent her most of the time.

He started to work on his project eagerly as soon as he got back to the apartment. And the more he sketched and painted, the more he wanted to keep at it. He found the process so absorbing that he even forgot about lunch.

As the afternoon wore on, he realized that a very strange thing had happened. He suddenly found himself perfectly at peace with himself and the world. The nagging anxiety about finding a job still lingered at the back of his mind, but all the black anger and bitterness that had whipped him up into a frenzy earlier in the day seemed to have ebbed away.

Time passed imperceptibly. When he looked up from his labors, he was shocked to see that the sun was about to set. It was almost time to set the table and heat the food, pending Rushmi's return.

* * *

When Rushmi returned from work, tired and irritable, he showed her the pictures he had painted.

"Very nice, dear," she said dryly. "But did you hear from any company? Did you send out any more resumes?"

"There is nothing in the paper," he told her. "The jobs have simply evaporated."

"Keep looking, keep trying," she said patiently. "You can't just give up."

"I know, I know," Dev moaned. "But all the companies are laying off people. The aeronautics industry is floundering. Semiconductors are sinking. And personal computers are in a real tailspin."

"Keep looking, sweetie," Rushmi responded. "You're too smart, too highly trained, too young to be wasting your life, sitting at home all day watching TV talk shows."

"I don't want to be sitting at home," Dev snapped back irritably.

And actually, he didn't.

* * *

Over the next few months, Dev kept up his job search. He sent out resumes in response to ads in the paper, called his friends and acquaintances to let them know he wanted a job, and scrutinized the want ads carefully. But at the same time, he kept on painting.

The painting proved to be a pressure-relief valve for him. He discovered a vast new source of creative energy within himself, an untapped reservoir that he didn't know he possessed. He bought books on art and on watercolors and began to teach himself how to sketch. With every picture he painted, he learned new tricks and techniques. With every picture he got better and better, more confident of his skills, more knowledgeable about the medium.

As summer turned into fall, Dev found out about a Mrs. Hammond, an experienced teacher, who gave lessons in watercolor painting. Mrs. Hammond held classes in a large workroom behind the artists' supplies store where he bought all the paper and paint and brushes he needed. Dev signed up with Mrs. Hammond and started attending a class that met on Mondays from 9 to 12. Rather nervous at first, he quickly shed his fears and began to pick up sophisticated techniques that seasoned professionals used.

Once in a while he'd go out on a job interview, but no one made him an offer. These interviews were like getting hit on the head with a sledge hammer. Again and again. You had to be a masochist to keep going through this futile and painful ritual. He got to feeling very discouraged and dispirited. But the joy he derived from his watercolors kept him moderately sane and cheerful through this grim period of disappointment and rejection. With each passing day he could see improvement in his work. Even Rushmi noticed his progress and kept encouraging him.

Then almost six months into his lessons, his neighbor, Sam Samudio, offered to buy a large painting he'd done of a single yellow rose. Dr. Samudio, a dentist by profession, loved classical music, expensive cognacs, and fine cigars.

"What are you charging for it?" Dr. Samudio asked.

"Oh, I don't know," said Dev. "I really don't know how much to ask."

"Well, give me an idea."

"How about a hundred dollars?"

"It's a deal," said the good doctor and held out his hand, grinning happily.

Giddy with joy, Dev rushed into the house to tell Rushmi that he'd sold his first painting. Rushmi could hardly trust her ears.

* * *

As he got better and better, Dev began to think seriously about trying to make a living as an artist. He started haunting commercial picture
galleries and talking to other watercolorists. But he soon realized that
none of the artists he met were able survive on art alone. They did other
work to supplement their incomes. But the involvement with art
enriched their lives. If he could sell just a few paintings a month, that
would do fine. With Rushmi bringing in a small but steady paycheck,
they needed just a little bit more to make life comfortable. Later on, as his
work started to sell, he would ask Rushmi to cut back on her hours and,
ultimately, give up the job altogether. This was another one of his daffy
dreams no doubt, but it felt good to be dreaming again, to experience the
pleasure of doing rewarding work.

Bob Wilson, out on bail, called once in a while to talk about their job-
related problems. Bob was also having a hard time finding work.

"How's Janet?" Dev asked him.

"Dunno," Bob said.

"Are you still seeing her?"

"Naaah," Bob said. "Can't afford her. Keeping her wined and dined
and recreated got to be too expensive. I could spend bucks like that when
I was bringing them in, but now—I'm barely able to feed myself and pay
the rent."

"I know," Dev said. "Same here. The only bright spot in my life is the
watercolors that I'm painting."

"I've gone golfing several times," Bob said. "But even that is more
than I can afford."

"Cheer up," Dev told him. "Things are bound to get better."

He tried to inject a note of enthusiasm into his voice. But he didn't
think he sounded very convincing.

"Bye, now," he said. "Hope I'll be seeing you soon."

And he did, but not the way he thought he would. Not many days
later, Dev flipped on the TV and saw Bob's face plastered on all the local
channels. Another crisis had erupted at Techware. Reporters were trans-
mitting special reports from the company parking lot.

"Shit!" said Dev, sitting down in front of the set. "I had a feeling this
might happen. Even a brain-damaged donkey could have predicted
this."

Bob had apparently flipped out again. He had barricaded himself
inside the building and was shooting at anything and everything he
could see from his position. A dozen or so Techware employees were still
in the building, being held as hostages. Dev heard the details repeated
over and over again on TV. All the area TV stations had commentators on
the scene, reporting on Bob's insane rampage, interspersed, of course,
with the usual inane commercial messages.

Bob had gone back to Techware as though he were the Lord of Death. He had taken a duffle bag filled with automatic rifles, shotguns, pistols, hand grenades, bandoliers of shotgun shells and bullets, and even a machete. Cameras with telephoto lenses caught him as he walked past glass windows, dressed in camouflage fatigues. Bent on doing the Rambo thing, he'd even gone to the trouble of dressing for the part.

The scene had an air of filmic unreality. Could the whole thing be a made-for-TV movie featuring lackluster talent picked up at random from some street corner?

Television tended to make even serious situations look like staged events with make-believe car crashes and pretend death scenes. Sane people knew that once the scenes had been played out, the actors would get up, dust themselves off, go take showers, and sit down to dinner with family members.

But this wasn't a low-budget movie. His churning guts, sweaty palms were all the proof he needed. A friend and colleague stood at the mouth of Hell. He could already have killed people—Dev had no doubt —and he wanted to be killed.

The cops now encircling the building were on hand to make sure that he got his wish.

Some workers had managed to escape, according to the TV commentators, but others were still trapped on the upper floors. A helicopter tried to land on the roof to evacuate them, but Bob fired at it from a balcony. The helicopter veered away sharply, started spinning out of control, and went careening to the ground. Fire engines and paramedics screamed toward the wreckage.

The TV crews were hard on their heels.

Dev wondered how long this would go on.

Professional negotiators had been sent for. Bob had asked for a TV newsman to come in and interview him so that he could tell his side of the story. For a doomed man to be so concerned that his final message to the world be reported right seemed rather odd to Dev.

Meanwhile, the SWAT teams busied themselves, positioning sharpshooters and setting up all kinds of equipment to prepare for an all-out assault. Obviously, they wanted to get the "situation" over with in a hurry. The longer the crisis continued, the more impotent and silly they looked. The matter had to be resolved, wrapped up, handled.

Dev wanted to turn off the TV, to somehow stop the nightmare as it unfolded with its own slow but irresistible logic. But he couldn't. A sick curiosity, a ghoulish need to see blood spilled, held him in an iron grip.

He wondered if Bob would listen to him if he raced over to Techware, commandeered a bullhorn, and begged him to surrender.

Bob, this is Dev, remember me? I had the cubicle next to yours. Stop this madness, Bob. Surrender. No matter how bad it is, I'm sure there is a way out. Please, Bob, listen to me. I beg you.

Or words to that effect.

Bob would probably respond with a volley of rifle fire. Fuck off, he'd probably say. I'm sick and tired of being pushed around. I've had it up to here. I don't give a shit what happens anymore. I'm already dead, so what the hell. Take this and this and this, you lousy bastards. You aren't going to catch me alive.

This is like the Wild West, Dev thought, just like the pioneer days. The time-honored tradition of dying in a hail of bullets. All we need is background music and this could be one of those Italian cowboy movies in which the slow-motion choreography of violence and death has a fateful inevitability.

By now the cops were lobbing tear gas canisters into the building. The SWAT team guys were running around in hideous pig-snout gas masks preparing to enter the building. Shots were fired at them from inside the building, but no one went down. Then a kind of silence fell over the scene. Even the firetrucks and ambulances stood silent, as if waiting for the next shot to be set up by the "Director."

With a supreme effort of will, Dev got up from the couch and turned off the TV. He'd seen enough. He already knew what would happen next. He went into the tiny guest bedroom that served as his studio and turned on the work light. He knew what the guys in white coats would find when they entered the building after the tear gas had dissipated. They'd find an actor who had been playing a role in a lousy movie. They wouldn't find Bob, his old friend and ex-colleague. Bob would be in some place far away.

Dev took out a fresh sheet of watercolor paper and quickly drew a single rose on the white surface. Then he picked up a No. 8 sable brush and started to add colors to the sketch, blending them carefully, letting them mix here and there to form new tints, slowly filling the blank emptiness in front of him with the image of a flower that would never wither, never die.

Sarita Sarvate

Statement: When I first came to this country as a young woman determined to build a "global village," being published as an Indian woman
writer in America seemed unthinkable. Now it seems possible. Much of
my writing is about people caught between cultures, between tradition
and liberation, between security and loneliness, between the mystical
and the modern. Many Americans have told me they can relate to my
writing because they can identify with the alienation and the loss of
innocence of my characters. Much of my writing is set in India and is
about the lives of modern Indian women. As a "citizen of the world"
who belongs nowhere, I feel the Bay Area is the perfect place for me to
live and write in.

In "The Law of Averages," Sarita Sarvate describes not only the terrible
pain and anger of a woman's loss of a child and a recognizable home but
also the discovery, in the end, of acceptance and of a family. Her step-
daughter's gift of a necklace echoes the Hindu tradition of the auspicious
marriage necklace, the *mangalasutra*, and the South Asian custom of presenting someone with a garland to signify honor, reverence, and love.

The Law of Averages

Meena cannot remember a time when she did not dread babies.
They creep up on her out of nowhere. As she walks out of her office, she
fishes inside her handbag for a pair of dark sunglasses, her protection
against the children from the daycare center walking around the courtyard in a crocodile. Even in the morning, riding the BART train, secure in
the company of other adults, she sometimes hears the cry of a baby deep
inside the car and quickly dons her dark glasses to hide the tears streaming down her cheeks.

Walking towards the train station in the middle of the afternoon,
she feels lightheaded. She has felt this way every since she woke up this
morning and realized her resolve. She has decided to kill herself. The
thought has been niggling at her for some time, since the miscarriage.

Last night, Milind came to her in a dream. He was five years old
and had long black hair. His body was slim and wiry, the dimples in his
face were gone. He stood in a lush green field dotted with manzanita

bushes, carrying an oversized beach ball. "Mommy, I need you," he said. Then he tossed the ball and ran away. She ran after him, peering through the maze of purple, black branches, but she could only hear a voice saying, "I am hiding, can you find me?" When she woke up with a start, she knew she had to go to her boy.

In Agatha Christie books, people die from the leaves of the yew tree or the seeds of the hemlock, but Meena is realizing how hard it is to die in real life. The only poisonous plant in her garden is the foxglove, but she is not sure just how poisonous it is. Even if she were to use the foxglove, she would have to stew it or grind it and prepare some sort of a witch's brew, and how is she supposed to do that with two stepdaughters and a husband lurking around the house all day?

Her husband, David, is unemployed and sits at his computer day and night, writing business proposals. Sometimes she wonders why he doesn't just put on his Reeboks and pound the streets looking for a job.

When she first came to America, people had told her, "You can find everything here in the yellow pages; life, death, marriage, babies, everything." So she looked in the yellow pages this morning, wondering only half in amusement if suicides were listed under s. She was really looking for a physician with a name like Chung or Wong or Yap. During the last few years, she has been so busy going to one gynecologist after another for infertility treatments, she has had no time to go to a regular doctor. She believes a Chinatown doctor will give her the drugs she needs. After all, six months ago, the therapist in Berkeley had practically pushed the sleeping pills on Meena, and when Meena had fended them off, the therapist had told her she didn't want to be helped.

The psychiatrist was a young woman named Zenobia with a mousy face and long blond hair. "I met David in Hawaii," Meena told her. "Hawaii was such a magical place, it was so easy to fall in love there. Afterwards, David offered to quit his job and move here. And I was such a fool, I let him do it." Meena broke into violent sobs. Zenobia looked bored. "When his ex-wife died in a car accident, what was I supposed to do? Tell the girls to stay on the streets until their Dad found a job?" Meena broke into a fresh wave of sobs.

For weeks, Meena told Zenobia the story of her life and for weeks Zenobia looked bored and irritated. Meena told Zenobia about men poking around her insides with sharp instruments as if she were the engine of a car. Meena told Zenobia about David's two blond girls, lying in wait at home like hungry cats.

At the end of her story, Zenobia said, "You've had so much bad luck it must be your turn to have some good luck now. You ought to buy lottery tickets; you'll probably win it."

Americans thought the law of averages applied to individual life, Meena thought. They thought that if you just tried hard enough, everything evened out in your lifetime. If you broke an arm, you sued someone and got a million dollars, if you contracted AIDS, you went on TV with the president. Basically, Americans thought everything was fair in life.

"Why don't you leave him?" Zenobia said abruptly one day in the middle of a session. "I mean, you're attractive, independent, you have a good job. Why do you need him?"

Meena burst into a new wave of sobs. "Do you know how it is to immigrate to a new country? I don't have anyone here." Meena knew Zenobia didn't know this. Americans always acted as if they were all alone, until they got pregnant, were run over by a car, or had a heart attack, Meena thought. Relatives popped out of the woodwork then, with baby clothes, strollers, and thermoses full of soup.

Zenobia said then what Meena expected her to say, "You can always find someone else!"

Americans believed in bumper stickers, Meena thought. They believed that *today was the first day of the rest of your life.* What nonsense! Today could not be the first day unless you could erase all memories, all scars, all knowledge. That day, Meena decided never to see Zenobia again.

Dr. Lee's office is a room on top of the Hong Kong market in Oakland's Chinatown. The fragrance of mangoes, jackfruit, and fresh fish wafts in through the window. She remembers walking here with David on Sunday afternoons after dim sum, picking bitter melons here, and peanut oil there.

She fills out the medical forms, and, under the headings "number of pregnancies" and "number of children," she puts two each.

She always knew she would not have the baby. She told no one about the pregnancy because she knew it was a hoax. She had sabotaged the baby by not celebrating its life. She thinks of the baby now as a blip on her basal body temperature chart. She knows the BBT chart was another way to jinx the baby. Every morning, she had compulsively studied the graphs, as if, without the charts, the egg and the sperm would not have known what to do.

Her chart and the blue stick from the pregnancy test are the only souvenirs left of the baby now. There was nothing left of the baby itself by the time they had driven to the hospital. It had been ejected into the toilet when Meena had doubled over with pain and had decided to go to the bathroom hoping it was just an attack of indigestion.

At the hospital, Dr. Hodge had arrived, looking perky in a blue surgical gown. He had given her a shot. "You're going to feel very good now. I've just given you a drug with the street-value of five hundred dollars," he had said. The drug made her float away among the clouds. Even with her dizzy, drugged head, she had marveled then at how Dr. Hodge knew the street value of the drug. She wondered if he was on drugs himself.

She remembers heavenly music. She is not sure if Dr. Hodge had played music in the surgery that night or if the drug had played it inside her head. David was rubbing her hand as Dr. Hodge vacuumed out her insides. She wishes she could go back to that moment, when pain was suspended, cordoned off at the door of the operating theater. She wishes to float to the accompaniment of that ethereal music, feel David's hand on her hand, and listen to the nurse's soothing voice saying it was nobody's fault.

They pulled into the driveway at home—her home since she was the one who paid the mortgage—and she got out, like an empty sailboat, her mast battered to bits, oars in shreds. Two beautiful children of David's slept inside her house while her baby lay dead in the toilet.

She walked around the office the next day, her breasts so full of milk that she had to remind herself continually that her womb was empty. She had told no one about the baby, and later, she told no one about its loss.

The Chinese doctor is a small, ageless man with tiny eyes blinking behind enormous spectacles. "I need sleeping pills," she tells him, "I have been working too hard." She pastes a winning smile on her face. In the windowpane, she can watch her own reflection. Her deep blue dress with dots of red and green and yellow fits snugly around her breasts and waist. Breasts unspoiled by breastfeeding! A waist without the blemish of stretch marks! This is how she thinks of her body now. The light catches in her long brown hair and makes it into a breeze.

The Chinese doctor breathes deeply, in and out, in and out. He looks like a yogi sitting under a banyan tree. "We have too much stress in this society," he says at last, shaking his head sadly, "far too much stress."

"Yes." The corners of her eyes begin to moisten.

"Have you tried the health food shops?" he says softly.

He knows everything, she realizes.

"You have two children?" he asks. She nods.

"Teenagers, hey?"

"One of them."

"They are difficult, I know. But they will outgrow this stage." He is talking about what he perceives to be her problem. But she has no desire to solve David's children's teenage angst. She has no desire to see them ever again if she can help it.

He writes the name of an over-the-counter sleep medication on a piece of paper, then gets up and touches her shoulder. "Don't worry so much, life is hard sometimes."

She decides to take the BART back and pick her car up at the station. She could drive to Monterey, stay in a motel on the beach, then walk into the waves, late at night, when no one is watching. She remembers being pulled by a current under the surf in Hawaii once. She remembers David and his daughters calling her from the shore. "Come back, come back," voices fading. David wading through the water and pulling her out. She remembers the soft feel of sand under her feet. She remembers the touch of Marsha's hot tears on her cheeks, the flutter of her tiny chest convulsing with sobs against her breasts. For a moment she has a desire to go home and see Marsha. Marsha who had once made her a Mother's Day card. Marsha who had taken her trick-or-treating one year because David wouldn't go with her. She remembers hearing people say at every door, "Give one to your Mom, too," and feeling angry at the stupidity of people who thought she had given birth to this miracle of peachy white complexion and corn-color hair. At this memory, she wishes she had been pulled under the waves in Hawaii.

Getting off the train and walking towards her car, she notices a tall, masculine figure out of the corner of her eye. It's David.

She is glad to be driven home. Her head is heavy, fatigued. He drives on to the freeway.

"Where are we going?" she asks.

"The Chinese doctor called me. They have a psychiatrist at Eden Hospital waiting for you." The deep lines in his tanned face are inscrutable, his blue eyes opaque.

"I am not going to a psychiatrist. He is probably some creep. All doctors are creeps." She notes David's expressionless profile. She wants him to cry for the baby. She wants him to scream, throw a tantrum, do anything, but he always says "what's the point" and shows no emotion.

"I hate you, I hate you," she pounds her fists on the window. In the next lane, three people in an Audi watch her contorted face with fascination. She wants to fling open the door and fall into the traffic. "I wish you had died instead of my baby." She is convulsing with sobs. "I hate your children. Do you hear? Get them out of my house! Now! Before I kill them. Do you realize how it is for me to see my baby die and then to have to look at the faces of your children every day?"

The woman at the reception desk has no curiosity about Meena; instead she is enchanted by a computer screen.

Dr. Whitfield is an obese man with gray hair and a large tummy. Arré Ram! What can he do for her? He looks like a man behind the counter of a bakery. His face is expressionless as she tells him her story. "Are you going to charge me a hundred dollars a week for the next ten years to tell me I chose David because I am a masochistic loser?" she asks him at the end.

"Why do you think I can't help you?" he asks.

She doesn't think anyone can help her. They can't give her the baby back, or all the years she has lost looking after David and his children. No one can give her time back. If someone could give her her childbearing years back, she would give them her career, her romances, her travels. But no one can give her what she has lost. People who get divorced after a couple of kids seem such happy people to her now. She used to think she would never bring a child into an unhappy marriage. She wishes she had had a child out of wedlock and given it up for adoption. Now, she could be looking for that child, her biological child. It would be in existence somewhere in the world instead of being dead in a toilet.

"I don't want to go home to David's children," she tells him.

"Why don't you stay here? You could be a voluntary patient. We could give you some intense therapy," he says.

At the psych ward a tall, thin nurse with prematurely gray hair shakes her head and enters her name into a chart. Another nurse shows her into a spacious room with an attached bathroom, a plush armchair, a coffee table, and a large picture window overlooking the valley. The nurse makes her sign for her jewelry. Meena stands at the window and looks at tiny houses with lush tropical gardens. She spots a plastic swimming pool beside a bed of calla lilies and two blond heads bobbing atop orange and green bicycles with training wheels. The sheet of glass separates her from life as ordinary people know it.

A blond nurse in jeans and a white T-shirt comes in and sits on the bed. "So what's the problem?" she asks. Her young pale face is streaked with freckles. Her eyes are ageless, as if somewhere, in another life, she has lived a century.

"I lost my baby," Meena says, realizing she is uttering these words for the first time.

"You ought to start a new life, leave your husband," the woman says at the end of Meena's story.

"But I don't hate him; he is a good man," Meena says. The nurse shakes her head.

At the group session in the hall, Meena sits on the edge of the circle, her face averted from the others. A man with a potato-head face is talking to the group. "I am going to get a pass to go out this Saturday. I know I can make it." He looks like a used-car salesman. He could be discussing a weekend game of golf with his business partner. The nurse looks perky in a flowery chintz dress. "I've got to get out this weekend!" As the man talks, his face flushes. Large green veins stand out in his forehead. He clenches his fists and his mouth froths. The nurse gets up and puts her arm around him. The muscles of his face relax. He no longer looks like a used-car salesman.

An ancient woman with a million wrinkles in her face sits with her back to the circle, staring at the wall across the room. "Yolanda, are we going to say anything today?" the nurse asks. The woman continues to stare at the wall. Meena leaves the room.

At night a nurse brings Meena sleeping pills. When Meena shakes her head, the nurse leaves the room and gets behind the counter. Meena follows her and watches her speak into the telephone. *If you didn't want to take the medications, why did you bother to come into the hospital*, her expression says. "He says you don't have to take it," the nurse shrugs her shoulders, putting the phone down.

It is midnight and Meena is wide awake. Her room is stuffy and the windows do not open. When the door creaks she feels nervous. Someone stands near her bed. A light flashes into her eyes. She sits up with a start and utters a muffled scream. It's a female orderly in a blue uniform. "Sh! We're supposed to check the patients."

"But why? I am not going to be able to rest this way."

"We have to make sure you're breathing."

Every hour, someone shines a beam of light in Meena's face, and even though Meena is wide awake, she pretends to be asleep.

As dawn is breaking, she sees Milind. He is holding Marsha's hand and together they walk around the maze of *suru* trees in the Maharajbag gardens in Nagpur. Seeing Meena, they freeze, watching her as if she is a stranger. Meena is startled to discover how alike they look, the same pointy jaw and large cheekbones, same blue eyes laced with dark lashes. "You don't love me and you wouldn't have loved him either," Marsha says. Then Marsha and Milind turn around and walk away hand in hand.

Meena puts her Reeboks on and runs out of the room. She hears the nurses' calls getting louder as she boards the elevator. On the first floor, she runs out the door and down the street past ticky-tacky houses, up the hill, through the parking lot, down the road to the lake. On the pier, she sits down, her feet dangling over water, and bites the blue hospital wand around her wrist into shreds. After hours of watching the waves, she walks home.

In the living room, ten-year-old Marsha is sitting on the sofa in pigtails and shorts. "Hi, Meena," she says, her brow in a deep frown. An antique wooden box engraved with mother-of-pearl is open in front of her and a few strands of pearls are flowing out.

"What are you doing?"

"I am playing with Mom's jewelry. Jenny and I divided it." Marsha holds up a long string of amber. "Here, you can have this."

"Where is everybody?" Meena asks.

"Remember Jenny turned sixteen yesterday? Dad took her to buy a car." *You mean while I have been in a loony bin, they have been busy spending some more of my money?* But Meena does not say this. Instead, she puts the string of amber around her neck and helps Marsha put the jewelry back in the box. As she puts her arm around Marsha's shoulders, she realizes the law of averages does apply after all.

Neila C. Seshachari

Statement: Waves after waves of dreamers are drawn to the shores of America and deposited into the heart of this cloud-cuckoo-land that they have visited over and over again in their imaginations. But the land and its people defy dreams. There are surprises and traumas lurking every-where—and, yes, heartaches and despair too. While this continent is a land of seeming opulence, it is also an inhumane, capitalistic system where immigrants can survive only if they can deliver more than others who are citizens. Thus, for immigrants, living in America becomes a perennial do-or die-game.

Within a week of immigrating to Utah in December 1969, I realized that I had become a second-class citizen, not so much because of my color—even though that mattered ultimately—as because of my gender. Utah, more than any other state, is covertly racist and sexist. Not belong-ing to the majority religion, Latter-day Saints (Mormons), can deprive the most competent immigrant of the highest opportunities. But the real-ly tough ones can more than survive. They can manage to live with grace.

For me, living in Utah has been both an exciting adventure and a frustrating prospect. My editorship of *Weber Studies: An Interdisciplinary Humanities Journal*, teaching, and professional and public service keep me busy and bring me a measure of recognition, but they leave me very little time to do creative writing. And there is plenty here to write about. Learning to balance the two—professional demands and personal needs —poses the biggest challenge for me.

"The Bride Comes Home" presents the same dilemma seen in at least one other story in this anthology, "The Dew and the Moon." The issue of unsuccessful family-arranged (and sometimes even self-arranged) mar-riages, usually between a South Asian man living in America and a South Asian woman who has not lived in America prior to the marriage, is not uncommon in the South Asian American community. It is an issue that is now being openly discussed in a variety of forums. The possible solution offered in this story may seem unusual, but the author has not only given a surprising twist to the story, she has also described an aspect of the family and religious life specific to a particular part of the United States.

The Bride Comes Home

When Rina's father announced that she would leave within the week for Salt Lake City to join her husband, her friends shrieked and clapped their hands with joy. Their laughter reverberated through the big house, and even the dog jumped and barked madly.

"How lucky you are!" squealed one in excitement. "I would sell my soul to be in the USA."

"I have a pediatrician cousin," said another, "who lives somewhere in Pennsylvania with her anesthesiologist husband. Their home is a palace, and they own two Cadillacs—*two Cadillacs*," she repeated, as if she were afraid Rina had missed the import.

"My nephew, who is only a student at the City University of New York, makes a thousand dollars a month busing dishes and cleaning tables at the university cafeteria," said a third.

"You will be stinking rich, Rina," they assured her.

Another friend studied her palm at length before she pronounced, "You will not work in the USA. Your stars are in the most auspicious cusp. You will be rich and happy."

They all helped her shop for the prettiest red silk sari with a foot-high gold border to wear on her journey. Most of her wedding saris were still new and unworn—she could wear any one of them—but they insisted that her journey to join her husband of six months was a good enough reason to buy another one. "Besides, would you be able to buy such a pretty sari in the USA?" they asked.

Rina tried to drown her anxieties in the prattle of her friends. Kris had not written her in two months. In fact, he had not written much at all since they were married. Most of his letters seemed to be written to convince her she ought to stay in Hyderabad and complete her master's degree before she came to Salt Lake City. It would take that long to get the visa anyway, he had written. But her father used his influence with the American Consulate and managed to get her the visa in record time.

"Krishna is going to be so surprised," her father said. "I am even tempted not to call him. Just imagine his beloved wife telephoning him from the Salt Lake International Airport to come and fetch her home! That would be a story to tell his children and grandchildren. Everyone needs exciting things to happen in their lives," he guffawed. "Like getting Rina's match, for instance—and the grand wedding with only four days to prepare for!"

"Appa," Rina interposed, "what if he is out of town? What would I do?"

"Get a taxi and go home. You know the address."

"And who will let me in?"

"Don't you remember Krishna saying that the apartment manager lives on the premises and fixes anything tenants need fixed—leaking faucets, burnt-out gas burners, anything? Ask him to let you in with his master key. You know we can't afford to send any escort with you."

The thought of the apartment manager calmed Rina considerably. She even began to feel it would be fun to surprise her husband. She had never traveled by air in all her life—in fact she'd traveled alone only once in her life by train, to attend a friend's wedding. But she was strangely elated that she would have to be brave and fly across the continents all by herself.

Rina boarded the plane amidst great celebration and ritual. At the Begumpet Airport, her cousins and friends gave farewell toasts, while her uncles and elders gave appropriate blessings. Her aunts dabbed dots on her forehead with auspicious red *kumkum* powder, as they put garlands of fragrant jasmine and roses round her neck. Her grandmother lit two wick-lamp *deepams* in a silver platter and circled the twin lights three times in front of Rina in a clockwise motion and blessed her in Sanskrit. They all stuffed sweetmeats into her mouth.

Her mother cried silently. "I'll come to see how you keep house in America without the help of a maid servant," her brother teased. Her sister moaned, "When will I ever see you again?" Her father strutted around with the satisfaction of one who had fulfilled his karma in life. He had married off his daughter and was sending her away to the land of riches and flowing milk. There were so many relatives and flower garlands at the airport, it was like getting married all over again.

Even as she boarded the plane, holding the pleats of her heavy silk sari and handbag in one hand and lugging her coat and overnighter in the other, she walked into what seemed a wedding hall. Soft sitar music and incense wafted into the air. The air hostess who welcomed passengers at the entrance was dressed as extravagantly as any bride she had seen. Suddenly, Rina felt calm. This luxury was all that her own life was about. This was the beginning of the good life the astrologer had predicted for her after comparing the two horoscopes—Kris's and hers—to determine if their union would be an auspicious one. "She will be brave as goddess Durga," the astrologer had foretold, "and wise as goddess Saraswati and rich as goddess Lakshmi. The stars are configurating in rare combinations in her chart." Rina wondered now if the burden of all the three goddesses was too much to bear.

She took her window seat and looked around. The interior of the plane was painted in soft pastel shades with gorgeous murals of Moghul miniatures all around—pictures of lovers in each other's arms, of brides looking coy as the grooms removed their bridal veils, of lovers with their eyes fixed on their beloveds' heaving breasts. Rina closed her eyes and abandoned herself to delicious daydreaming.

The rest of Rina's flight unfolded like a picture-book journey. The stops at Helsinki, Paris, and London were uneventful. Customs at New York was a breeze. And Rina found herself flying the "friendly skies" to Salt Lake City and wondering if Kris had received the telegram her father had sent.

How would it be to have total privacy with him? In the brief three days Kris had been with her after their wedding, Rina had hardly got to know her husband. The house was full of lingering guests and confusion. Her father had coaxed the newlyweds not to go away on a honeymoon. It was more important for them to take care of her immigration application. "It will be one long honeymoon for you both when she gets to Utah," he had roared happily as he winked at his son-in-law. Before Kris left for the United States, custom demanded the bridal couple visit his parents at least for a day. The hundred-mile journey in a taxi cramped with three other relatives had taken four hours each way. The summer heat had been unbearable, and they had both ended up with headaches.

Rina was happy to leave her relatives behind in India. She looked out of the window, fascinated at the myriad lights of Salt Lake City as the plane gently bumped on the runway and taxied to a stop. This is the city where I meet my future, she mused, as she picked up her coat and bags and started walking down the aisle and on to the jetway. I'm in Salt Lake City—I am in America!—she kept thinking.

At the lounge outside the gate, she stood searching for Kris's face among the people who had flocked to the airport to receive their loved ones, but he was not there.

She took out her diary and reread the instructions her uncle had given her. She got her American coins out, studied them twice over, and called Kris from a public telephone booth. No Kris; only the long wails of the telephone ringing across the wires.

Rina shivered. For the first time since she had glimpsed her first snow and seen the bitter cold on the steamy breaths and red noses of airport ground workers in Paris en route, she became aware of the weather. The snow was thick and sparkling all around. It glowed beneath all those bright airport lights.

Passengers donned their gloves and coats as they got ready for the walk to the baggage claim. Their loved ones talked and laughed around them. Rina tucked the loose ends of her sari at her waist and slipped into the coat with shabby rabbit fur on the collar—it belonged to her aunt who had bought it in England two decades earlier. She wondered if it looked incongruous over her rich sari. She suddenly realized that she herself, bedecked in red and gold, was incongruous in the brisk and businesslike mood of the airport. Even as she started walking toward the baggage claim, she knew that her red leather thongs, fancy and gold-lined to match her sari, were most unsuitable to protect her feet from the cold snow outside.

There were no porters to help her take her bags off the revolving baggage-claim rack. Lugging her bags into one corner, she took out her diary again and called Kris. The same familiar ring of the telephone echoing in his apartment. But no Kris.

A worker at the information booth got her a luggage cart and offered to help her get a taxicab. A biting wind cut through Rina's ears as she stepped outside the air terminal. Her eyes stung and her fingers turned red and numb. She could see her breath come out in great white puffs. She quite forgot to notice—until she got into the taxicab—that her toes curled as her thin leather thongs touched the subzero temperatures of the curb.

The cab driver had no trouble taking Rina to her husband's apartment complex in Salt Lake City. She sought out the manager's apartment first. She had neither dollars to pay for the cab nor keys to get into the apartment. Rina felt secure that the manager could take care of those essentials.

Hank, the manager, eyed her minutely as he dialed Kris's number again. "He's not home, lady," he said.

Rina took out her passport to prove that she was Kris's wife.

"Okay, I'll take you to the apartment," he said finally, still eyeing her.

They carried the bags up one flight of stairs. Hank threw open the door and gestured to Rina to step in as he started pulling her bags inside.

The living room was quietly lit. Some strange rock music thumped from the adjacent room, and Rina felt relieved that Kris could not really be away for long. Perhaps he had just received the telegram and rushed to the airport.

As she turned to the manager to thank him, she saw a sudden bewildered look in his eyes, and she turned her head back with lightning speed.

Kris, half clad, was standing in the doorway inside. "What the fuck is going on?" he shouted at the manager. "How dare you break into my apartment?"

Then his eyes fell on Rina. "You, h—here?" he stammered, as he stepped back momentarily. Then he collected himself and fell into a rage. "Who asked you to come here?" he yelled. "You didn't even have the courtesy to inform me." Then he glared at Hank. "Why the hell didn't you call me before bringing her here?"

Rina stepped back just as a disheveled woman walked out of the bedroom, wrapping her robe around her.

What a moment! All hell is breaking loose on me, Rina thought, as she flopped to the floor cupping her ears in her palms and burying her face in her knees.

She heard Hank say, "I sure called you, Kris, just before I brought her, but you didn't answer."

"Don't you dare lie to me," Kris hollered.

"Honey, I'm sorry," said the woman, "I turned the ringer off on the telephone yesterday and forgot to turn it on again."

Rina raised her head above her knees and looked up. "Didn't you get Appa's telegram? We sent it three days ago."

"Damn! The ringer off!" said Kris. "Now the telegram will come tomorrow by mail."

Hank had disappeared by now. The woman retreated back into the bedroom. Kris rushed into the bedroom after her and rolled a bundle toward Rina.

"I can't deal with all this now," he said. "Here is a sleeping bag for you to use tonight. The bathroom is right there," he pointed out. "You will have to go back to your father as soon as possible—perhaps even tomorrow, if connecting international flights are available. Let's talk about it in the morning before I go to work."

He vanished into the bedroom, banging the door after him. She could hear the two of them whispering inside. At times the whispers reached urgent crescendos, but she could not understand what they were saying. She was too tired to care. She lay on the sleeping bag, looking at the ceiling with tinsel flecks that seemed to glower at her. She did not turn off the light. All alone, she needed the light.

Rina rolled up the sleeping bag feverishly when she heard noises inside the bedroom next morning. She straightened out her crumpled sari, ran her fingers through her hair as a comb, and rebraided her hair.

Kris walked out of the bedroom, fully dressed for work. He put a cereal box and a bowl on the dining table. "Here's your breakfast," he said tersely. "There is milk in the refrigerator. The tea bags are in the cupboard somewhere. Make yourself comfortable. I'll reserve your return flight today. You'll need sleep to get over your jet lag anyway."

"I am not going back," Rina heard herself say. "I am here now. I can't go back."

Kris banged a fist on the table. "I don't have time to talk to you now," he said, "but you'll have to go. It serves them right for forcing me to get married during my two-week visit to India. Damn! What a mess!"

"I'll stay, even if I have to make a police case," she said. "I can't go back now. I am married to you."

Kris beckoned to the woman inside the bedroom, and they walked out. She did not even look at Rina.

Rina was in deep slumber when the doorbell rang insistently. She woke up with a start and peered through the viewer eye. A young blonde woman was standing with a brown paper bag in her hand. Rina opened the door cautiously as the woman smiled.

"My name is Linda," said the stranger as she stretched out her hand toward Rina. "I live in these apartments, one floor above. Hank told me you arrived last night. I have brought a little casserole to welcome you."

The two women stood inspecting each other. Rina felt assured by the stranger's warmth. She pressed the outstretched hand in hers and asked the visitor to step in. Suddenly she felt all her strength and resolve ebb out of her. Even as she closed the door and asked Linda to take a seat, she broke into a sob. Then she sobbed and sobbed uncontrollably as Linda comforted her.

"I am so sorry," said Linda gently. "Hank told me."

Rina was grateful she didn't have to explain.

"What are you going to do now?" inquired Linda.

"First I have to send my father a telegram to say I have reached Utah safely and that I am very happy," smiled Rina bitterly. "Please, can you help me?"

"No problem," said Linda. "I sent telegrams to my brother when he was in Lima on a mission for the Church of Jesus Christ of Latter-day Saints."

While they ate the macaroni and tuna casserole, they composed the message Linda was to send through Western Union. Linda was very perplexed about the previous night's episode. "I don't understand why Kris married you in the first place," she said, "if he didn't want you to come here."

Every now and then, she shook her head in disbelief, as if she were still trying to figure out a puzzle. "Mindy has been living here for the last two months at least," she confided. And before she left, Linda promised to visit her again the next afternoon.

As Rina waited for Kris to come home, her lips chanted silent hymns to goddess Durga. She needed to be brave first. The other two goddesses, Saraswati and Lakshmi, could wait—she didn't need to be wise or rich right away.

A little before six o'clock, Kris and Mindy walked into the house. Mindy made a beeline for the bedroom. Kris faced Rina.

"Look," he said, "I have made arrangements for your return flight. There is a direct flight from Salt Lake leaving at 2:00 p.m. tomorrow that will take you into New York in time to catch Air India."

"You heard me this morning," she said. "I am not leaving."

"The hell you are not," Kris banged his fist on the table.

With a lightning impulse, Rina banged her fist harder on the table. The tinkle of her green glass bangles, given to her as bridal fertility symbols, echoed through the air as three of them shattered and careened all over the kitchen floor.

"Two people can bang fists," she said. "Why don't we sit and talk? Tell me how you plan to get us out of this mess."

Kris reluctantly sat down to talk. He finally agreed to accommodate her. "Okay, okay," he said. "I'll let you move into the second bedroom—which I see you have already occupied. But don't get ideas. This won't work. I never wanted to marry you. I'll have to divorce you as soon as possible. I have no obligations to you of any kind—not even for alimony."

"Can you help me get admission at the university for a master's degree?"

Kris shook his head. "Nope," he said tersely. "You can't make it here. You will squirm until you are ready to fly home." He looked at her for a long time before he got up from his chair. "I'll force you to go home, one way or another," he said under his breath as he walked to his bedroom.

Back in her room, Rina pulled out the aerogram she had found on the table that afternoon. She began writing to her parents:

Dear Amma and Appa,

Trust the telegram we sent has reached you by now. I had a very good and comfortable journey all the way.

Dear husband was at the airport to receive me. We are very happy. He is busy at work and will get even busier—he was just promoted to a higher position in his company today! He says it is all due to my auspicious arrival.

The long journey here gave me time to think of all that you both have done for me—my education at the exclusive St. Ann's High School and Osmania University. And all that expense for my wedding! How can I ever thank you enough?

I plan to continue my education. I want to get a master's in business administration. Dear husband wants me to do anything I please. How lucky I am.

In the next two or three years, we plan to send you tickets to visit us. Will you come see me? Please tell my friends I will write to them in due time. Our love to all at home. Ask Pinky and Babbu to write.

Your affectionate daughter,
Rina

For the first time since she arrived in Salt Lake City, Rina drew the drapes of her windows and looked out. Under a full moon, the entire valley stretched out supine below the mountains. Strange shapes stood out against the sky in the clear light of the moon or clustered around the floor of the valley. The bright moon had banished most of the little stars, but the city streetlights sparkled in parallel rows up to the horizon. Long icicles hung down from the eaves of the windows like the flowing beard of some ancient watchman. In time she would have to befriend these shapes and learn to love them, she mused. She picked up the only book that was in the room—*Vector Analysis*—and read herself to sleep.

When she woke up at 9:00 in the morning, the house was empty. The sink was full of breakfast dishes. The *Salt Lake Tribune* lay unopened on the table. She poured herself some cereal and milk and started to read the newspaper. The gas heater kept puffing out warm air into the apartment, keeping at bay the frigid cold invading from outside. In spite of her own anxieties, Rina admired the ingenuity of the American way of life. She waited for Linda to visit.

"Can you help me get admission to the University of Utah?" Rina asked her that afternoon.

"How will you pay your tuition and fees?"

"I can work at the cafeteria and make a thousand dollars a month."

"A thousand dollars at the cafeteria?" laughed Linda. "Who told you that? It would take you three months of work to collect a thousand dollars. And who will admit you before you pay your tuition?"

Rina sighed.

"I can help you get work at K-Mart," said Linda. "I used to work there. But you'll have to buy some work clothes. Do you have money to buy clothes?" Linda did not have any to lend her. Her husband was away for two weeks. Rina cried silently.

Not knowing how to cheer her up, Linda took her for a spin around the city. Rina thought Salt Lake City was beautiful. So clean. She looked wistfully at the buildings as they drove around the university. *She* would have sold her soul to change places with any of those college students, she thought. And the mall! She could not imagine how all the stores were wide open, with goods lying everywhere for anybody to walk out with! How she coveted a couple of pairs of jeans and a few blouses to tide her over until she got a job.

Linda and Rina had to go to Hank to enter Rina's apartment. "Can't you give her another key?" Linda asked him.

"In return for what?" he asked, looking at Rina. "Oh, well, not until Kris asks me to," he added.

"What if he doesn't?" Linda asked.

Hank laughed and shrugged his shoulders as he descended the stairs.

It was Friday and Linda was to visit her parents and a sister in Bountiful, ten miles away, over the weekend. She promised to see Rina again on Monday. She had brought her some books to read. Rina was afraid of facing Kris and Mindy over the weekend. She had so far avoided seeing them altogether. She came out of her room in the mornings only after they left. She took refuge in her room before they came home, and she never came out for anything until they had retired for the night. The weekend, Rina knew, was going to be difficult. How was she going to · avoid seeing them?

On Saturday morning Rina lay in bed as long as she could. She heard noises in the kitchen for a while and then the noises ceased. When she finally ventured out into the kitchen, there was nobody in the house. The table had not been cleared. The milk was still on the counter. Rina ate her breakfast cereal, read the newspaper, and settled down to watch TV.

The day was long without Linda's visit.

Around 9:00 p.m., the doorbell rang and Rina peeped out with apprehension. It was Hank. She told him nobody was home. He had come to give her a message, he said. Kris and Mindy had left in the morning to spend a weekend at Alta Lodge, the ski resort.

"So you need money to get started?" he said, as he entered the apartment. "Linda told me everything," he said. "I am here to help you. I don't have much money, but I'll give you what I can. Repay me in whatever way you can."

Rina mumbled her thanks as he put a wad of bills on the coffee table.

"No interest for you, honey," he said, looking at Rina intently. "I'll take your friendship instead. I like you. I am here to help you."

He thrust his arm toward Rina, but she pulled away, and his arm grabbed the air.

"You want money; don't you, honey?" he said with deliberation. "You need a job. I am your friend. I'll help you."

Hank walked slowly toward Rina, who had pulled herself against the wall, and put his arms gently round her. "Don't be afraid of me, honey," he said, as he pulled her to him. "I won't harm you. That husband of yours is a rat. He doesn't deserve you. I like you so much, I could fall in love with you." He started kissing her, gently at first, then passionately all over her body. Rina closed her eyes tightly and clenched her fists as, there on the living room carpet, he pressed her down and lifted her sari and made love to her.

Rina's tears brimmed over her closed eyes and ran down her temples. "Please don't cry," said Hank, alarmed. "I don't want to hurt you.

Please stop crying." Later, before he left, he assured her, "I'll buy you some work clothes tomorrow."

He came again the next morning with a couple of cinnamon rolls and an appetite for sex. "I'll give you everything you need, honey," he said.

Rina spent the morning in a daze as he took her out shopping and helped her buy inexpensive snow boots, gloves, and a couple of outfits on sale. He drove her to McDonald's for lunch and showered her with kindness. When he brought her home, he even presented her with a key to the apartment. Rina was grateful.

Things seemed to move fast after that. With Linda's help, Rina got a job at K-Mart and started working right away.

It was past 9:00 p.m. when Rina walked the city block back to the apartment from her first day at work. Kris and Mindy were watching TV in the living room. Kris was aghast to see Rina walk in wearing pants and a sweater.

"Where the hell have you been so late?" Kris shouted. "And in these Western clothes? Whom are you going out with? Have you no shame?"

"Not any more than you do," she said. "I am working now. Have to make a living."

Mindy retreated in haste as Kris motioned her to leave them alone. He wanted to talk to Rina. "Tell me, where are you working? How did you get the job? Who helped you?" he asked.

"That is hardly of interest to you, is it?" she said. "I'll make enough to take care of myself."

"I have no choice now but to divorce you and throw you out as soon as possible," he said. "I want to marry Mindy."

Linda had the strangest solution to Rina's crisis. "Tell him to go ahead and marry Mindy," she said. "You could all three live together happily. Bigamy is an offense only under law," she smiled. "Nobody gets punished for bigamy."

"You are so inventive," Rina laughed. "How can you think of such outlandish ideas?"

On Rina's day off, they went to visit Linda's sister. The snow was falling lightly as they started out. The city fell behind them abruptly and the countryside lay ahead, pristine and alluring. They drove close to the mountains, crossing a number of snow-clad apple, peach, and cherry orchards. Linda showed her Sister Rochelle's home from a distance. It lay sprawling on a wide expanse of acreage. A small orchard nestled close to the house at the foot of the mountain. What appeared to be a flowing creek behind the house lay frozen into a picture of stillness for the season.

Rochelle, heavy and very pregnant, came out to greet them. Two little children trailed after her and looked at Rina shyly from behind their mother's apron. The home was furnished sparingly. The smell of fresh-baked bread wafted into Rina's nostrils. It reminded her of Royal Bakery just behind her parents' home in Hyderabad. Entering a home—a real home with a mother and children in it—overwhelmed Rina momentarily. She blinked back her tears as she bent down and picked up the little girl. Rochelle led them to the kitchen, where a rustic-looking table was laid out with six place settings.

"Sister Rochelle is a great cook," said Linda. After a while, she added, "Are you surprised I call her Sister Rochelle?"

"No," said Rina. "We do it in India, too. My brother and sister call me 'Rina Didi'—didi means older sister."

Rochelle and Linda looked at each other but didn't say anything. Just then Rochelle's husband came home from work.

"This is our husband, Rulon," said Sister Rochelle. "Our husband?" repeated Rina in her mind but didn't have time to think about the matter. Rochelle pulled out the rolls from the oven, and Rulon strapped the children in their high chairs. He said grace in a beautiful voice. He thanked the Lord for the nourishing food, for all that he had, for Rochelle and the children, and Linda, and Rina too. It was a good meal and the talk was congenial.

Rina felt very at home in their company. It was obvious from the conversation that Linda had been prudent enough to let her family know Rina's circumstances. Neither Rochelle nor Rulon asked her uncomfortable questions. They only asked her about her life in India and her family back home.

After dinner Rulon said he would show her their home and surrounding property while Rochelle and Linda did the dishes. He told her about his job and his very comfortable salary. He talked about his religion, too. He belonged to a group that had broken away from the main Church of Jesus Christ of Latter-day Saints, because the church had moved away from divinely ordained family values.

"We meet in different private homes every week," he told her. "Please visit us with Linda next Sunday. The services will be held here in our home," he said.

Rina had to decline because she worked that weekend.

Rulon was a handsome and God-fearing man who spoke of Rochelle and Linda with great affection. "You are truly like a sister to them," he said. "Even I would like to make you one of us. The Lord wills it so." Rina had been warned about the missionary zeal of Utahans and was not surprised.

On the way back, Linda asked Rina if she liked her husband.

"You know I have not met him yet, Linda," said Rina.

"Sister Rochelle and I are both lucky to be married to Rulon," Linda said in a whisper.

Nobody spoke for a long while after that. The whir of the wheels and the hum of the engine were almost too much for Rina to bear. *That's why Linda suggested Kris could marry Mindy and all three of us could live happily in the same home thereafter*, she thought. How strange! Did Rulon live two weeks with Rochelle and the other two with Linda? Was that why he was away from her even though he worked in town? Rina shuddered as she gave an involuntary sigh.

"It is very nice to be a plural wife," said Linda softly.

"What?" said Rina.

"We got married only five months ago," Linda continued. "Rulon is going to add another wing to the home, so I could live there too. I am going to have a baby at the end of summer, Rina." Her eyes glistened in the dark as she continued to pour forth what was on her mind. "Would you like to come and live with us? Rulon would like to add two wings —one for you and one for me—if you are willing. You won't ever have to work again. Rulon is a wonderful husband and provider. He will love you as much as he loves us."

They were just pulling into the carport by then. They both got out of the car in total silence and started climbing the stairs. At the top of the stairs, Rina held Linda's hands. "You've been a wonderful friend," she said. "How can I thank you enough for everything?"

Then she started walking down the long corridor to her apartment, fumbling into her handbag for her key, dreading to face another night and another day.

Moazzam Sheikh

Statement: What draws us to Canada and the United States, and what we find for ourselves in America while we overlook or forget that this country was founded on genocide and slavery, is very perplexing to me. I wonder how future South Asian Americans will interact with the members of other races and colors. I also wonder if we South Asians as a community are being used as a buffer zone between the dominant Euro-American society and the minority communities in the making of an American society. I ask myself if we should keep our South Asian cultures alive in the United States or should we assimilate. I constantly run into a figurative brick wall constructed of these questions. And so I write. Yet although this land of opportunities and freedom (I will not argue with that) provides many of us with better space and air, the systematic sterility, political or literary, can dry up our pens and make us suffocate. The Turkish poet Nazim Hikmet says that the point is not to give up.

The wry humor of "Kissing the Holy Land" tends to soften the frustration, the pain, and the shock of the encounter between cultures experienced by the protagonist of the story. It is interesting to note that the South Asian narrator as well as the Americans he encounters at the airport indulge in the stereotyping of one another. The protagonist's early excitement of being in America is very quickly marred by his discovery that his money has been stolen by one of the "American President–looking" men he has been admiring earlier. "Kissing the Holy Land" and the selection from Bapsi Sidhwa's *An American Brat* are amusing and informative variations on the autobiographical selection from Ved Mehta's *Sound-Shadows of the New World*.

Kissing the Holy Land

The bitter taste of coffee was still in my mouth when the captain announced the landing. I felt the invisible coffee grains on the tip of my tongue and feeling irritated I spat them out between my right armrest and the window, making sure no one was witnessing this. My cousin, Sultana, was famous for reading coffee cups. In mine she had seen a bear with wings, green mountains, and an ocean. It all made sense now; I was going to California. I had arrived in New York, my port of entry, from

Pakistan on a TWA plane and was now bound for San Francisco. This was the first time I had ever left my country.

My father had lived in New York for two years in the early fifties, and since then he had always been in love with the Big Apple. He took great delight in telling us about his stay in New York. He told his stories over and over again, driving everyone nuts. One of his favorite tales was about his arrival at the Hotel Ambassador. A tall, handsome white man in his twenties, with blue eyes and blonde hair, stood waiting in his crisp clothes for my father. He advanced in my dad's direction to take charge of his suitcases. It was as if the East India Company had invaded again. My father felt unprepared for this. He simply was not ready to let a white man who resembled his ex-master carry his luggage. My father thought that all whites were related. On seeing the white man bend his knees to take the suitcases, my father felt as if someone had dropped a *fanoos*, a huge chandelier, on his head. Pulling his suitcases closer to himself, he shrank with fear.

"Good morning, sir. You must be Mr. Malik," the bellboy said with a smile. My father at last understood that this man was not directly related to the Queen of England.

Things have changed. My mother warned me strictly against taking a stroll in any inch of New York City. People who came told stories of what could happen to them in cities like New York, Detroit, or Los Angeles. With all these thoughts I shuffled out of the plane onto the land that was famous for the Statue of Liberty.

I, along with other non-Americans, was going to be interviewed by an immigration officer. I was nervous. I had known a man back home who was deported twice from the States. He did not give up and got in the third time. He had told me that he hated people who worked for immigration. Finally my turn came, and it seemed as if the officer did not like my face to begin with. He asked me stupid questions about why I had come to this country and how I got the visa and so on. I was about to choke and pass out under the barrage of questions when he let me go with a sarcastic nod. I was discouraged by his lack of hospitality.

I was flying to San Francisco from New York in three hours, and I had to spend those hours at the airport. I walked from one airline counter to another, one waiting area to a different one, establishing imaginary friendships, nodding my head in approving gestures as if it were okay with me if strangers wanted to share the same roof of the airport with me. I had put my luggage in a locker and was free to move unencumbered through Kennedy Airport. I admired American presidents.

I was thinking of Mr. Kennedy at the time I happened to walk by an American family. The man looked surprisingly like John F. Kennedy. He had the same seductive eyes, tempting lips, and arched eyebrows. His sons looked like little Kennedys to me. I must have been staring at them for some time when I noticed that one of the little Kennedys was noticing me. I quickly turned my eyes to a TV screen about six inches away from the boy's head, pretending that I had not noticed him. I thought that this Kennedy family did not want any media attention.

People said "excuse me" or "pardon me" every time they bumped into me. My hand reached into my pocket to see if my wallet was still there. But I was getting better at dodging people, who seemed to be deliberately taking aim at my shoulders. I reached the big cafeteria section, and with a look of confidence I started to read the menu beneath the neon signs. I searched for familiar dishes. I must have stood in one position for a good fifteen minutes reading the menu up and down, left and right, getting more and more indecisive. A young woman behind the cash register noticed my confusion and asked, "May I help you, sir?" I was mesmerized by her voice and I looked in her direction. She repeated her question. "Why did she not work for immigration?" I wondered. I mumbled something to her that she could not make any sense of. I tried mumbling again, but this time the sound did not come out. She gave up on me, as a new customer walked up to her. My fear transformed my English into some kind of an ancient language. Becoming embarrassed, I left.

But her face was stuck in my head. Her face grew like a small red apple with two grapelike eyes. A light blue ribbon curled around her ponytail. I still hung out in the same lobby. I hid behind a gigantic pillar. I was good at hiding from women I liked and desired. The image of her face increased my hunger. I went back to the restaurant. The name tag on her shirt said "McDonald's . . . Tasha . . . Have a nice day." I was not sure whether her name was McDonald's or Tasha.

"May I help you?"

My ears waited for her to finish the sentence, but she repeated the same thing, "May I help you?" Nervous, I said, "I . . . would . . ." She leaned forward, resting one hand on the counter in order to hear me better. Her leaning made me feel very uncomfortable about my ability to speak English. I raised my finger in the direction of the menu, as if in protest. The line was piling up behind me. She turned, like a ballerina, to look where my finger pointed and got me a cup of coffee. My first cup of coffee in America. "Why did she not call me sir this time?" I was puzzled.

Holding my coffee, I walked away from her, dejectedly. A man almost knocked the coffee out of my hands, but I dodged him. He smiled and said, "Pardon me, sir." A gush of blood ran through my arteries. I took a good look at his face as he scooted past me. Astonishingly, he resembled the late president Lincoln. The same beard and the freckled cheeks. I thought he must be related to President Lincoln's family. I felt lucky to run into people from distinguished families. I stole a seat in the corner of a lounge and, as I sipped my coffee, thought about Tasha or McDonald's. I checked my money. It was still there.

I was looking at a woman who sat opposite me. She seemed to be in her early twenties, and her face was as fresh as a newly blossomed flower. She crossed her legs and looked in my direction. As I was slicing my heart for her, a man showed up and sat next to her. He had two beer bottles in his hands. I had seen beer before. She took one from his hand and clinked it with his before she sipped from her bottle. It made me a little depressed. But I was impressed by the fact that one could drink alcohol at such places. That was not possible in Pakistan. In Pakistan one could not even drink in one's own living room. I understood the value of freedom to drink. I wanted a beer. I wanted to celebrate. I wanted a beer to celebrate my first day in America.

I got myself a chilled Dutch beer and searched for a nice and comfortable place to sit down and enjoy my first drink. I chose a seat next to a big window through which I could see one side of the runway. I watched the planes land and take off. The beer had a strange taste at first, as if rotten fruits were crushed inside. But with a few gulps, as my stomach cried "fire," I started to feel good. I had heard that people could get drunk if they did not stop in time. I was curious to know what it would be like being drunk. The Koran declared that drinking was a sin. I remembered that my mother and the mullah in the mosque backed it up. "Too much of everything is bad." I promised myself to stick to only one bottle. I felt relaxed.

I remember what else I felt: I felt that the world and its people were beautiful. Their eyes, noses, and lips and the sounds they made were beautiful. Their clothes, shoes, and the cars they drove, the McDonald's neon signs and the animals and the sounds they uttered were beautiful. The people who worked for immigration and the people who were deported were beautiful. Armies were beautiful and the towns and the people they wiped out were also beautiful. I felt my head was spinning a little faster now. The movies, actors, actresses, directors and writers, composers and singers, stunt fighters, the extras, and the audiences were beautiful. The presidents of America and of other countries, the students, the teachers, the editors, the newscasters, the milkmen, the postmen, the Olympic stars, the businessmen, and smugglers and the federal security officers who were hired to catch the smugglers were all beautiful. I thought New York, all fruits, vegetables, all meats, lentils, rice, wheat, rye, corn, and the entire concept of eating were beautiful. The concept of love and all the love stories . . . and I thought money . . . yes, money was beautiful, very beautiful.

The first bottle of beer had been consumed to its full extent and justified. I do not remember getting up and buying myself another beer. I simply do not. My head was spinning like an atom in a smasher, and my bladder informed the atom upstairs that it was going to explode any moment. Just one and a half bottles had knocked all the senses out of my switcher. I got scared. So I did a little praying to God and myself and tried to channel all the energy from different pressure points of my body to one focus, my knees, and I said, "You can do it."

My knees showed some strength and dignity, and my hips elevated my existence about six inches from the seat. I stayed in that position for two minutes as if I had frozen in a snowstorm.

"You can do it," I repeated and fell back to where I had been two minutes before. I felt a jolt in my head. The beer ice-skated inside my skull furiously and tried to seep out through the joints. I thought I had fallen from grace. My head spun in the opposite direction now, and a feeling of nausea overcame me. I was worried. I rose up with some effort and whispered, "You can do it, you can do it."

The good news was that I was walking, walking towards the restroom, and nobody was bumping into me. No one was saying "I am sorry" or "pardon me" or "excuse me." As I had just thought of opening the door, it opened by itself. Actually, a man who looked like a carbon copy of Nixon was walking out. He saw my face and preferred to stand aside, making room for me. I slipped in. It was hard to walk straight with a spinning head. My bladder guided me to the urinal. I rested my head against the water pipe while I unzipped. The water pipe was as cold as the chilled beer. I took a piss and fell asleep, resting my head against the pipe. But a man's laughter sent a tremor up my spine as it undazed me. His face looked extremely familiar. But before I could figure anything out, he was out of sight. I zipped up and began to walk out.

Once again, a man opened the door just before I could touch the handle. The man facing me looked worried as soon as he saw me. My knees betrayed me as I passed him. I fell like an eagle shot down.

"Are you all right?" I heard his concerned voice. I was so ashamed that I refused to understand his language. I tried to get up, but the armies of will power had been crushed. However, involuntarily, my hand reached for my pocket. It was as if my hand moved into the zone of void. There was nothing. The money was gone, the entire wallet vanished. My hand groped for the slightest trace of money, helplessly. The empty pocket felt very tragic. I began crying hysterically. "Which president's relative could have stolen my money?" By now my body had converted into an elegant arc from hips to head, with the admirers around. I rested my head on the carpet and cried and cried.

I heard the same voice: "Are you okay?" The man put his hand on my shoulder. "He seems sick; let me call a doctor."

Right then I heard another voice: "No! No, no, no . . . He's kissing his new homeland. He's happy; he's crying with emotions, I think. I did the same ten years ago. Right, pal? He's not sick. He's kissing the holy land. Hey, man! Welcome to America." The man delivered his speech with spark and passion, and left.

An older man, with an accent, bent next to me and whispered in my left ear, "You must love this country. Welcome, young man. Whoever pays taxes, this country belongs to him."

Ranbir Sidhu

Statement: The author writes that his writings speak for him.

The title of this story, "Border Song," could be an apt title for this anthology. We see a South Asian woman's introduction to the different aspects of American life and her adjustment to her new homeland through the eyes of her young nephew. As we see the South Asian American family in this story living in America, we gradually hear the memories that the aunt has carried with her in the form of stories and songs as she crossed political and geographical borders. She recalls the violence and the sorrow that accompanied the 1947 partition of India into India and Pakistan. As she explains why she sings all the time, we realize that her experience of her first border crossing, away from her village to another part of India, is still a vital part of her life in America. Through her stories she passes on to her nephew the memories of India's political and historical past.

Border Song

Bikram sang. Usually old Punjabi or Hindi movie tunes, but her repertoire had expanded since moving to California. She had learned the theme to M*A*S*H and all the songs on Abba's *Greatest Hits Volume One*. She sang all the time. Her voice echoed the rhythm of frogs that had invaded her childhood nights with their persistent croaking. She filled up the spaces of the house with her songs, and she let her songs breathe outside—in the garden, in the busy, cramped aisles at the Safeway, during those hours she spent alone, when everyone was out, gone to work or to school. Song was gold jewelry that she carried with her from country to country, across freshly painted borders. Now it seemed an heirloom, an artifact of some previous life.

Her nephew, Ravi, when he was young, believed she sang only for him. She had a beautiful voice then. High and sharp and full of force and energy. It belied her small, self-effacing frame always covered by an old silk sari and one of the many new jackets Harbans often brought back for her from the store. These were 49ers jackets, or Charlie's Angels or The Who tour jackets; all promotionals that had been sent to one of Harbans' convenience stores. Bikram almost never talked. She expressed herself through the long silences of her songs, and only reverted to Punjabi or English, often a mixture, when a song wouldn't say it.

Some years later, when Ravi was older, he would see how she always sang, or hummed or muttered to herself, and it would seem a betrayal. Always to herself, and never to another person. He saw that it wasn't for him, had never been for him. His aunt wasn't his private songster. Bikram became somehow defective, and her voice the manifestation of a person unhinged or askew.

Almost the only times she stopped singing willingly was to tell a story. Ravi treasured such times. His aunt became real. His own mother never told stories. She worked late and was always gone when he fell asleep, often to the thickening night of his aunt's voice.

When Bikram spoke, her body stirred to the rhythm of her singing. You could see it in the way her lips moved—they were trying to sing, trying to reform words into melody. But her voice was far from songlike. It was awkward and uneven, disturbed by the strange junctures that existed in speech. A word became unreal on her tongue—it only lost this weight of speech when connected to a tune, when it slowly merged into the next word of a song.

Every story she told was different, mutated from a previous version. A leopard in one story became a frog in another. A crow slighted in one became the antagonist in the next. The roles of alligator and bird reversed; in one, the alligator ate the bird, but in a future version, the bird, like a snake, unhinged its jaw and swallowed the writhing, snapping form of the alligator, right down to the struggling tail. Ravi was never disturbed by these inconsistencies, or at least he never showed any surprise at the transubstantiation of mouse into elephant or tiger into hyena. They were no more curious than an aunt, mad, who sang, and one, sane, who told stories.

One day Bikram told the story of the dying King and his three children.

The old King knew he was dying, and he was unsure of who among his children, two sons and a daughter, would succeed him. He decided to hold a contest. He gave each child a hundred pieces of gold, and the one who filled the hundred rooms and the great hall of the palace completely by using just this money would be the future ruler. The eldest son quickly took his money off to the market. This was no problem for him. He spent all the money on sacks of coal, and soon there was a procession of donkey carts leading up to the palace. But the unloaded coal barely filled a quarter of the great hall and left all the other rooms quite empty— and it made a mess and took several days to clean up. The second eldest, the other son, laughed at his brother's mistake. He also walked down the hill to the market and spent his one hundred pieces of gold on sacks of wool. A far longer procession than the previous soon wound its way up to the palace. But the

*unloaded wool only filled the great hall, and left the rest of the palace empty —
and it was even harder to clean all the small tufts of wool from the carpets and
the chairs and the tapestries and from behind the chairs and from the lamps on
the walls and ceiling. The youngest, the daughter, thought about her brothers'
mistakes and soon she disappeared and was not seen again. The two brothers
laughed. They told the King that their sister had run away in fear and taken the
money for herself. But the King told his sons to hold judgment. After some time
the daughter reappeared, and behind her there was a procession of one hundred
men and women. The brothers laughed again. Surely they had won now, if this
was all she could muster. They had already decided to split the kingdom between
themselves when the old man died. The daughter, however, placed a single person in each of the hundred rooms of the palace, and she placed herself in the great
hall. On her word every single person began to sing, and the palace was filled
completely with their voices. She had won the right to become Queen. She didn't
become Queen, however. When the King died, the two brothers conspired and
murdered their sister and split the Kingdom between themselves. For the rest of
their lives the two new Kingdoms were ever at war, and all singing was banned.*

It was 1964 when Bikram and Harbans left India and moved to
California. Bikram didn't know why they moved. She didn't want to, but
then, a new bride, one who had been so hard to find a husband for, she
was told not to ask. All her friends, her whole family, told her through
their parting tears to be happy, to rejoice. She was going to where they all
wanted to go. She didn't ask then why they were all crying as though she
were a corpse, as though this parting was only the start of long years of
mourning.

For two years they lived in Oakland, by Lake Merritt. She could see
it from the single window of their apartment. In the summer, the sunsets
glistened red and orange and sometimes pink. Harbans spent most of his
hours away. He said he was trying to start a business, though he never
told her what kind of business. He said he was having "meetings," "discussions," and that soon they would be "in the money." Every day
Bikram walked the two blocks down to the grocery store where she
could find nothing she wanted and so had to buy everything she didn't
want. Once she walked out to the lake but found that the people stared
harshly at her in her sari, and when she looked down into the water it
was dirty. Gasoline and oil stained the lake surface and Coca-Cola bottles
and tin cans bobbed like dead fish.

One day Harbans said that they were now "in the money." They
moved out of Oakland and into the hills where there were almost no
houses yet, and Bikram could no longer walk to the grocery store but
instead had to rely on Harbans or travel with him once a week on
Saturdays. Eventually, she learned how to drive, but this was years later
when her sister-in-law Jyoti taught her. Jyoti had come from England.

Her husband had died. Her husband had been Harbans' younger brother, and so Harbans offered Jyoti a home for herself and her two children, Ravi and Meena.

Before Jyoti arrived the house had been unfurnished. They hadn't the money to buy furniture yet. It would be some time, Harbans told her. Instead, Bikram filled the rooms with her voice. She spent her days roaming from empty room to empty room singing or telling stories to herself. There was a single step that led down into the living room from the hallway. It seemed such a luxury, this single step. Sometimes for a whole hour she would sit on it, staring at the far blank wall, humming blandly, only occasionally standing up to relish the step fully by stepping down and then back up into the hallway.

It was several years before she came to be on talking terms with the neighbors. For Harbans, it had been much sooner. Some of the men had come up to him early on, running an admiring palm across the smooth, clean curves of his new Chevrolet. When Harbans was gone, no one ever padded in sneakers up the laid-stone path that bifurcated the balanced halves of the front lawn. Instead, when Bikram was out watering the lawn or planting bulbs or herbs, she would notice the neighbors only by the slight darkened triangle of a pushed-back curtain. In the triangle, the vague shape of a face appeared, not moving. Sometimes there were as many as five or six such triangles with dark moon hidden faces peering suspiciously through the freshly cleaned glass.

It was Ravi who changed this. He had a bursting energy that couldn't be contained by the low brick wall at the bottom of the front lawn. His body found itself in neighbors' gardens, or playing in the backs of their trucks. Occasionally he would have to be brought home, lost, confused. He might have wandered into an unfamiliar house thinking it his own or hurt himself playing with a neighbor's kid. And when the neighbors walked him home, they had to stop to chat, to ask how the rose-bushes were coming this year and whether Bikram was having trouble with skunks or gophers. They told her about the new freeway coming through and that soon many more houses would be built up in the hills where everybody knew the ground was unstable and liable to slide.

After a couple of years of drought, deer started appearing in the street late at night. Harbans would come home telling of a deer he almost collided with on the new freeway off-ramp. Bikram would see them in the mottled, predawn hours. She still always woke early, before anyone else in the house. It was instinctive, she felt, this early rising. She no longer had cows to milk or chickens to feed, but her childhood habit had stayed with her.

The deer had looked like outlines from her dreams the first time she saw them. She hadn't expected deer in California, in suburban California. This was the civilized world where animals and people were kept separated. But she guessed that the deer didn't know this. When dawn silhouetted the backs of the houses visible through the kitchen window, she noticed that her roses had disappeared. Just the flowers were gone. They were all eaten by the deer.

Bikram had inspected the neatly cut stalks. The deer had left few traces. Their hoofs left only slight scars, indistinct chevrons in the moist, dew-spotted soil. She covered up the tracks with her own hands, smudging them with her fingers until all that was left were lines from her hands. Back inside in the kitchen, she diligently washed her fingertips first, and then her hands and last her forearms.

She wasn't surprised when she heard the rifle shots, not too far away. Every morning for two weeks she heard them. Twice she saw the carcasses of the deer, no longer shadows or dream shapes, lying on the crisp, golden hillside where she sometimes took an afternoon walk. Their mouths gaped open and their bodies looked ugly, beginning to swell in the heat. The smell didn't affect her. She had approached one carcass and examined it closely. Around the gums and teeth flies and bugs and maggots already swarmed. The hide was full of holes where it had been eaten away. The eyes bulged yellow. Puss escaped from the sockets.

One evening she sat Ravi down beside her on the single step that led down from the hallway and into the living room. The living room was now furnished. A sofa and love seat faced a color RCA TV set. There was an imported Persian rug on the floor, and on the wall was a wide-view portrait of the Golden Temple. Bikram asked Ravi if he wanted to hear the real story of how she had begun to sing, and Ravi nodded, though he asked Auntiji to be quick, for the new episode of *Lost in Space* was about to be on.

"This is how it happened," she said. She had never claimed this before. Outside it was cool. A bright orange scarf of muslin clouds half hid the setting sun, half showed it, as though the day itself was ambivalent about its own nature. Bikram wasn't sure if she really knew what happened, or how she did in fact begin to sing. The memories were all confused now. They had merged with songs and the different versions she had told, versions she knew were false but now was unable to wholly extricate from her memory of those days before the rupture. "It was dawn. No, before dawn. One morning dawn broke early, before it should have, and that was how it all started. Dawn broke on the west side of the village, the side where I'd take the buffalo down to the creek for her afternoon drink and where the Mantos had a house. Mrs. Manto would call me in as I walked by and hand me a glass of lychee if it was hot. It always tasted so sweet, so freshening. There was nothing like it. Still not. You can't make real lychee from the milk you buy at Fry's."

In the mornings she listened to the birds and the frogs, to the shuffling of the cows and the three goats, and to the soft squawks of the chickens. Her favorite task was to walk over to where the chickens were kept and search for freshly laid eggs. That dawn she pattered across the mud courtyard. It was warm, and she could hear the chickens protesting the weather already. The air clung to her skin. She walked down to the well to pull up some fresh water and doused her flaming skin. The dark, rounded dome that covered the well reminded her of the ruined temple, an ancient one that stood alone in a far corner of Papaji's sugarcane fields. The temple was fairly engulfed those days by creepers, and only monkeys and snakes visited it. She never did.

The water splashed and spilled from its bucket when she pulled it up. She crouched down onto the ground and splashed small handfuls onto herself. The warm breeze now cooled her skin. Only then did she see it. Or perhaps she had sensed it first in the distant scuffles in the animal pen, in a random dog barking, in the faint smell of burning thatch. She looked up and saw the false dawn, bloody, spilled across the wrong side of the world. She thought she saw the bloodied outline of the temple on the horizon. The west rose, red fingers spidering into the engulfing bowl of night. Not far away houses were burning. She could smell it on the air.

The family fled with nothing. They just took their clothes and some bags of flour, and Mamaji carried her bag of gold jewelry and that was all. Only later when they became part of that vast carnival, that artery pumping people across new borders, did they learn of how the world had been split in half. Indiapakistan became two words with no tunes that might link them in song.

"I began to sing on the road. Every day I sang to cheer up Mother and Father, who were both sad. They lost many friends. So did I. And as we crossed the new border I was singing, and I think my voice got stuck at that border and because of that I always sing. If I had been chattering, maybe I would always be chattering, and if I had been silent, I would never have said another word. What we did at that border, that is how our lives continued, and what we didn't do, we could never do again. Maybe one day our lives will be released, but only if the border goes."

It was time for *Lost in Space*, and before Bikram could even shoo Ravi away, he was at the controls of the television. Bikram began to hum *"Mera joota hai Japani."* My shoes are Japanese.*

---

*A well–known Indian film song in which the singer catalogues the foreign clothes he is wearing. He concludes with the statement that his real self is Hindustani.

Bapsi Sidhwa

Statement: From V. S. Maniam, "Houstonian Novelist Projects a Friendship Forum," *Voice of Asia,* January 1994:
What evidently matters to her is that people from the Indian sub-continent and around, who have settled here [America], should be brought together. . . . [Underlining] the importance of such coming together, she mentions: "We are so vulnerable. We are poor countries. . . . We depend upon each other. Whatever is said and done, we are human-beings." She pauses, then adds: "To the First World, we are not. . . . Every writer, whether you like it or not, becomes political, develops a strong political consciousness. In fact, this is also why a person becomes a writer."

An American Brat is Bapsi Sidhwa's first novel set in the United States. It begins in Pakistan, when the Parsi family of Feroza Ginwalla, disturbed when Feroza reflects the influence of Pakistani Islamic fundamentalism in her growing tendency toward conservatism, decides to send her off to visit her Uncle Manek, who is studying at MIT. Feroza's discovery of the brighter and the darker sides of the United States, the lessons in survival her young uncle and her American roommate teach her, her first love affair, and a visit by her mother lead to her gradual discovery of her own identity and strength. The excerpt included here is important because it reminds us of the selection from Ved Mehta's memoir *Sound-Shadows of the New World* and Moazzam Sheikh's "Kissing the Holy Land." It also gives us a flavor of the humor and the underlying seriousness of *An American Brat.*

An American Brat

Her wide-open eyes soaking in the new impressions as she pushed the cart, a strange awareness seeped into Feroza: She knew no one, and no one knew her! It was a heady feeling to be suddenly so free—for the moment, at least—of the thousand constraints that governed her life.

The two panels of a heavy exit door at the far end opened to allow a stack of crates to pass, and, suddenly, Feroza saw Manek leaning against the demarcation railing just outside the exit. One ankle comfortably crossed over the other, arms patiently folded, Manek had peered into the abruptly revealed interior also.

After an initial start, and without the slightest change in his laid-back posture, he at once contorted his features to display a gamut of scatty emotions—surprise, confusion, helplessness—to reflect Feroza's presumed condition. At the same time, he raised a languid forearm from the elbow and waved his hand from side to side like a mechanical paw.

Feroza squealed and waved her whole arm and, with a huge grin on her face, steered the cart towards him. She was so excited, and also relieved, to see him. Even from the distance, his skin looked lighter, his face fuller. He had grown a mustache. Knowing him as she did, his deliberate insouciance and the regal wave of the mechanical paw filled her with delight. He hadn't changed as much as her mother had imagined. He was the same old Manek, except he was really glad to see her. Three years of separation have a mellowing effect, make remembered ways dearer. Feroza's heart filled with affection for her former tormentor. Having no brothers, she hadn't realized how much she missed him.

A woman in a blue uniform, stationed at a counter to the left of Feroza's path, checked her. "Hey! You can't leave the terminal. Your passport, please." She held out her hand.

The woman read the white slip inserted in the passport. She looked sternly at Feroza. "You must go for secondary inspection." Again the cryptic instruction.

The woman said something to a man in a white shirt and navy pants standing by her. She showed him the slip and gave him Feroza's passport.

Feroza noticed the "Immigration" badge pinned to the man's shirt. He motioned to her.

As she followed him, Feroza quickly glanced back at the exit to see if Manek was still there, but the heavy metal panels were closed. An inset door in one of the panels opened just enough to let the passengers and their carts through, one at a time.

Feroza followed the immigration officer past the row of ribbonlike wooden counters. A few open suitcases lay on them at uneven distances. These were being searched by absorbed customs inspectors who acted as if they had all the time in the world at their disposal. The weary passengers standing before their disarrayed possessions looked subdued and, as happens when law-abiding citizens are accosted with unwarranted suspicion, unaccountably guilty.

The man led her to the very last counter and told her to place her bags on it.

Applying leverage with her legs, struggling with the stiff leather straps that bound the suitcases, Feroza hoisted the bags, one by one, to the counter.

"Are you a student?" he asked.

"What?" The officer leaned forward in response to Feroza's nervous mumbling and cupped his ear. He had slightly bulging, watery blue eyes and a moist, pale face that called to Feroza's mind images of soft-boiled eggs.

"What're you speaking—English? Do you want an interpreter?"

"No." Feroza shook her head and, managing a somewhat louder pitch, breathlessly repeated, "I'm a tourist."

"I'm an officer of the United States Immigration and Naturalization Service, authorized by law to take testimony."

The man spoke gravely, and it took Feroza a while to realize he was reciting something he must have parroted hundreds of times.

"I desire to take your sworn statement regarding your application for entering the United States. Are you willing to answer my questions at this time?"

"Y-es," Feroza stammered, her voice a doubtful quaver.

Why was she being asked to give sworn statements? Was it normal procedure?

"Do you swear that all the statements you are about to make will be the truth, the whole truth, and nothing but the truth, so help you God?"

Feroza looked at the man, speechless, then numbly nodded. "Yes."

"If you give false testimony in this proceeding, you may be prosecuted for perjury. If you are convicted of perjury, you can be fined two thousand dollars or imprisoned for not more than five years, or both. Do you understand?"

"Y-yes." By now Feroza's pulse was throbbing.

"Please speak up. What is your complete and correct name?"

"Feroza Cyrus Ginwalla."

"Are you known by any other name?"

"No."

"What is your date of birth?"

"November 19, 1961."

He asked her where she was born, what her nationality was, her Pakistan address, her parents' address. Had her parents ever applied for U.S. citizenship? Was she single or married? Did she have any relatives in the United States? Anyone else besides her uncle?

"How long do you wish to stay in the United States?"

"Two or three months."

"What'll it be? Two months or three months? Don't you know?"

"Probably three months."

"Probably?"

The officer had placed a trim, booted foot on the counter; her green passport was open on his knee. His soft-boiled, lashless eyes were looking at Feroza with such humiliating mistrust that Feroza's posture instinctively assumed the stolid sheath of dignity that had served her so well since childhood.

"Where will you reside in the United States?" The officer appeared edgy, provoked by her haughty air.

An olive-skinned Hispanic customs inspector in a pale gray uniform sauntered up to them. He had rebellious, straight black hair that fell over his narrow, close-set eyes.

"With my uncle," Feroza said.

"*Where will you* stay . . . What is the *address?*"

The officer spoke with exaggerated patience, as if asking the question for the tenth time of an idiot.

"I don't know," Feroza answered, her offended expression concealing how stupid she felt, how intimidated.

"You don't know?" The man appeared to be suddenly in a rage. "You should know!"

But why was he so angry?

The Hispanic customs inspector with the unruly hair indicated a suitcase with a thrust of his chin. "Open it." He sounded crude and discomfitingly foreign to Feroza.

Rummaging in her handbag, Feroza withdrew a tiny key and tried clumsily to fit it into the lock.

"What is your uncle's occupation?" her interrogator asked. "Can he support you?"

"He's a student. But he also works at two other jobs to make extra money."

She had stepped into the trap. Didn't she know it was a crime for foreign students to work, he asked. Her uncle would be hauled before an immigration judge and, most likely, deported. She would have to go back on the next available flight. He knew she was a liar. She had no uncle in America. Her so-called "uncle" was in fact her fiancé. He wished to point out that she was making false statements; would she now speak the truth?

Feroza could not credit what her ears heard. Her eyes were smarting. The fear that had lain dormant during the flight, manifesting itself only in an unnoticed flutter of her heart, now sprang into her consciousness like a wild beast and made her heart pound. "I'm telling you the truth," she said shakily.

Sensing that some people were staring at them, Feroza cast her eyes down and took a small step, backing away from the luggage, wishing to disassociate herself from the intolerable scene the man was creating. The key dangled in the tiny lock.

"Open your bags," the customs inspector said, intent on his duty. He sounded hostile.

Feroza fumbled with the lock again. She unbuckled the leather straps, pressed open the snaps, and lifted the lid. She opened the other suitcase.

The contents had been neatly packed by Zareen, and Feroza drew courage from the well-ordered stacks of clothes, the neat parcels containing her shoes, the little plastic pouches holding her toiletries.

Like a shark attacking in calm waters, the customs inspector with the discomfiting accent plunged his hands into one suitcase after the other and rummaged callously among the contents. Odd bits of clothing spilled over the sides: a slippery stack of nylon underwear, a cardigan.

The man held up one of the parcels: "What's this?"

"Shoes."

He dug out copper wall plaques, heavy onyx bookends and ashtrays, the books and magazines Manek had asked for, a sanitary pad. He felt it as if searching for something concealed in it.

He brutally caricatured Feroza's shocked expression.

Feroza shut her mouth and looked steadily at the inspector—but hers was the steadfast gaze of a mesmerized kitten.

The man fished out and examined small vests, a brassiere.

Feroza became hatefully conscious of the tears sliding down her burning cheeks.

"What's the matter, officer? Can I help you?"

It was Manek. He was accompanied by another immigration officer.

"Who're you?"

"He's my uncle," Feroza said, gasping on an intake of air that was like a shuddering sigh. Faint with relief to have Manek with her, she gave his arm a squeeze and clung to it.

How was Feroza to know that Manek had been paged, his name announced over the loudspeakers in the reception lobby, interrogated? She sensed, though, that she had unwittingly incriminated him with her naive answers to the questions fired at her, and she was petrified.

"He's your uncle?" Feroza's cross-examiner looked incredulous. He turned to the officer with Manek, a moist-skinned, oval-faced man with a scanty thatch of damp blond hair. They could be brothers. "Does he look like her uncle?"

The officer with Manek twisted his glistening lips in a fastidious grimace: "No."

"I'm her uncle, officer," Manek asserted. He appeared composed, reliable, trustworthy.

Feroza was amazed. She could never have expected the Manek she knew to project these sterling qualities. And, at the same time, she was unutterably glad to have this confidence-inspiring new manifestation of her uncle at her side.

"No, you're not. You're too young to be her uncle. You're her fiancé. How old are you?"

"I'm twenty-two, officer." There he was again: meek, composed, worthy.

"What's the status of your visa?"

"I'm a student, sir. At MIT. I'm studying chemical engineering. I have an F-1 visa."

From his manner of speaking, Feroza guessed that he had been separately questioned. She was appalled at the official perfidy, and at herself for not having sensed it earlier.

"This woman just told me you work at two different jobs. The F-1 visa does not permit you to work. You have broken the law. You will have to face charges . . . You'll be deported."

"I work in the university cafeteria and at other odd jobs there, officer. She's just arrived, she doesn't know. I receive enough money from home for my tuition and living expenses. I can show you my bank drafts and statements to prove it. I can get a letter from my university. I work only for them. I'm permitted that."

The officer was skeptical. He turned to Feroza and, at the sight of her, at once reverted to his aspect of demon prosecutor.

"You are not eligible to enter the United States. You and your 'uncle' have concealed the truth. You're both lying. Isn't this man your fiancé? Aren't you here to marry him?"

Bewildered and scared, Feroza could not fathom what it was about her that got this pale man with his soft-boiled eyes so riled. She stared at him with her mesmerized kitten's eyes and shook her head.

"She's lying." The officer shifted his righteous, watery blue stare to his colleague, seeking confirmation.

His colleague nodded grimly.

"Aren't you engaged to him? Come on . . . you've come to the United States to marry your fiancé! You both plan to live here illegally. We know how to get at the truth. Stop lying!"

"I'm her uncle, officer. I cannot marry my niece."

"Are you kidding? We know y'all marry your cousins."

"Yes, officer; but not our nieces."

Feroza was crying again. Her whole body shook with her sobs and the effort to contain them: to restrict the ugly scene to their small circle and not advertise her misery and humiliation.

Meanwhile the customs inspector was holding up a lacy pink nylon nightie he had fished out of the bag. It looked obscene pinched between his spatulate fingers.

"Ah-ha!" Feroza's interrogator sounded triumphant. "The wedding negligee!"

Both immigration officers leered at the nightgown Zareen had packed at the last minute as if it was an incriminating weapon discovered at the scene of a crime.

"It's no use, your lying. Here's the evidence!"

The inspector repeatedly stabbed a soggy-looking, tapered finger at the offending garment.

Feroza, who had only heard of seeing "red," felt a crimson rush of blood blur her vision. Her tears, scorched by her rage, dried up. In a swift, feline gesture, she snatched her mother's nightgown from the Hispanic's stubby, desecrating fingers and said, "To hell with you and your damn country. I'll go back!"

Feroza flung the soft pink apparel into the bag and began stashing her other belongings on the swollen mound of disheveled clothes.

The inspector, who had displayed the nightdress and had it snatched from his hand, turned as if what was happening was no concern of his and drifted away.

Feroza's immigration officer had surprise stamped all over his soft, shiny face. By the looks of it, he might have exceeded his bounds.

"*Choop kar*," Manek hissed into Feroza's ear, warning his niece to shut up.

"Look, officer, I guarantee she'll go back at the end of three months, or whenever her visa finishes." Manek turned to the immigration officer who had accompanied him. "I can get a letter certifying she's my niece. Here's my visiting card. I promise to send you a copy of my passport and visa and a letter from the university stating I don't work anywhere else. I will send you copies of the bank drafts from Pakistan."

The officer took the proffered card. Manek signed a form acknowledging that his statements had been correctly recorded. He was sternly advised to provide proof of his assertions as soon as possible.

Feroza also signed a form. The officer who had treated her so vilely just a few moments back was now conciliatory. Shaken by the yellow blaze of fury emanating from the eyes Feroza had inherited from Khutlibai, and confounded by the fierce dignity imparted to her genes by Soonamai, he even stashed a few of her belongings into her turbulent suitcase.

Once all the contents were back in, the officer brought the lid forward, marked it with chalk, and, after stamping Feroza's passport, handed it back to her.

As the taxi drove out of Kennedy Airport, speaking in Gujrati Manek said, "You're the same old *uloo*. That was a damn silly way to behave. What if those chaps had packed us back to Lahore? You're in America now: you have to learn to control your temper. There are no grannies or mummy-daddies here to bail you out!"

What rubbish! Feroza thought. What had she ever done that might require her grandmothers or parents to bail her out of prison?

Aloud she said, "He insulted my mother! I couldn't stand the way that creep handled her nightgown."

"You'll have to learn to stand a lot of things in this world."

"Look. You didn't stand up for your sister's honor. So don't shout at me for defending her *izzat*."

"I'm not shouting," said Manek, managing with difficulty to keep his voice low and sound reasonable. "And you'd better forget this honor-shonor business. Nobody bothers about that here."

They remained silent in their respective places in the rear of the taxi. Feroza's profile, silhouetted against the wintry night outside, was a study in aristocratic umbrage.

"So, how's everyone at home?" Manek asked, after a while.

"Fine."

"Look, I've missed you all," Manek said. "Talk to me properly."

Impulsively he sought Feroza's hand in the dark and gripped it. It was icy cold and surprisingly soft, almost fragile.

Manek did something else he had never done before—he put his arm, stiff and awkward, round her shoulders.

"Are you feeling cold? Look, don't worry," he said with unaccustomed kindness, "it's all right. Immigration gives everyone a hard time. You should hear some of the stories! But that's behind us. We're going to have a great time. You'll love New York. I've planned it so we can spend a week here. Then we'll get back to Cambridge. If I get the time, we'll even go to Disneyland."

Immediately Feroza noticed the garlands of lights outlining the iron rhythm of the bridge they were racing along, the sumptuous red tail-lights of the cars ahead. Then she realized they had driven over other bridges, equally long.

"*Vekh! Vekh! Sher-di-batian!*" Feroza said in exuberant Punjabi, mimicking excited yokels pointing out the bright city lights from bullock carts. It was an old joke they shared with their young friends and cousins, except she now used it to express her own excitement at the extravagant display.

Feroza couldn't credit everything her eyes saw. And, as excitement gripped her, she laughed, a clear laugh with modulations that suddenly informed Manek, more than the bodily changes he had noticed, that Feroza had grown into a woman—a desirable and passionate woman—in the three years he'd been away, and he'd have to look out for her.

He felt proud of his niece, happy and awkward. And then they were climbing into a futuristic spaghetti of curving and incredibly suspended roads, mile upon looping mile of wide highway that weaved in and out of the sky at all angles so that sometimes they descended to the level of the horizon of lights in the distance that Manek told her was Manhattan, and sometimes they appeared to be aiming at the sky. Feroza saw ships in an incredible river. How deep the river must be to hold the ships.

The sky and the air appeared to her to be lit up in a perennial glow that dispelled night and darkness and sleep, banished all things that did not participate in the happy, wakeful celebration of life.

It was almost two in the morning by the time the taxi deposited Manek and Feroza at the YMCA on Broadway.

Once they were in their room on the fifteenth floor, Manek, utterly exhausted, got into his pajamas and slipped into bed.

Feroza pushed the heavier of the two suitcases against the wall. "I don't need to open this till we get to Cambridge. It's got lots of gifts and things for you, but you'll have to wait."

Manek agreed: he had no wish to see its contents strewn about in the tiny room, or to repack the bulky suitcase. He knew what he'd asked for and the gifts could wait.

Feroza unzipped a canvas carryall, removed a nightdress and her robe, and began rummaging through its contents.

"Look, don't be so *pora-chora* at this time of night," he said, slipping into his old bullying tone. "Turn off the light and go to sleep. You can unpack in the morning."

Feroza fished out an intricately patterned fawn-and-blue cardigan and, saying, "Catch, it's for you," threw it to Manek.

Manek sat up in bed and spread it out on his comforter. "Not bad," he said.

"Your sister got swollen eyes knitting the Fair Isle pattern for you, and all you can say is 'Not bad'?"

"Very nice," Manek said, running his hand appreciatively over the soft wool; it had been a long time since anyone had bothered to pamper him.

Feroza, who had expected him to make disparaging comments, checked a caustic remark and tried not to show how surprised she was by his uncharacteristic behavior. She switched off the light and discreetly changed into her nightdress.

Just before getting into bed, Feroza slipped a gray-and-white snakeskin wallet under Manek's pillow. "It's from your mother," she said, but Manek was already asleep.

Outside their room, the night was full of unfamiliar smells and alien sounds that kept Feroza's eyes wide awake and her breath tentative. She fell asleep to the shrill, eerie cry of the sirens that patrol New York, just when she was convinced she would never sleep at all.

Neera Kuckreja Sohoni

Statement: I have lived in America variously as student, worker, home-maker, and mother. Each phase has been enriching in some ways and alienating in others. But the experience of being here has never been dull or ambivalent. It has made me more willing to try out uncharted territory.

The protagonist of "Close Encounter" is fully aware of the choices she has made as a resident of the United States and of the contrast between the life she could have led in India and the sometimes frustrating adventures of the life she has chosen in America. The vignette about a middle-aged South Asian American woman who stands in a long line to get into a concert and is gently accosted by a young man who could have been her son juxtaposes not only her life in the two countries but also the woman's past and present. Neera Sohoni skillfully shows how memory is constantly woven into everyday life.

Close Encounter

The line outside the ticket counter at Shoreline Amphitheater had barely moved. Nisha felt trapped there. Concerts are less compelling when you are a mother of three teenagers. Her desire to retreat seemed less overwhelming after she had ascertained that there were others around her who were not allowing their age to overrule their persistence. As she stood there, she found herself not necessarily counting chickens but in fact using the waiting period to test whether she could accurately recall the recently learned *shloka* from her daily prayer. She had never been too religious and could count on her fingertips the number of religious verses or prayers she knew. But motherhood, multiculturalism, and age—in that sequence—had inhibited her hours of sleep and accentuated her decibels of stress. Since she lacked the concentration to meditate and the discipline to take advantage of yoga, she had to turn to alternative medicine: homeopathy and religious recitation had for some time now held the top two slots on her list of prescribed sleep-enhancing remedies.

But memory is easy to lose and slow to recover. And so she found herself blinking, stumbling, and eventually blanked out over the fifteenth line of the mantra. By that time, of course, her impatience with herself had grown, far exceeding even its customary low threshold level.

Once impatience sets in, it needs no time or rational reason to explode or expand. Nisha began slowly but desperately to peel off her brittle, mostly chipped nails. "These bloody nail hardeners are worth nothing. They do nothing for my Asian nails," she griped. "Probably all Revlon product testing is done on slender white Caucasian nails."

The sun was chipping away at her energy and tolerance. She felt hot and cluttered. Suddenly, the scenario around her seemed pitiful. At age fifty, her mother or sister would never have had to stand in a line to buy their tickets or ride a bike to do so. Their families treat them like porcelain, she whined to herself. They don't walk to a car. The driver always brings it around to where they are standing. Their servants stand in line to buy their concert and cinema tickets. Even their children and grandchildren have never had to bike to school. "What the hell am I doing here?" she thought. "Where is my car, my driver, my husband?"

Ooooo, husband? She should never have thought of him. "His is the most precious absence in my life," she mused. "For the twenty odd years that we have been married, his home has been a plane or a hotel or an airport lounge. Marketing and venture capitalism are the new frontier trades that Californians engage in. Silicon Valley's protagonists carry a bag full of money to try and marry it to a whole bunch of start-up companies. As each company takes off, if the stock price bloats, it whets your greed for more. This is the gold rush of our times. It's all so stressful. . . ."

Though distressed, she did not feel the need to give up her standing in the line. "This is my only standing after all," she thought gloomily. "Here, in front of the ticket counter, I can know finally exactly how many people are ahead of me and how many overtaken by me." Even as she ruminated, her impatience started to revive. "Why is it always important to me to compare? Why do I seek my gratification only in relationship to others? Why cannot I let myself alone?"

While she was thus begrudging her self to herself, she suddenly became aware of a pair of gray-blue eyes looking curiously at her. The face surrounding the eyes seemed cheery and friendly and suggestive of a mouthful of a grin. After staring at her for several minutes, which left Nisha feeling most uncomfortable and possibly pale, the young man moved cautiously toward her and said haltingly, "Excuse me, are you Indian?"

She never resented being asked that question. It somehow vivified her entity. In this case, aware that she was wearing a *bindi*, she felt a bit cross at his naiveté. But suppressing her impatience, she said, "Surely the red dot should define my identity beyond doubt," not knowing exactly why she chose to sound pompous. But his reply caused her to reconsider her stance. "Oh sure, your *bindi* tells me that you are Hindu, but you could be from India or from any of its neighboring countries, or for that matter from Fiji, Africa, or even the U.K."

Nisha was impressed. In the increasingly parochial nineties, such a discerning worldview, notwithstanding the hogwash of multicultural-ism, was more than she had trained herself to expect. What a refreshing throwback to the refined knowledgeability of the sixties! Is he a flower-child, she wondered, or the child of a flowerchild? Aloud she asked politely, possibly even reverently, "Forgive me if I sounded abrasive. But the times are not exactly conducive to making us immigrants feel secure. And my children will tell you that I need no provocation to blow my fuse or to confuse the micro with the macro, that is, the indi-vidual with the societal. That is how you became a scapegoat. Do you understand?"

The smile, which was quizzical, came ever so slowly. Once again, Nisha saw the promise of a mouthful of a grin. She even felt a sense of déjà vu. His tousled red hair, his squarish build. . . .

Before she could say anything else, he looked at her closely, as though sizing her up against a portrait he may have seen somewhere, "Can I ask you your name?"

"Why? Of what possible use can it be to you?" she asked, borrowing his quizzical look.

"I just . . . well, it's because. . . ." But Nisha cut him short. "Is it for some sick survey of immigrants?" she asked brusquely. "Really, I am fed up of being treated as a statistic. I have no interest in adding more grim numbers to Governor Wilson's immigration phobia. I see myself as a vic-tim of immigrant backlash. If you need to earn your ten dollars hourly by grilling overworked, dehydrated, concert-queue-standing immigrant women, please seek out someone else. Or here, better still, take ten dol-lars from me and tear up that dumb questionnaire!"

"Wait a minute, you are getting this all wrong. I am not a survey hand or Mr. Wilson's political lackey. I am merely curious about your name."

But finding her unreceptive to his curiosity about her and observing her resistance to reveal anything more to him, he stepped in to resolve the impasse.

"Doesn't your name mean night?" he ventured with the right amount of respectful distance in his tone.

Nisha felt stumped. How could this person have known her name, much less its meaning? Had she dropped her wallet or maybe just her business card? She looked hurriedly through her bag, that old tote bag that, similar to her life, was like a well into whose bottom everything just sank, with its mirror-inlay embroidery whose threads had begun to tar-nish like her hair.

Even as her fumbling fingers stumbled upon her wallet, she felt a gentle restraining hand. Impishly he said, "Gosh, it's incredible! But for your gray hair and expanded midriff, you look very much like you did in the photographs I have seen of you from thirty years ago. Worse, you are exactly as Dad described you . . . even down to your paranoia!"

And then suddenly it dawned on her. He was no stranger. He was the son she would have had if she had dared to follow her heart.

Jyotsna Sreenivasan

Statement: I was born and raised in the United States, and I've been writing stories since I was seven. But it wasn't until I got to graduate school that I started writing stories with Indian American characters! Before that it never even occurred to me that I had something to say about my cultural and ethnic experiences, probably because most of the stories and novels I read were about white Americans or Europeans. The first book I read by an Asian American was *The Woman Warrior* by Maxine Hong Kingston. I loved it and identified with many of the Asian American culture-clash problems it described. But still, I didn't feel my race or culture was different enough from mainstream white culture to comment on. I wasn't the victim of blatant racism; my parents spoke fluent English, as did most of my relatives; and we were financially well off. Finally in graduate school I started experimenting with Indian American characters. I had to figure out what part of my experience was due to my ethnic background and what was just me as an individual. I think "The Peacock's Mirrored Eyes" is my most successful story with an Indian American protagonist.

One thing I want to do with my writing is to show that just because you're a "person of color," doesn't mean your race is your only interest. I am, of course, interested in Indian culture, but I am also interested in lots of other things: feminism, folk music, old books, herbal remedies, and organic gardening, to name a few. Through my writing I'd like to help people deal with others as individuals, not just as members of a particular race.

In this story a young woman tells of her somewhat reluctant friendship with a classmate who has recently arrived from India. The attempt to understand one's own culture and to explain it to others is an important theme in the works of second-generation South Asian American writers.

The Peacock's Mirrored Eyes

My grandmother went back to India this summer. She stayed with us for a year. She used to walk around the block with her nine-yard sari wrapped around her bowed legs. She was short and bony, with a pot belly, and she tottered when she walked. I'm supposed to look like her.

All the kids on the block knew she was my grandmother, and they'd ask these questions like, "Can't she speak English?" and "Why does she wear that red mark on her forehead?" My grandmother made comments about my friends, too: "She'd be pretty if her eyes weren't so pale," and "Don't they feel ashamed to wear those clothes?" She tried to get my mother to make me wear a long skirt to school.

Now she's gone. I'm going to a new school, too, where no one knows I have a grandmother like that. It's a prep school, and I got my hair permed and I got two pairs of Levi's. Erica, my friend with the pale eyes, is actually envious of me. She's pretty popular in school, not like me. But not incredibly *popular*, because we're both brains.

The first day after classes at my new school, I got a chance to show off a little bit. Except it didn't work exactly the way I wanted. I signed up to be on the field hockey team (every student here has to play sports), and the coach took us out for a run on the cross-country hills. Erica and I had jogged over the summer, and I could run three miles. But now I lagged far behind all the other girls. I would've been last except for Radha, a girl who had just come from India a few months before. Her forearms and calves swung out from her body—she ran like an adult lady. She was probably moving slower than a walker. Just before the end of the course, in one of the dips between hills, I waited for her to catch up, and we ran in together. I hated for everyone to think of us as the "slow Indians"—I'd worked so hard to build up my endurance over the summer! Still, I thought it wasn't very nice to let her be last.

Radha turned up everywhere I was after that. In my art class she sat beside me. It made my neck itch to have her looking over my shoulder and asking me softly whether I thought her drawing was "a good likeness." It felt like having my mother in class with me! I tried to draw with my body twisted around my paper, but not so much that she'd think I was being rude. Our teacher, this tall, kind of flabby man with white hair, waved his arms in the air and said, "Passion! Freedom! Be loose and open! Draw with your whole body and your heart!" He drew a big arc on the easel up front—he threw himself at it like a dancer, almost. Radha kept her eyes on her paper and became very still when he did that. What did she think of these crazy Americans? I felt it was somehow my fault that she might be scared or offended.

Most frustrating of all was that everyone else at school thought it was perfectly normal that Radha and I should hang out together. "So you've found each other!" said my English teacher. She smiled encouragingly as she hurried by. Even Sylvia, a really nice girl I met from registration, seemed to be more cool, and kept her distance. I admit I didn't make a big effort to talk to Sylvia all the time. Radha needed me so much more—she seemed so lost sometimes, especially when boys talked to her.

She just looked away and giggled, and I had to explain to the guy, who was probably feeling pretty awkward talking to a girl anyway, that girls in India weren't used to speaking to boys.

Radha sat by me at lunch and waited for me to walk to the gym with her to change into our sweats for practice. She made sure to stand beside me during hockey drills, and if another girl was beside me first, she'd say, "Please excuse me," and squeeze in between us. After a while the other girls started standing farther away from me. Radha had her locker switched so it was closer to mine. After practice one day she saw one of the sophomore girls take her clothes off and hold a towel over her front to go take a shower. Radha looked at me, her eyes wide, and giggled with her hand over her mouth. I tried to smile with her, but I wanted to be bold like that girl, too, and walk to the shower without any underwear on, not caring who saw me. But how could I with Radha always next to me?

My mother was very concerned about how Radha was "adjusting to life here," as she told Radha's mother. Mom invited Radha's family over for a Deepavali celebration at our house, at the end of October. Well, at least Radha could help me keep an eye on the younger kids—we were expecting five other families.

Mom cooked all day, mixing dough and peeling potatoes and stirring the milk and sugar for *burfi*. I helped by grating carrots for a salad made with lemon juice and hot chilies. Mom doesn't let me cut chilies or onions because they would hurt my eyes.

Dad was outside lining up little paper bags filled with sand in the grass along the edges of the driveway. We were going to put a candle in each one to light when it got dark. Deepavali is the festival of lights. "If everyone on our street was Indian, it would look so beautiful!" Mom said. "Just like at Christmas."

Dad came banging in through the side door. "It's cold. Let's have a fire tonight. Do we have a log?"

"Look in the hall closet," Mom said. We used those chemically treated logs wrapped in glossy paper you buy at the store. When we first moved here the contractors had left us a pile of cut wood out back. We'd be able to have a real fire, just like on *The Waltons*! But the wood had gotten wet or something. Dad spent almost an hour one day crumpling paper in the fireplace with the wood and lighting it, only to have the fire go out the minute the paper turned to ashes. Ever since, my parents bought fake logs.

The fire flared and crackled, and Mom rustled busily in her bright green and gold silk sari, placing cotton wicks in the tall brass lamps we took out only once a year. I came downstairs wearing a new pink and maroon *salwar-kameez* and gold bangles and a small black dot on my forehead. Mom exclaimed, "Aaah! That looks very pretty! Do you want to wear my necklace with the red stones and pearls? Go up and get it!" I didn't really care whether I wore the necklace, but Mom loved to see me in jewelry, so I put it on.

The doorbell started ringing. Shoes clomped in the entranceway, lots of smiles and loud voices speaking Kannada and English, lots of coats to take upstairs to the guest room, lots of bright silk colors and gold and ruffles on little girls and miniature ties on little boys. Radha and her parents arrived, and as I took the coats upstairs I heard them talking about how Radha's *salwar-kameez* was "the latest style in India" and how my mother would ask friends going to India to bring me one like it.

When I came back down, Radha was in the family room with the other women, answering everyone's questions about school in fluent Kannada. Now Radha's soft-spokenness and her reserved manner seemed so appropriate—the model of a good Indian daughter! She was pretty according to Indian tastes—light tan skin, well-filled arms and cheeks, black eyes, and a thick, long black braid. I felt scrawny next to her, with my thin hair loose. The long scarf of my outfit kept slipping off my shoulders.

"How do you find life here?" someone asked Radha.

"It's nice. I like all the TV programs, and the streets are so clean. But I miss my friends in India, and my grandmother." She smiled, and all the other women nodded and agreed.

"Soon you'll make friends here and we won't recognize you!" cackled Mrs. Patel, who wore bright red lipstick, short hair done in large curls, heavy gold earrings the size of half-dollars, and bangles jingling almost to her elbows. "You'll be wearing mini-skirts and going to rock concerts!"

"Oh, no," giggled Radha softly.

"Oh, yes, just wait and see," Mrs. Patel insisted loudly and laughed.

"God forbid, I hope not!" said Radha's mother, laughing. "Radha is saying she wants to go back to India to stay with her grandmother and finish school there."

"That's a good idea," said my mother encouragingly. "That way you won't have all this peer pressure to date and stay out late and drink. But your mother will miss you."

"I don't want her to go back," said Radha's mother, "but my mother is telling me to send her back, and they'll find a boy for her once she finishes school."

"Then she can always join you here for further studies," added my mother.

I looked at Radha to see how she was reacting to all these plans for her future. She was gazing down into her cup of punch with a slight

smile and seemed to be blushing. Was this something I'd enjoy too—
having Mom and Dad make plans for my husband and college? But
they had never mentioned anything to me. I didn't think I'd be
allowed to go out with guys. And even if I could, no boy seemed to
like me anyway.

After dinner Mom asked me and Radha to take the kids onto the
back porch to burn sparklers.

"Do you want to study together tomorrow?" asked Radha. I was trying to make sure none of the kids touched the pretty spray of sparks
coming from their silver sticks.

I never like studying with other people—it seems to take longer, and
I end up tutoring them. "I think we might be going out tomorrow," I lied.

"How can you go out when there's a test the next day!" Radha
exclaimed. We had a Spanish test on Monday, but we'd drilled so much
for it during the week I had no plans to study for it.

"Well, I'll ask my mother," I said.

I had a dream that night. I was carrying Radha's book bag, which is
made of black cloth embroidered with turquoise and green and yellow
peacocks with little mirrors set into the tail feathers for the eyes. I was
walking through the town where our school is, past Merkle's Drugstore,
past the old brick church with ivy growing all over it, past Aunt Molly's
Attic, where they have used books and old jewelry. I turned down the
street toward campus. The book bag was bulging with heavy books, and
the strap broke. I had to lift it up and carry it in both arms, like a baby. I
turned back and walked away from campus, down the highway toward
my house in Misty Creek Acres.

When I woke up I realized what the dream meant. But what could I
do? I knew how it felt to be lonely. I didn't want to reject Radha and
make her feel that way. But was it right for me to continue being her best
friend when I felt she was a burden to me? Maybe she'd just go back to
India soon and I wouldn't have to worry about it.

Radha said she'd be over at 2:00. I knew I had to do something.
Sylvia was in our Spanish class, too. What was she doing today? Maybe I
should call her up and invite her to study with us. I ran upstairs to look
for our school phone directory, shoved aside the papers and books on my
desk till I found it, then bounded into my parents' bedroom to call her.
"Hello, Sylvia? How are you? I was wondering—you know that Spanish
test we're having tomorrow? Do you want to come over today and study
with me and Radha?"

"Oh, wow, I wish I could but I told my Mom I'd go shopping with
her for a present for my grandmother. Mom says she can't decide what
to get her because if she doesn't have it already, she doesn't want it!"
Sylvia laughed and I laughed too.

"So are you and Radha really good friends now?" asked Sylvia after a small pause. She called her "Radda."

"Yeah, I guess. I don't know how I got into it, though. I feel like she follows me everywhere!" I was glad Mom was out in the garden and Dad was in the basement.

"You mean you don't really like her?"

"Well. . . ." I didn't want to say anything bad about Radha. "I think she's not my type. If we were in India we probably wouldn't be friends at all! You know, she'd have her group and I'd have mine. But I think she's lonely here, so she just follows me around."

"She seems really shy."

"I think girls in India are taught to be quieter than we are here. She thinks all the girls here are loud and that we have too many expressions on our faces. Like we act things out—if we want to tell someone how our mother yelled at us, we'll put this sour expression on our faces and exaggerate the tone of voice. She thinks that's strange."

"Sometimes it's hard for me to tell what she's thinking because she always has the same expression!" said Sylvia.

"Yeah. Sometimes I don't know if Radha really likes me or if I'm just all she has. She talks so much about her old friends in India, I feel like I'm just there to listen."

"There's another girl in our class who reminds me of Radha," said Sylvia. "You know Miriam? She's from Senegal. She's really quiet, but really nice, too. I think she's lonely, though. Maybe we should get the two of them together!"

That sounded like a great idea to me! That's what Radha needed—another friend. Then I'd be off the hook. "But how should we do it?"

That Friday, all four of us signed out from lunch and went to this really good pizza place in town. Before we ordered, Radha wanted to make sure none of her slices had meat on them, so we had to explain what pepperoni and anchovies were. Sylvia said she'd go in with Radha on a vegetarian pizza so Radha wouldn't have to worry about stray pieces of meat on her half. Radha smiled and said, "Oh no, please don't worry about me," but Sylvia said, "No, really, I like vegetables."

"But you must want to eat at least a little meat," insisted Radha.

"Oh, no, not a bit. Before we even got here I was just telling myself I wanted onions and green peppers."

"But you mustn't do it just for me."

"Don't be silly. It'll be great!"

The difference between me and Sylvia was that Radha's protesting drove me crazy—why couldn't she just say what she really felt?

Miriam hardly said a word at first. I started asking her questions about Senegal and her family. She had a heavy foreign accent, but I'm pretty good at understanding all sorts of accents. It turned out she lives in an apartment complex right by these horse stables, and she was going to take horse-riding lessons. She invited me to come out one day and ride around on the trail with the guide!

After that lunch, Radha and Miriam didn't become best friends. But all four of us started to hang out together, and we've been a group ever since. We do some exciting things together, like go skating and horseback riding. But mostly we just meet each other in the student lounge and sit at the same lunch table and call each other on the phone. Radha switched to the tennis team after Sylvia told her the workouts were shorter than for hockey. Sylvia and I talk to each other in private sometimes about how our foreign friends are fitting in. Radha still bugs me in art class, but I'm trying to ignore her presence there.

Now it's almost the end of freshman year. Radha's going to India over the summer. She can't decide if she's coming back or not. She still talks about her Indian friends, but less often. One of Radha's cousins is even pen pals with Sylvia. Her cousin wanted a "real" American to write to.

Radha doesn't follow me around now because she has other people. And she is learning to be a little more American—she's actually starting to get a midwestern accent! But I still feel responsible or guilty if she doesn't like something American. The other day she told me it was "so sad" how Mr. and Mrs. Stone, who are the physics teacher and the dance teacher, are getting divorced and how it's all because "love marriages" never last anyway. I felt like I should defend American marriages or something. I told Sylvia about how I felt guilty, and she thinks I'm crazy. So maybe I should stop feeling that way. Still, it would be easier for me if Radha stayed in India. I have a feeling she won't, though. It would be too hard to leave her parents. Besides, I think America is already part of her in some way, and she's already part of America.

Rajini Srikanth

Statement: Motherhood has had a great influence both on my scholarship and my creative writing. Questions of identity, home, cultural border spaces, memory, and loss—all of which I explore in my work—are invested with emotional urgency as I watch and participate in my two daughters' lives.

"You Live on Your Side" portrays the tensions not between the dominating culture and South Asian Americans but between two South Asian American families and mainly between two women. Although the tensions arise for a number of subtle and explicit reasons, the core of the story upon which the tensions rest and which gives rise to the different shadings of emotions is memory. And the memory central to this story is that of the mother who has come from India to visit her daughter in America. It is not the memory of traditions and rituals, as in Tahira Naqvi's "All Is Not Lost," or the memories that have to be kept hidden, as in Panna Naik's "Illegal Alien," or the memories of a possible comfortable life in India in Neera Kuckreja Sohoni's "Close Encounter." It is the memory of a mother's terrible grief at the loss of her child.

You Live on Your Side

Tara, who should know better, says my Mother is mad. I don't entirely disagree, but it's the venom Tara packs into the word that bothers me. "Mad!" she says, spitting the sound out into my face. "Crazy!" she hisses. And because she's angry and scared, I think Tara is going to do something about Mother.

About a year ago, when Tara and Rajeev moved in across the street from us, I was ecstatic. I envisioned walking up to their front door, empty bowl in hand, laughing apologetically because I'd allowed myself to run out of sugar, and asking if I could please borrow some. And I thought Tara would run to our house some morning because she was out of milk for tea or bread for breakfast. But Tara, I soon learned, is very organized. She pencils things into a weekly planner. Grocery shopping is penciled in for Thursdays, on her way back from work, before she picks up Shiv from the babysitter. Rajeev told me that, proud and somewhat awestruck by her efficiency.

When I did go over one morning to borrow sugar, Tara stood at the door, meticulously dressed in a burgundy suit, two slender lace ruffles flaring out from under the sleeves of her jacket. On the wall behind her hung two large paintings, one, a market scene in an Indian village, people milling around stalls of fruit and vegetables; the other, a festival parade, heat and dust rising around the decorated elephants.

Rajeev's smile beckoned me in. "You like them?" He gestured to the paintings. "I did them." In the kitchen, he poured a stream of sugar into my bowl and I watched as it settled in a soft and low mound. Sugar dust hung heavy around my nose and mouth. "Come anytime," he said. "Don't be a stranger."

I invited them for dinner a few weeks after Mother came to visit. I should have known when Mother first saw Rajeev and gasped, her eyes widening in sudden recognition, that something would happen. Tara spoke that evening of how she had gone to high school in Pittsburgh and then to Bryn Mawr, holding herself like a little porcelain doll while Sunil leaned forward and listened, playing the polite and gracious host. "My family came here from Bombay when I was five years old, but I feel like I was born here," I heard her say. On the other side of the room, Rajeev told Mother he grew up in Mysore. I moved in and out of their conversations, filling the emptying bowls of peanuts and chips. Then Mother said, "I had a son who died in a shipwreck near Chittagong. You remind me so much of him." Her head trembled a little as she spoke.

I laughed quickly before the awkwardness could settle, like you briskly shake a picnic blanket to clear it of ants, and said, "You know what they say, Mother? That there are at least seven people in the world who look like each other." Tara sensibly picked up my idea and told us that she'd once met a woman who sounded so much like her that when they both spoke it seemed like the room was filled with echoes.

But that evening was the beginning of Mother's madness. She didn't plunge into it in a cataclysmic way like jumping off a cliff. It was more like she crawled into a tunnel with no end and, bit by bit, started to creep away from the light into the darkness.

She began by peering through the blinds like a nosy neighbor. She'd open the slats and part them wide enough to get a good view of Rajeev mowing his lawn. She'd know he was out there because you could hear the whine of the motor and smell the grass as he cut it. Some days he'd come home early to get this chore done. Tara worries about a shabby lawn.

If Mother were content with just watching Rajeev, we wouldn't have a problem. But she wants more. Just the other evening, we were sitting together on the front porch laughing about relatives. Mother is a good mimic, and she had me shaking with her imitations of Ramu Uncle interviewing prospective bridegrooms for his ever so accomplished daughter. "Well, young man, where did you get your first degree?" Mother spoke for him, her voice pitched low and deliberately forbidding. Of course it was understood that the young man had more than a bachelor's degree; that's why the "first." And if the candidate mentioned the name of some second-tier college, Ramu Uncle would make no secret of his disappointment. He'd stand up, signalling the end of the interview, not even bothering to offer the visitor a cup of coffee. Mother stood up to show me the closing scene: the young man, his head bent downward, looking at the patterned tiles on the floor, then Uncle, his long back held straight, booming on about his daughter's superb appointment at the Indian Space Research center, and literally shooing the rejected suitor out the front door. She had just finished her act and was getting ready to sit back down, when suddenly her body became still. I followed the direction of her eyes and saw that Rajeev was putting Shiv in the stroller, getting ready to take a walk. "Let's go in for tea, mother," I offered quickly. But she just smiled and started to walk down the porch steps toward the street.

Rajeev hadn't seen her yet; he was still struggling with the safety belt on the stroller. I waited and watched. When he realized she was beside him, he exchanged the usual greetings and spoke to her for a few minutes. Mother bent once to stroke Shiv's hair. They stood under a birch, its already yellow leaves hanging low and almost encircling their heads. Mother's face was bright. Then Rajeev bid her goodbye and turned to start on his walk. "That was simple," I thought, relieved. But Mother turned with him and walked along on the other side of the stroller. I looked to see if Tara had observed this little drama. If she had, she didn't respond. Perhaps she was in the back of the house.

There is no gracious way to tell your mother that she's being a terrible nuisance and that she should go back to her own home. It's particularly difficult if you've spent a year writing letters to convince her to come and visit. We'd promised the usual delights. We drove up north with her, where the colors on the mountains burst upon the windscreen of our car like a fiery vision. She responded with polite wonder. In the museum of glass flowers, I coaxed her to marvel at the hair-thin strands of glass pulled into pistils and stamens. But the fragile forms under their glass cases held little magic for her.

She is finding her pleasures in other things. Like the surprise walks around the neighborhood with Rajeev. I've learned to accept these because they seem to be doing no harm, probably because Tara hasn't found out as yet. But Mother's latest plan has me worried. She wants to cook her special treats for Rajeev. Oh, she doesn't say they'll be for him. She pretends that she'd like to make them for Sunil and Preethi and me, because *chaklis* and *kodbales* and *burfis* are too complicated and laborious to prepare without adequate planning. But then she adds, "And we'll send some across to Rajeev, I'm sure he misses Indian snacks." I am petrified at what Tara's reaction will be.

Yesterday, Mother spent three hours in the kitchen putting her plan to work. At the end of the frying and stirring, when all the snacks were ready, she wanted to walk across with Preethi and deliver the goodies herself. But I knew this was unwise. "I'll take them," I told her. "Tara's fussy about fried foods." I arranged the snacks on a large china platter and covered them with a pale blue organdy hand-embroidered napkin. Presentation is important to Tara, and I wanted to impress her before I made the offering. I went over when I knew that both of them would be in. I didn't want Tara to get the impression that we were feeding her husband behind her back. She accepted the platter and carried it to the dining table. Her skirt squished gracefully around her legs. The napkin lay over the food like a fine gauze. Rajeev, who followed her, pulled the napkin off with undisguised delight, and tossed a *burfi* whole into his mouth. Tara picked up the napkin and neatly folded it into a square. Her face was motionless as she watched Rajeev chewing.

Sunil is absolutely right. In bed last night, after I'd told him about the snacks, he said to me, "Anjali, we have to send her back. This obsession of hers will lead to who knows what. And in this country, . . . they won't try to understand. They'll say she's a potential threat to the neighborhood. Even worse, some righteous thinker will say she's unfit to be around children. Before you know it, we'll have a social worker on our doorstep."

Or a police officer, I thought. I was beginning to find out that police officers these days are like counselors and psychiatrists. I read in the town newspaper's police log that a policewoman had to help the parents of a high school kid because he wouldn't do his homework and was abusive to them. And there was a lady at the town pool who refused to wear a bathing cap and argued with the lifeguards, so they called the police because they didn't know how to handle her. Perhaps Mother's case will further sharpen police skills. I can see the entry in the log: "Visiting mother of Packard Road resident advised to stop harassing neighbor who she says reminds her of dead son." It wouldn't surprise me if Tara has already called the police.

This evening, she pulled up in her Volvo to our front door. She must have thought about what she would say as she drove back from work. A little breathlessly, her eyes flashing in her coffee-colored face, she came, ready for a confrontation. She did manage to fling the words "mad" and "crazy" into my face, but she had to restrain herself and edit extempore because Preethi, who's twelve and very inquisitive, came up to the door.

Tara did well, considering her earlier frenzy. "Rajeev and I would like to discuss a little matter with you. Could we meet somewhere? The deli in the center, perhaps?" At least, I thought thankfully, even if she did grow up here, she still believes that some things should be kept from children.

Yes, Mother is mad. But hers is not the madness that pulls a trigger or wields a knife. Hers is the madness of walking in a fog as thick as sooty cotton candy and not wishing for better visibility.

Tonight I see that there is a light rain. Gossamer-like, it falls on the tall hemlock trees that rise to my bedroom window on the second floor. Mother is in her room downstairs. Preethi and Sunil are fast asleep. It is not late, only 9:30, but we are all tired.

The doorbell wakes me. It is still dark and the clock on the VCR says 11:00. I shake Sunil and we both go downstairs. Before we can reach the door, the bell rings again, and through the panes in the door I can see shadows moving. "Who is there?" Sunil asks loudly. The response from the other side chills me. "Police."

We open the door only halfway, cautiously herding up our words for the answers we will have to give. I stare at the figures in blue and feel, and know that Sunil feels as well, like the sheath of our anonymity has suddenly been slashed open. Under the casing of our respectability and moderate success, I see ourselves as they must see us: shivering and cold, cringing foreigners, the house behind us rapidly falling and crumbling into dust. Behind us, the wet land rolls away into darkness.

With as much aplomb as I can summon, I ask, taking the lead in the conversation, attempting to preempt their declarations: "Yes, what's the problem?"

"Ma'am, you have a visitor, your mother, I believe? She was found trespassing on the property across the street, looking in through the windows."

I now notice Mother's sandals by the front door, drizzle-soaked, her shawl flung on the chair by the foyer, the fabric dark in patches where the light rain has seeped through.

"My Mother's asleep, officer. What makes the people from across so sure that they saw her?"

"The gentleman claims that a lady in a sari"—he pronounces it "sorry," and with considerable hesitation, glancing at his notes as he does so —"walked up to this driveway when he went up to the window."

In the pause, I stand, wondering what we're going to say. I dare not look at Sunil to see whether he is defiant or ashamed or angry at this intrusion. Sunil has spent years cultivating his anonymity in this town. A good citizen, he votes in town elections, pays his taxes, maintains his property. He is angry, I'm sure. Angry at me, angry at Tara, angry at the cops. "Speak," I shout inside myself to him, willing him to say something.

But the officer is already talking again. "No formal charges of trespassing have been filed. However, if it's not inconvenient, we'd like to speak to the lady in question."

Sunil springs up. "Officer, my wife's mother barely speaks English." I'm glad that Preethi is asleep and cannot hear her father lie. "It would be quite useless to try to talk to her."

"Well, sir, we can't force you to get her. Your neighbors haven't filed formal charges. But it seems to me that another occurrence could lead to a legal matter." His tone is slightly more belligerent than before, perhaps because he senses the falseness in Sunil's words.

As their shoes click down the driveway and we shut the door behind them, Sunil turns to me, his face streaked with anger and pain. "Send her back," he says. Then he walks up the stairs and shuts himself in our room.

Sunil was right not to let the officers speak to Mother. He may have done what he did for his own reasons. But I knew why I would never expose her to their probing. Their trained and practiced questions would pull her pain out from within her and force her to confront it. But she could never survive such a harsh scrutiny of her grief. Hers is a pain that, like some treasured memento, needs to be covered in diaphanous material, half hidden and half visible, something she can run her fingers over and feel the shape of, know that it's there, and yet not have to look at to see its every detail of form and color.

I wonder what I'll say to Mother and how I'll keep her away from Rajeev and Tara. I know that it's because of Rajeev that no charges have been filed. But he will not be able to stop Tara from doing it the next time. He himself could have a change of heart. I enter Mother's room and stroke her hand as she lies in bed. She is not asleep.

"What happened?" I ask.

She sits up. Her voice is soft, almost a whisper. "I've caused you so much trouble, I'm sorry. Anjali, it's frightening; I don't know what came over me. I was lying here and thinking about Mohan when suddenly I felt I had to see Rajeev."

"Mother, Rajeev is not Mohan. He doesn't even look like Mohan."

"Not to you, he may not." Her words were firmer now, louder. "You don't remember the way Mohan smiled or the way his arms hung down. Of course Rajeev doesn't have Mohan's features, I know that. But when I see him, I see Mohan's spirit inside him."

Her talk was getting dangerous. She was beginning to sound like she did in the months following Mohan's drowning. In those days she was convinced that Mohan was still alive because his body hadn't been found. She had visited every fortune-teller and astrologist and palm-reader in Bangalore to find out about Mohan. Finally some madman, some opium-smoking, self-proclaimed seer had confirmed her suspicions. Mohan was alive he said, running scared and lonely in the jungles of Chittagong.

"Mother, how did the police see you?"

"It was not the police. I was standing on their porch, looking in. Rajeev and Tara were sitting on the couch, Shiv was between them. They looked so comfortable and happy. I saw those two paintings you've told me about. He's a fine artist. I was just getting ready to leave, when a car or something turned onto the road. The headlights fell on me."

The rest I can imagine. Mother is bathed in light. Tara looks up from whatever she is doing at precisely that moment and sees a silhouette against the window. She screams and rushes to the phone, and Rajeev dashes to the window to catch a glimpse of Mother's figure under the streetlamp as she heads up the driveway of our house.

"Mother, it's against the law here to do what you did. You could have been in serious trouble."

Even as I say the words, speaking to her as if to a child, I realize how ridiculous I sound. I think of all the mad men and women I have known growing up in India. Some of them would shake their fists at us as we ran past the houses in which they lived, part giggling, part scared. Or they would wave their walking sticks, threatening to bring them down upon our heads, muttering their curses as we taunted them with childish rhymes. There was one woman, I remember, in particular. She sat on a stone bench in the compound of her daughter's house, huddled into herself, a green shawl wrapped around her in any kind of weather. As I walked with my friends to and from college, she would beckon to us, a clutch of flowers in her hand. The first time we saw her, we looked the other way and walked faster. But over time we grew brave enough to accept her flowers and to watch her face crack open into a wide and toothless smile. Rajeev, I'm sure, had encountered the same kind of mad men and women in Mysore. But something had scared him tonight, scared him into thinking that this old woman, my mother, had become something evil and malignant.

"Anjali, I think I should go home. Who knows what else I might do? I don't want to cause you any trouble."

I feel that I should protest, but I cannot bring myself to say the words that will keep her here. Back in her home, amid the clamor and clutter of people, she hears only dimly the cries of her pain, only faintly the sounds of her disbelief. Here, in the still quiet of a crisp fall day, as she looks at the empty streets and hears only the cheep of the cardinals, here her suffering swells to a loudness she cannot bear. And then she does things she cannot understand.

"I'll make the reservations tomorrow," I say. "I'll let Arun know you're coming."

"There's one thing I'd like before I go. Please don't be angry. Can you ask Rajeev to come over one last time?"

I want to scream, to shake her, to tell her that she's crazy. But I just curl my fingers and dig into the mattress. "I'll try. I don't know if he'll come." Then I leave the room.

Rajeev does come. But not because I ask him. Before I've come up with a plan to approach him, he arrives at our doorstep, apologizing for what's happened, explaining how scared Tara is. I want to tell him it's anger she feels, not fear, but I am grateful for his visit. He agrees to speak to Mother. I leave them in the living room together. They spend a long time talking.

On the day of Mother's departure, we are sitting in the kitchen drinking our last cup of tea together. The steam curls up around our faces and Mother looks calm. Rajeev makes another visit, but this time he just hands her a long cardboard tube. He gives me an envelope, as well. I am about to read what's inside, but Mother begins to talk.

"I told Rajeev all about Mohan to explain what I had done that night. He listened and then he told me about his aunt. Her son died of meningitis when he was twelve years old. Rajeev was scared at the time, because he was twelve, too. But after a while he stopped being scared about dying and started to get scared about the way his aunt looked at him. He would be sitting in the same room with her, because she stayed with his parents for a while after the tragedy, and he would know that her eyes were on him. Suddenly he'd feel like his face was curling up and twisting itself into a new shape, as if he were losing his face and a new one was being pushed up from under the surface—the face of his dead cousin."

The hot tea eases down my throat, and I am slowly beginning to get angry with Rajeev. Mother continues, "He started to avoid his aunt, he was so afraid that she would touch him and really work some magic on how he looked. Of course, he feels terrible now for the way he acted, and he hasn't seen his aunt in over seventeen years."

By now, I am tired of Rajeev's easy words and angry with Mother for being soothed by his nostalgic story. Mother has forgotten what her own children did for her when Mohan died, her surviving children, that is. All of us, all five of us, had pushed down our own grief to help with hers. Perhaps in the process, we'd forgotten how to feel sad, so anxious were we to stop Mother from tormenting herself into thinking that Mohan might be alive somewhere, lost, and in need of help.

Mother is pulling an ivory-colored scroll from inside the long tube. She unrolls it and exclaims, "Beautiful. Unbelievable." I rise from my chair to look over her shoulder and I gasp at what I see. The strokes and colors are bold and strong. In the foreground is a listing ship, the waves around it dark and tall; in the background, in the depth of the painting, lies a thick growth of foliage, long and narrow bamboo trees clumped in profusion. In their midst, I discern a dim figure in the act of running, arms thrown out, body leaning toward the viewer.

The painting is unsigned. Perhaps Rajeev meant it not as a remembrance of him but as an acknowledgment of Mother's hope, her dream. "You must save it carefully," I say, somewhat superfluously.

It is only after Mother leaves that I remember Rajeev's envelope. It is a brief note to thank me for my friendship. "But it would be best for both our families if we kept our distance from each other." There is no mention of Tara, but her name hangs heavy over the letter. "No more sugar borrowing," he writes, half in jest, half seriously. "For the time being, you live your life on your side of the street, we'll live our life on our side." Before I turn on the lights, I pull down the blinds and turn the slats shut.

About the Contributors

Qiron Adhikary

Qiron Adhikary is a Southeast Asian writer of South Asian descent who currently lives in the United States. Unashamedly feminist, Qiron grew up with no fear of the *rotan* (the disciplining cane) despite a childhood spent in (comparatively) strict Singapore. She has worked variously as a journalist, copywriter, screenwriter, technical writer, law clerk, office manager, and blackjack dealer. She is a lawyer by training.

Qiron has been writing since her childhood, though disparaging friends and family brushed away her early efforts as "mere graffiti." Her short stories have been published in a collection used to teach Singapore University students about Third World writers writing in English. In her many years as a commercial writer, Qiron has written for highly technical magazines, books, and papers as well as for what she terms "low-brow" entertainment media preferred by her immediate family and friends.

Qiron lives in Piedmont, California. She has written three novels, one of which contains the earlier adventures of Nosey Nakshitka. She has also written several books of short stories, including two books of feminist folktales for children. One of her short stories, "The Marriage of Minoo Mashi," appears in *Our Feet Walk the Sky: Women of the South Asian Diaspora* (1993).

Meena Alexander

Born in Allahabad, India, on February 17, 1951, Meena Alexander has lived and studied in the Sudan, England, and India. One of the leading Indian poets writing in English as well as one of the most important South Asian American writers, she is also an essayist and a novelist. She is professor of English and women's studies at the Graduate Center at Hunter College, City University of New York, and teaches a poetry workshop at Columbia University. She lives in New York with her family. The titles and dates of some of her important works can be found in her statement in the text headnotes.

Agha Shahid Ali

Agha Shahid Ali, considered one of the most important and influential American poets of South Asian descent, was born in New Delhi on February 4, 1954, and was raised in Kashmir. He came to the United States for graduate work in 1976 and earned a Ph. D. in English from Pennsylvania State University and an M.F.A. in poetry writing from the University of Arizona. His six volumes of verse include *The Half-Inch Himalayas* (1987), *A Walk Through the Yellow Pages* (1987), and *A Nostalgist's Map of America* (1991). He is also the translator of *The Rebel's Silhoutte/Faiz Ahmed Faiz* (1991) and the author of a scholarly work, *T.S. Eliot as Editor* (1986).

Indran Amirthanayagam

Indran Amirthanayagam was born in 1960. He is from the Jaffna peninsula of Sri Lanka and spent much of his childhood in Colombo. He has a B.A. from Haverford College and an M.A. in journalism from Columbia University. He has lived in New York City and has worked as a poet, teacher, and theater critic. His poems have been published in journals such as *Grand Street, The Kenyon Review, The Massachusetts Review, Exquisite Corpse, The Graham House Review, The New York Times,* and *New York/Newsday* and have been included in *The Open Boat: Poems from Asian America* (1993). His first book of poems, *The Elephants of Reckoning* (1993), won the Patterson Poetry Prize. He received a New York Foundation for the Arts fellowship in 1993 and will be featured on a national PBS television series, *The United States of Poetry,* to be aired in 1995. He is presently a U.S. diplomat posted in South America.

G. S. Sharat Chandra

G. S. Sharat Chandra was born in May 1938 in the village of Nanjangud in Mysore, India. Educated as a lawyer, he left India in 1963 and abandoned his legal career in 1966. He received degrees in English and creative writing from the University of Iowa and has been a professor of creative writing and literature since 1968 at the University of Missouri in Kansas City. His writings have appeared internationally and have influenced a number of South Asian and South Asian American writers. His collections of poetry include *Family of Mirrors* (1993), which was nominated for the 1994 Pulitzer Prize for Poetry, and *Immigrants of Loss* (1994), which has been nominated for the Commonwealth Poetry prize and the T. S. Eliot Prize.

Darius Cooper

Darius Cooper was born in Pune, India, in 1949 and came to the United States in the fall of 1980 on a scholarship to pursue a doctorate in literature and film in the English Department at the University of Southern California, Los Angeles. He holds a B.A. in English and French from St. Xavier's College, Bombay; an M.A. in English and aesthetics from Bombay University; an M.A. in English from the University of Southern California; and a Ph.D. in literature and film from the University of Southern California. His essays on Indian cinema have been published in *Film Quarterly, The East-West Film Journal,* and *The Bombay Literary Review.* He has presented papers on Indian cinema at the Cinema Studies Conference at New Orleans, the Film-Video Conference at the University of Southern California, and the Commonwealth and Post-Colonial Conference at Statesboro, Georgia. His poems and short stories have appeared in American journals such as *The Greenwood Review, Chelsea, Helix,* and *The Massachusetts Review* and several Indian literary journals. His essays on the world-renowned Indian film director, Satyajit Ray, are to be included in the forthcoming anthology *Nation and Nation-Making* and in the *Journal of Arts and Ideas* (Delhi, India). Darius Cooper is professor of literature and film in the Department of English at San Diego Mesa College.

Rienzi Crusz

Rienzi Crusz, a widely published South Asian Canadian poet, was born in Galle, Sri Lanka, and came to Canada in 1965. He was educated at the universities of Ceylon, London, Toronto, and Waterloo. He was a Colombo Plan Scholar at the University of London in 1951 and is the author of six volumes of verse, *Flesh and Thorn* (1975), *Elephant and Ice* (1980), *Singing Against the Wind* (1984), *A Time for Loving* (1989), *Still Close to the Raven* (1990), and *The Rain Does Not Know Me Any More* (1992). He has published in several journals such as *The New York Quarterly*, *Prairie Schooner*, *Canadian Literature*, *Malahat Review*, *Descant*, and *Dalhousie Review*. His works have appeared in *Anthology of Magazine Verse and Yearbook of American Poetry* (1985), *Relations: Family Portraits* (1987), *Another Way to Dance* (1989), *The Geography of Voice: Canadian Literature of the South Asian Diaspora* (1992), *The Indian Diaspora* (1992), and *Something to Declare: Selections from International Literature* (1994). He has won competitive grants from the Canada Council, Department of State, Multicultural Directorate, and was awarded the KW Cultural Award for Writing in 1993. He worked as a collections and reference librarian at the University of Waterloo, Canada, from 1967 to 1993.

Boman Desai

Boman Desai was born in Bombay in 1950 and arrived in the United States in 1969. He has studied architecture and received his degree in psychology. He writes that he has "had some schooling, worked some jobs, published some articles, some stories, won some prizes." He has published a novel, *The Memory of Elephants* (1988), which has little to do with elephants and is currently working on his second novel, *The Black Elephant*. Boman Desai lives in Chicago.

Chitra Divakaruni

Chitra Divakaruni was born in 1953 in Calcutta, India, and educated at Calcutta University, Wright State (Ohio). She has a Ph.D. in English from the University of California at Berkeley and teaches English and creative writing at Foothill College in California, where she is the director of the annual multicultural creative writing conference. Her poems have appeared in publications such as *The Beloit Poetry Journal*, *Chelsea*, *The Colorado Review*, *Ms*, *The Threepenny Review*, and *Blood into Ink: South Asian and Middle Eastern Women Write War* (Westview Press, 1994). She has published three books of poetry, *Dark Like the River* (1987), *The Reason for Nasturtiums* (1990), and *Black Candle* (1991). She has also edited *Multitude: Cross-Cultural Readings for Writers* (1993). She was nominated twice for the Pushcart Prize and has received a Gerbode Foundation award. She lives in the San Francisco Bay Area with her husband and son and is actively involved in women's issues. She is a volunteer for the Mid-Peninsula Support Network Women's Shelter and is the coordinator of Maitri, a Bay Area help line for South Asian women.

Lakshmi Gill

Lakshmi Gill was born in Manila, Philippines, in 1943 and arrived in San Francisco in 1959 to begin her university studies. She attended the San Francisco College for Women, College of Notre Dame in Belmont, California, and Western Washington University, where she obtained her B.A. in English. Her M.A. is from the University of British Columbia in Vancouver, and her B.Ed. is from Mt. Allison University in Sackville, New Brunswick. Since 1965 she has taught all levels from grade one to university classes. Her works have appeared in such publications as the *Toronto South Asia Review* and *The Geography of Voice: Canadian Literature of the South Asian Diaspora* (1992). Her novel, *The Third Infinitive*, was published in 1994.

Anu Gupta

Anu Gupta was born and raised in New York. She attended Brown University and majored in English and American literature with a focus in Asian American literature. She received honors for her thesis on the emergence of South Asian American literature in the canon of Asian American and American literature. She currently attends the Yale School of Medicine and will receive her M.D. in 1997. She is continuing her study of South Asian American literature, and "Crystal Quince" is her first story to be published.

Minal Hajratwala

Minal Hajratwala was born in 1971 in San Francisco and was raised in New Zealand and Michigan by a father from Gujarat, India, and a Gujarati mother born in the Fiji Islands. She graduated from Stanford University and now works as a journalist in San Jose, California. Her writings have been published in two anthologies, *Our Feet Walk the Sky: Women of the South Asian Diaspora* (1993) and *The Very Inside* (1994) as well as literary journals, including *Bottomfish*, *The Rag*, *Sunflower*, and *Writing for Our Lives*.

Naseem A. Hines

Born in Raipur, Madhya Pradesh, India, Naseem Hines came to the United States in 1980. She has a B.A. from Osmania University, Hyderabad, where she studied Sanskrit, Hindi, and sociology. Her B.A. in English literature and her M.A. in South Asian languages and literature are from the University of Washington. She has traveled widely and is very interested in Sufi literature and Indian classical music. Her publications include an article in Hindi in the magazine *Dharmayuga* (1993) and the Foreword in an Urdu monograph, *Jaras-I-Caravan* (1994). She teaches Hindi and Urdu languages and literatures at the University of Washington, where she is also pursuing a Ph.D. in early Indo-Sufi literature.

Litu Kabir

Litu Kabir was born in Bangladesh in 1959. He came to the United States when he was seventeen years old and has studied, lived, and worked in different parts of the country. Development and grassroots projects in Bangladesh take him on frequent and extended trips to Bangladesh, which he considers his home, along with Cambridge, Massachusetts. He is currently working as a software engineer in the Boston area.

Anuradha Mannar

Anuradha Mannar was born in Bangalore, India, in 1971 and came to Rhode Island right after her first birthday. She grew up in Knoxville, Tennessee, and went to school at the University of North Carolina at Chapel Hill. She graduated in 1992 with a B.A. in journalism and is now working as a copy editor for the *News and Record* in Greensboro. She has published short narratives and poetry in *Sanyog*, a South Asian studies magazine at Duke University.

Diane S. Mehta

Born in Frankfurt, Germany, Diane Mehta grew up in Bombay and moved to the United States in 1973. She was a poetry fellow at Boston University, where she earned her M.A. in English and creative writing. She won honorable mention in the Academy of American Poets Prize for Boston University in 1993 and was semifinalist for the Discovery/The Nation contest in 1994. She recently won the 1993 Joel Climenhaga Creative Writing Award in poetry from Kansas State University. Her poems have appeared in *The Formalist* and *Hum Magazine*. She works as an associate reviews editor for *InfoWorld*.

Ved (Parkash) Mehta

Born on March 21, 1934, in Lahore, India (Pakistan after 1947), Ved Mehta suffered meningitis at the age of three, which left him blind. He came to the United States in 1949 to attend the School for the Blind in Little Rock, Arkansas. He received his B.A. from Pomona College, California, in 1956; a B.A. from Balliol College, Oxford, in 1959; an M.A. from Harvard University in 1961; and an M.A. from Balliol College in 1962. He has been a staff writer for *The New Yorker* since 1961 and has taught at Bard College, Sarah Lawrence, Balliol College, New York University, and Yale University. His writings include a series of autobiographical works that began with *Face to Face* (1957) and continued with *Daddyji* (1972), *Sound-Shadows of the New World* (1986), and *The Stolen Light* (1989). He has also written a number of books on India; a novel, *Delinquent Chacha* (1976); and a collection of short stories, *Three Stories of the Raj* (1986).

Tara Menon

Tara Menon was born in the southern tip of India in 1961. As a child she lived abroad in many different countries and attended American schools. She returned to India to do her B.A. and M.A. in English literature. Her short stories have appeared in *ELF: Eclectic Literay Forum*, *The Asian/ Pacific American Journal*, and the *South Carolina Review*. She lives in Lexington, Massachusetts, with her husband.

Panna Naik

Panna Naik, one of the leading Indian feminist poets writing in Gujarati, was born in Bombay in 1933 and emigrated to the United States in 1960. She has an M.A. in South Asian studies from the University of Bombay, an M.S. in library science from Drexel University, and an M.A. in South Asian studies from the University of Pennsylvania. Since 1964 she has worked as a librarian at the Van Pelt Library, University of Pennsylvania. She has published seven collections of poems in Gujarati, including *Philadelphia* (1980); three of the collections have been adopted as texts in Indian universities and colleges.

Tahira Naqvi

Tahira Naqvi is a leading Pakistani American short story writer. She was born in 1945 in Iran to Pakistani parents and as a child returned to Lahore, Pakistan, where she received her education. She has an M.A. in psychology from Government College, Lahore, and an M.S. in English education from Western Connecticut State University, Danbury, where she now teaches English. She is active in the Islamic Center, which she helped to organize in Connecticut.

Her short stories have been published in journals and anthologies such as *Journal of South Asian Literature, The Massachusetts Review, The Forbidden Stitch: An Asian American Women's Anthology* (1989), and *Imagining America: Stories from the Promised Land* (1991). Her translations of well-known Urdu writers such as Manto, Hijab Imtiaz Ali, Ahmed Ali, and Ismat Chugtai have been published in the United States, Europe, and South Asia. She is at present working on a translation of Ismat Chugtai's novel, *Terhi Lakir*, and compiling a collection of her short stories, *Memories of a Lahore Childhood*. Her first collection of short stories, *Attar of Roses and Other Stories*, was published by Three Continents Press in 1995.

Kirin Narayan

Kirin Narayan was born in Bombay in 1959 and began to inscribe stories in lined notebooks as soon as she learned to write. She first came to the United States on a scholarship to Sarah Lawrence College when she was sixteen. Although she took several creative writing classes in college, she decided that she did not have the courage to depend on her creative writing to support herself and therefore went to graduate school in anthropology at the University of California at Berkeley. She received her Ph.D. in 1987. Since then she has taught at Middlebury College, Hampshire College, and the University of Wisconsin at Madison, where she is now an associate professor of anthropology and South Asian studies. Her first book, *Storytellers, Saints and Scoundrels: Folk Narrative in Hindu Religious Teaching* (1990), won the 1990 Victor Turner Prize for ethnographic writing. The book examines the didactic tales used by an old Swamiji in Nasik; some of these tales are incorporated in her novel *Love, Stars, and All That* (1994).

Usha Nilsson

Usha Nilsson, who often uses Usha Priyamvada as her nom de plume, is one of the foremost South Asian American women writers of fiction in Hindi. She was born in Kanpur, India, into a family of doctors and journalists who were very active in India's Freedom Movement. After her father's death, when she was very young, her financially impoverished family continued to be politically active and to encourage her to read as widely as possible. Usha Nilsson has a B.A., an M.A., and a Ph.D. in English literature from Allahabad University, where she minored in Hindi language and literature. She did postdoctoral studies in American and comparative literature at Indiana University. She has been a professor in the Department of South Asian Studies at the University of Wisconsin at Madison since 1977.

Rajesh C. Oza

Rajesh C. Oza—descendant from Rajasthan, born in Bombay in 1960, reared in Canada, and educated in Chicago—now lives with his family in California. He is a manager for Hewlett-Packard. He was a contributing books editor for *India Currents Magazine*.

Uma Parameswaran

Uma Parameswaran was born in Tamilnadu and educated in Madhya Pradesh and Maharashtra. She has lived in Winnipeg, Canada, since 1966 and has been on the faculty of the University of Winnipeg since 1967. She completed her Ph.D. at Michigan State University in 1972. Her areas of research and specialization are the English Romantics and postcolonial literatures. Her critical works include *A Study of Representative Indo-English Novelists* (1976), *Commonwealth in Canada* (editor, 1982), and *The Perforated Sheet: A Study of Salman Rushdie's Fiction* (1988). She is the author of three books of creative writing, *Trishanku* (1987), *Rootless but Green Are the Boulevard Trees* (1988), and *The Door I Shut Behind Me* (1990).

Saleem Peeradina

Saleem Peeradina was born on October 5, 1944, in Bombay, India, and came to the United States in 1988. He received an M.A. from Bombay University and another M.A. from Wake Forest University. He has been teaching and conducting creative writing workshops for twenty years and has been a recipient of a Fulbright travel grant and a British Council writers grant. He is an artist and a photographer in his spare time.

He has written *First Offence* (1980) and *Group Portrait* (1992) and edited *Contemporary Indian Poetry in English* (1972) and *Cultural Forces Shaping India* (1988). A volume of his poetry, *Meditations on Desire*, and a memoir, *The Ocean in My Yard*, are forthcoming. His poems have been included in anthologies such as *Young Poets of India* (1972), *Poems from India, Sri Lanka, Malaysia and Singapore* (1979), *India—An Anthology of Contemporary Writing* (1982), and *Poetry of India in English* (1990).

Javaid Qazi

Javaid Qazi was born in Sahiwal, Pakistan, in 1947. He attended Aitchison College in Lahore and obtained his B.A. in 1967 from Government College, Lahore (University of the Punjab). He came to the United States to continue his studies in 1968. He has an M.A. in English literature from the University of Missouri at Kansas City and a Ph.D. in English literature from Arizona State University. He has also studied at the University of Chicago in the Department of South East Asian Languages and Civilizations. His short stories have appeared in several magazines, including *Kansas Quarterly, Sequoia, The Toronto South Asian Review, Chelsea, Anaïs Nin International Journal,* and *The Massachusetts Review.* He lives in San Jose, California, where he works as a high technology public relations specialist and a technical writer for the computer industry. He also paints in watercolors.

Jyotsna Sanzgiri

Jyotsna Sanzgiri was born in Bombay and came to the United States in 1971. She received her M.B.A. from Tulane University in 1973 and her Ph.D. in business administration from the University of Pittsburgh in 1977; her areas of specialization are Organization Development and Strategic Planning. Her poetry, short stories, and book reviews have appeared in *Synthesis, Calapooya Collage, Korone, Quest: A Feminist Quarterly, The Santa Monica Review, Blind Date, The Haven, The Book of Contemporary Myth, The Americas Review, Modern Short Stories,* the *San Francisco Chronicle,* and *India Currents Magazine.* Her poem, "Colonial Times," won first prize in a national competition sponsored by *The Americas Review.*

Sarita Sarvate

A native of Nagpur, India, Sarita Sarvate came to the United States in 1976 to attend graduate school in energy policy at the University of California at Berkeley. Since then, she has lived in Hawaii and New Zealand and is currently employed as a senior analyst at the California Public Utilities Commission in San Francisco. She has written for the *San Francisco Chronicle,* the *Oakland Tribune,* and other Bay Area newspapers. Her fiction and essays have appeared in *India Currents Magazine, Chabot Review, Insight,* and *New Outlook.* She lives in San Leandro, California, with her husband and two children.

Neila C. Seshachari

Neila C. Seshachari was born in 1934 in Belgaum, India, and emigrated with her family to Ogden, Utah, in 1969 from Hyderabad, India, where she was a lecturer in English at Osmania University. She received her Ph.D. in English from the University of Utah in 1975 and is currently Professor of English and editor of *Weber Studies: An Interdisciplinary Humanities Journal* at Weber State University. She has been a Danforth Faculty Associate, has won an NEH summer seminar award, and has received two statewide "Woman of the Year" awards and a recent award for editing a special issue of *Weber Studies.* Her publications include articles, fiction, and poems in a number of journals and books; her interviews with Ann Beattie, Alan Cheuse, May Sarton, and Maxine Hong Kingston have appeared in *Weber Studies*. In 1995 she will become the first female president of the Utah Academy of Sciences, Arts, and Letters since its inception in 1908. She lives with her husband and three children in Ogden, Utah.

Rashmi Sharma

Rashmi Sharma was born in Delhi in 1952 and received her M.A. from Delhi University in 1974. Married for over twenty years to a dedicated scientist, she tried her hand at various activities—morning coffees and afternoon teas, demonstrating Indian cooking and Indian fashions, volunteering, serving as managing editor of a local, nonprofit monthly newspaper, PTA President, SIP Chair, etc.— until she found her niche as curriculum developer.

In 1990 she established Vidya Books, a small publishing company dedicated to preserving a noncolonial perspective on India and Indians. Since 1991 she has been researching, writing, and publishing supplementary educational materials and presenting teacher workshops at various conferences in California and at the national level for K-12 educators.

Moazzam Sheikh

Moazzam Sheikh was born in Lahore in 1962 and moved to the United States in 1985. He has a degree in business from the University of the Punjab and has studied film at San Francisco State University for three years. He left the university in order to continue his vocation, reading and writing. He lives in San Francisco and in the past nine years has held a variety of jobs to enable him to continue to write. Moazzam Sheikh writes in Urdu and English. His story "Rains of the Monsoon" was published in *The Adobe Anthology* (1993) and another one titled "Kamla" was published in *The Milvia St. Journal* (1993).

Ranbir Sidhu

Ranbir Sidhu's Punjabi Sikh parents moved to London in the late 1950s; Ranbir Sidhu was born in England. He has lived for twelve years in the San Francisco Bay Area and has a degree in anthropology from the University of California, Berkeley. He is at present working in the M.F.A. program in fiction at the University of Arizona. His short stories have appeared in magazines such as *Zyzzyva* and *The Toronto South Asia Review*. He has completed a collection of short stories, *Dispatches from the New World Order*, which he hopes will be accepted for publication.

Bapsi Sidhwa

Bapsi Sidhwa, one of the best-known Pakistani American writers, was born in Karachi in 1938. Because she had polio as a child she was educated mainly at her family home in Lahore. She has stated that the oral tradition of storytelling, especially as practiced by the women of her family and community, was an important influence on her as a child, as a young woman, and as a writer. It was Louisa May Alcott's *Little Women*, presented to her on her eleventh birthday, that opened up the world of Western novels for her. She has written four novels, *The Crow Eaters* (1978, reprinted 1992), *The Bride* (1984), *Cracking India* (1992), and *An American Brat* (1994). She has won numerous prizes and awards including the Pakistan Academy's National Award (1985), Sitara-I-Imtiaz (Pakistan, 1991), the Bunting Fellowship at the Mary Ingraham Institute of Radcliffe College (1986–1987), and the Lila Wallace–Reader's Digest Writers Award (1994).

Neera Kuckreja Sohoni

Neera Sohoni was born in Delhi in 1943. She came to America in 1964 to get her master's in public administration at Syracuse University. She had already received her master's in history from Delhi University. She received her Ph.D. in economics from Gokhale Institute of Politics and Economics, Pune University India.

From 1965 to 1991 Neera Sohoni worked with a variety of national and multinational nonprofit organizations, including UNICEF, the Ford Foundation, and the International Council on Social Welfare's regional office for Asia and the Pacific. She was also a consultant for the government of India. She is at present an affiliated scholar at Stanford University's Institute for Research on Women and Gender. Her published works include *Women Behind Bars: A Sociodemographic Study of Women Prisoners* (1986), *People in Action* (1990), *Status of Girls in Developing Strategies* (1994), *The Burden of Girlhood: A Global Perspective* (1994), and a translation of Mahadevi Varma's *Ateet Ke Chalchitra, Sketches from My Past* (1994). In her monthly column for *India Currents Magazine*, she discusses political, social, and cultural issues.

Jyotsna Sreenivasan

Jyotsna Sreenivasan was born in Ohio in 1964. She has an M.A. in English from the University of Michigan and is the author of *The Moon Over Crete* (1994), a feminist adventure novel for children age eight and older. She works as a writer and editor at the Feminist Majority in Arlington, Virginia.

Rajini Srikanth

Born in Bombay in 1957, Rajini Srikanth came to the United States in 1976. She received her Ph.D. in English in 1987 from the State University of New York at Buffalo. She teaches in the English department at Tufts University. Her training is in American literature (she wrote her dissertation on William Faulkner), but her interests make her into what she calls "something of an intellectual nomad." Her essay on R. K. Narayan has been published in *R. K. Narayan: Contemporary Critical Perspectives* (1994). She has delivered several conference papers and has organized and chaired conference panels on Asian American writers for Asian American studies conferences (1993, 1994, and 1995) and for the Modern Language Association conference (1994). She is currently exploring the effect of gender on images of home in diasporic literature.

Amita Vasudeva

Amita Vasudeva is the daughter of post–1965 Indian immigrants. She was born and raised in the Midwest along with two older brothers. Committed to social justice issues, she is currently working with an immigrants' rights organization in San Francisco, California. After studying Hindi and Punjabi in India for a year, she plans to study law and work for immigrant workers' rights. She has published "Can You Talk Mexican?" and other works in *Our Feet Walk the Sky: Women of the South Asian Diaspora* (1994).

About the Book
and Editor

Perceptions and realities of life in North America are interwoven with memories of South Asia in this first anthology of literary works focusing on South Asian American perspectives on the United States and Canada. Most of the short stories and poems deal explicitly with South Asian American experiences, but the evocative themes of love, loss, exile, nostalgia, loneliness, and renewal are present throughout.

Living in America is a stimulating compilation of established authors such as Meena Alexander, Agha Shahid Ali, G. S. Sharat Chandra, Rienzi Crusz, Chitra Divakaruni, Ved Mehta, and Bapsi Sidhwa and talented writers as yet undiscovered by general readers. The diversity and strength of these South Asian American voices illuminate the wide range of South Asian history and traditions as well as the complexity of cultures—Asian as well as American—that undergird the work of authors of South Asian descent.

The book includes both a historical introduction and one exploring South Asian literary traditions and the concept of the collection. The editor has also provided detailed headnotes to place each individual work in context and discuss its literary nuances.

Roshni Rustomji-Kerns is emerita professor, Hutchins School of Liberal Studies and the India Studies Program, at Sonoma State University, California.